THEOLOGY AS THANKSGIVING

THEOLOGY AS THANKSGIVING

From Israel's Psalms to the Church's Eucharist

BY HARVEY H. GUTHRIE, JR.

THE SEABURY PRESS · NEW YORK

1981
The Seabury Press
815 Second Avenue
New York, N.Y. 10017

Printed in the United States of America

Library of Congress Cataloging in Publication Data

Guthrie, Harvey H
Theology as thanksgiving.

1. Gratitude. 2. Worship in the Bible.
3. Lord's Supper. I. Title.
BV4647.G8G87 264'.36 80-27012
ISBN 0-8164-0486-0

To Students, Staff, Faculty, and Trustees
of the Episcopal Divinity School, 1974–1980,
Companions in Transition and Turbulence for Whom
Thanksgiving is in Order

Contents

Preface

THIS book began in different areas of my life and work and experience. I am a student and teacher of the Old Testament whose work through the last decade or so has focussed on the Psalter. I have also been interested in and fascinated by the way in which the Wisdom Literature of the Old Testament became so theologically important in Israel during and after the exilic period. Moreover, I have been increasingly impressed by the extent to which the earliest Christian Church's understanding of itself was rooted in Israel's life and history and theology. On the other hand, through the last decade I have been not only a professor of Old Testament, but a dean responsible for the administrative and pastoral and liturgical oversight of a theological seminary. In particular, the liturgical aspect of those responsibilities, in a time of liturgical renewal and reform, has resulted in an awareness of the history of Christian liturgy and all the issues connected with that history. Finally, I have continued to be influenced by a conviction picked up from Marshall McLuhan back in the sixties. "The medium," I too believe, is "the message." Cult and song and all kinds of in-between-the-lines things, I am convinced, often reveal more about what is really going on in a community of faith than do theological treatises and conciliar pronouncements.

All these things converged in a growing certainty that the *forms* of Israel's worship and praise of God are theologically significant, that exploration of those forms may lead to a more profound understanding of the nature of Israel's faith than study concentrated on the content transmitted through the forms. That growing certainty was accompanied by another: that those forms, inherited from Israel's cultic life, were lived in, were unconsciously just *there* for Jesus of Nazareth and for the earliest Christian Church. The thesis of this book grew out of those things.

The thesis, then, is that the doing of Eucharist—that act which is the Christian Church's normative way of identifying itself liturgically for what it is—is very deeply rooted in ancient Israel's forms of worship. My thesis is that those forms were appropriated by the earliest Church, not necessarily consciously but almost inevitably, because of the way in which the earliest Church's experience paralleled that of ancient Israel. Further, the *kanon*—the measuring rod, the standard, the norm—by which both ancient Israel and the early Church weighed the adequacy of theological statements was not one involving the content of those statements as such. On the contrary, that *kanon* was based on what emerged from liturgical forms, from cultic actions. It was based on what a community of faith knew and experienced and was involved in as it proclaimed its identity in worship. That form, that action, was one denoted by the Hebrew word *todah,* by the Greek word *eucharistia.* Their English equivalent is *thanksgiving.*

The sense in which they both mean "thanksgiving," however, and the background out of which they mean "thanksgiving" require an exploration of Israel's cultic life against the background of the culture of the ancient Near East, the setting of ancient Israel's life and history. They require a search for what "thanksgiving" originally meant in concrete terms. They require, then, a tracing of how Wisdom supplanted "thanksgiving" as a norm for Israel's understanding of the nature of its relationship to God in a period in which there seemed to be nothing to give thanks for. They require showing how the earliest Christian community found itself undergoing an experience which, once again, made "thanksgiving" rather than Wisdom normative for theological understanding. What *todah, eucharistia,* as a norm for theology means requires taking liturgy seriously in a theological sense, and not regarding liturgy simply as that which is done to express the theological content of faith once that content has been determined on other grounds. To a considerable extent the thesis of this book is like that of Louis Bouyer's book, *Eucharist.* Bouyer's significant treatment of the central act of Christian worship traces the origins of the Eucharist back to the *berakoth,* the blessings used in the synagogue and especially at meals by Jews. This book goes on from there, however, and pursues the way in which the tradition underlying the *berakoth,* and therefore the tradition underlying the form of the Christian Eucharist, goes back much further than that. The thesis is that the roots of the Eucharist go back to the utilization by ancient Israel of the *todah,* or thanksgiving, form of cultic worship as the form most appropriate for praising the God with whom Israel found itself involved in its life and history.

For the opportunity to organize and think through what is written down in this book, I am grateful to St. John's College, Auckland, and to the Church of the Province of New Zealand for doing me the honor of appointing me to the George Augustus Selwyn lectureship for the summer (winter from their point of view) of 1977. For the time away from regular duties to do the writing, I am grateful to the trustees of the Episcopal Divinity School for a leave in the winter of 1978–79. For letting me have the use of a place where, far from my telephone and mailbox, I could actually get the writing done, I am grateful to the Fuller Theological

Seminary and to the warmth and concern of Inez Smith. For encouragement and support along the way I am grateful to the Society of St. John the Evangelist, under whose sponsorship the content was given in a shorter form that helped me focus my ideas, and especially to the community that is the Episcopal Divinity School in which and with which the doing of Eucharist is a reality for me. Finally, I am grateful for Doris who continually keeps me aware that the ultimate reality must be a Some*one,* not a theological abstraction.

It should be noted that the translations of biblical passages in this book are my own and that they have been made to emphasize the way in which I believe them to embody what is being set forth in this book. They also, in line with the style of the book as a whole, avoid usage which implies that God and the human community are exclusively male. It should also be noted that there is no way to avoid painful historical realities in the choice of words to denote the land in which ancient Israel lived and in which the earliest Church came into being. I use the word ''Palestine'' simply in a traditional way to denote an area larger than the contemporary state of Israel and the occupied territory on the west bank of the Jordan.

Harvey H. Guthrie, Jr.

1

Hymn and Thanksgiving: The Transformation of a Myth

FORM criticism is that discipline through which biblical scholars seek to understand a given piece of literature in terms of the function it served in the human community that produced it. The line of thought that led to what this book sets forth originated in form critical study of the Old Testament psalms, particularly of the psalms of praise. Form criticism is really no esoteric, arcane property of scholars alone. It is something we all engage in every time we stop to browse in a bookstore. Without even realizing it consciously, we classify a book we pick up according to its *genre*, its type, its form. Our mind automatically recognizes one book as a novel, another as a biography, another as a work of history. We do that in order to read a book in the way its author intended. If we were to read a novel as if it were history, or an editorial as if it were a news story, or a biography as if it were a fairy story, we would be in difficulty. We do not, for we are acquainted with our culture's literary forms. Without being conscious of it, every one of us engages in form criticism all the time.

To do so is to engage in an easy enough undertaking when we are dealing with the literature of our own culture. When, however, we begin to deal with the literature of a culture of which we are not natives, and the forms of whose literature are foreign to us, then form criticism has to become a much more self-conscious and disciplined task. Under those circumstances, form criticism involves careful examination of as much of the literature of a culture as possible, so as to classify the various writings under the forms underlying their different types. It involves studying the literature of neighboring peoples and cultures to find what will help in that classification. Then, when the different forms have been defined in terms of their formal characteristics, form criticism involves examining all the aspects of the culture in question in order to gain some understanding of the function served for the human community by the various literary forms. Obviously, especially when we are dealing with the literature of a culture far removed from us in space and time and ethos, form criticism has to be more of an art than a science. Criticism of the discipline for the way in which its practitioners sometimes arrive at different conclusions about the same piece of literature overlooks that fact.

Form Criticism and the Psalms of Praise

Hermann Gunkel was the scholar who first applied form criticism to the Psalter in such a thorough way as to make his classification of the psalms into types the starting point from which all subsequent work has proceeded and to which all subsequent classifications refer.[1] In working with those psalms whose content was manifestly the praise of God, Gunkel discerned two types: the hymn (the word, as we will see, has a more specific meaning here than it does in normal English usage) and the thanksgiving. Subsequent study, starting from Gunkel's basic distinction of the two types, has produced further and more detailed explanations of how the types originated, what functions they served in the community that produced them, what specific cultic occasions might have been the settings in which the two types of song were sung, and what were the theological presuppositions of each of the two types.[2]

The hymn, of which Psalm 29 is as pure an example as there is, has very definite formal characteristics. It begins with a series of plural imperatives. Hebrew, unlike English but like many other languages, distinguishes between whether a command is being given to one person or to more than one person. The imperatives with which hymns begin, commanding that God be praised, are in the plural:

Ascribe to Yahweh,[3] *all you divine beings,*
Ascribe to Yahweh importance and power,
Ascribe to Yahweh the importance consonant with Yahweh's fame,
Do obeisance to Yahweh vested in sacred array.
(Ps. 29:1–2)

The imperative introduction to hymns is followed by the main body of the song in which, in poetic and mythological imagery, the characteristics of the god that warrant hymnic praise are set forth:

Yahweh's sound (is louder than) the waters,
The really important God is one who thunders,
Yahweh (is a dominator of) the primeval waters.
Yahweh's sound is powerful,
Yahweh's sound is awe inspiring.
Yahweh's sound is something that shatters cedars—
Yes, Yahweh has shattered even the cedars of Lebanon.
Yes, Yahweh has made Lebanon skip like a calf,
Sirion like a wild ox.
Yahweh's sound is something accompanied by fiery flames
Yahweh's sound makes the desert writhe around,
Yahweh makes even Kadesh's desert writhe around.
Yahweh's sound scares hinds into calving.
Makes kids be born prematurely.
(Ps. 29:3–9a)

While it is impossible to convey it in a consistent way in translation, the form of the Hebrew verb normally employed in hymns is not narrative, not recitative. It is a form of the verb (classified as participle in Hebrew grammars) which denotes the *doer* of the action the verb describes. What is said, usually, is not, "God *does* (or *did*) so and so," but, "God is the one who characteristically does so and so." In the canons of form criticism, the use of that verb form in hymns is one of the principal things that distinguishes hymns from thanksgivings. A rereading of the translation of Psalm 29:3–9 given above will indicate the extent to which the body of the hymn describes Israel's God as the One who characteristically manifests power in rain and thunder and lightning and in the bringing of fertility to the earth, and does not *narrate* some particular occasion on which those actions have taken place.

The conclusion of a hymn may speak of how those to whom the imperative at the beginning of the hymn was addressed have obeyed it, often speaks of the enthronement of the god in question as cosmic sovereign, may assert how that god will continue to be victorious, rounds off the hymn with praise:

> *In Yahweh's heavenly palace . . . (some words probably missing)*
> *They all* are *proclaiming Yahweh's importance.*
> *Yahweh, over potential watery chaos is enthroned,*
> *Yes, Yahweh reigns over all the ages.*
> *Yahweh* will *strengthen the people who are Yahweh's,*
> *Will bless Yahweh's people with* shalom.
>
> (Ps. 29:9b–11)

The origin of the hymn seems to lie in the world view of the culture into which Israel emerged as a people toward the end of the second millenium before the Christian era. Literature in which that world view finds expression has been recovered from Mesopotamia, from Egypt, and from the area into which Israel came.[4] That world view has been characterized as mythopoeic in character.[5] In that world view the realm of existence that really mattered was not the earth on which human life was lived. What happened on earth was only a derivative of, dependent on, and reflective of what transpired in the heavenly realm inhabited by the assembly of heavenly beings. The realities of life experienced by human beings, particularly the annual cycle of nature upon which the human community was so dependent for survival and sustenance, were accounted for in mythical narratives of what transpired in the divine realm above and beyond the realm of nature and history in which human beings lived.

Those mythical narratives followed a certain pattern. They spoke of a primeval conflict in the divine realm in which the forces of life and light and good and order had been pitted against the forces of death and darkness and evil and chaos. That conflict obviously accounted for what the human community experienced as the crisis of the annual cycle of nature came around: in Mesopotamia as the spring floods threatened to destroy everything and then receded to allow life to continue; in Palestine as the summer drought threatened life and fertility and then gave way to the vitality made possible by the fall rains.[6] That conflict was seen as also recurring in the monthly lunar cycle, as well as in the daily cycle focussed on the setting and rising of the sun. There was always the possibility that the flood or the drought might be the end of everything, that the moon might go in never to come out, that the sun might set never to rise again.

Those mythical narratives always accounted for the victory of life over death, of order over chaos, by recounting how a hero god had taken on the destructive and rebellious divine beings and defeated them. That was their way of accounting for why the god of a given people had come to be the cosmic ruler of the universe. It is quite probable that those narratives served as scripts for the cultic drama in which the cosmic struggle was reenacted year by year, with the human king most probably representing the cosmic ruler. Cultic dramas of that kind seem to have taken place at appropriate times in the cycles of nature: annually, for reasons connected with the climates of the two areas, at the spring equinox in Mesopotamia and at the fall equinox in Palestine; but also, on less grand scales, at such other appropriate times as new moon or sunrise.

It is likely that the climax of the cultic drama for which those mythical narratives served as scripts involved both the offering of sacrifice and the singing of praise. The sacrifice offered on such public celebrations of the continuance of life in the universe to the god who had made the continuance of life possible was what is called in Hebrew *'olah* (literally "what goes up"), the whole burnt offering, in which every bit of the animal sacrificed was consumed by fire to make its way upward to the god. The song of praise was the hymn. Given the setting in which the hymn originated and was sung, the formal characteristics of the hymn are easily understood. The reason for the imperatives in the hymn's introduction is that the human community is calling upon the divine community to acclaim as sovereign that god who has brought the rebellious forces into check and who, therefore, rules over both the gods and the human community and the world in which it exists. The reason for the form of the verb used in the body of the hymn, that form which does not recount the actions of the god but describes the nature of the god, is that hymns were not narrations of what had happened on one, specific occasion. They were acclamations of what turned out to be the nature of the god on the basis of annual and monthly and daily realities in the cycles of nature.

The thanksgiving, like the hymn, also has definite formal characteristics. Psalm 30 provides a good example of this type of psalm, the introduction to which is characterized by a verb in the first person singular in which the singer praises a god who has delivered the singer from suffering and distress:

I exalt you, Yahweh, because you rescued me from the depths,
Removed cause for my enemies to rejoice over me.
(Ps. 30:1)

While the verb in the introduction to Psalm 30 is "I will exalt," the verb that predominates in the introductions—and in the conclusions—of thanksgivings is "I will give thanks," the form of the verb from which the noun *todah*, thanksgiving, is derived.

The body of a thanksgiving is narrative in form, a recital of how the one giving thanks cried out to his or her divine protector in distress and was heard and delivered:

Yahweh, my God, I cried out to you for help,
And you healed me.
Yahweh, you pulled my life back up from Sheol,
Made me alive again rather than an inhabitant of the Pit . . .
Foolish me, I said when things were going well for me,
"I shall never be overwhelmed by chaos!"
Yahweh, because it pleased you, you made me like a strong mountain;
But when you weren't obviously blessing me, I fell all apart.
To you, Yahweh, I cried out,
Yes, to a powerful One made supplication:
"What good would be served by my death,
By my descent to the nether regions?
Can dust give todah, *or testify to your trustworthiness?*
Hear, O Yahweh, and deal graciously with me,
Yahweh, please be my helper!"
So you turned my mourning into dancing,
Stripped off my sackcloth and dressed me up in joy!
(Ps. 30:2–3, 6–11)

The verbs in the body of a thanksgiving, in contrast to the verbs in the body of a hymn, are characteristically in a finite form. They do not denote what the god's normal mode of activity is, what the nature of the god is, as do the verbs in hymns. The verbs in the bodies of thanksgivings describe what the god *has done* for a specific suppliant in a specific situation. They are recitative, narrative in form. The body of a thanksgiving often alludes to the lament voiced by the god's devotee in distress (cf. Ps. 30:2a, 9–11),[7] may speak of a night spent at a holy place in penitence and solemn supplication:

> *In the evening weeping sets in,*
> *But what characterizes the morning is joy!*
> (Ps. 30:5b)

The body of a thanksgiving quite often contains hyperbole in which the deliverance accomplished by the god is likened to rescue from death and annihilation themselves (cf. Ps. 30:3). The conclusion of a thanksgiving usually takes up the wording and the theme of the introduction once again, promising that by giving thanks continually, engaging constantly in the offering of *todah*, the devotee will remain a witness to the goodness and power of the god in question:

> *So that the fame of what has happened may redound to your praise and not fade away,*
> *O Yahweh my God, as long as time shall last will I do* todah *for you!*
> (Ps. 30:12)

It may very well be that the cultic situation out of which lament and thanksgiving arose as a human being in need and distress called upon a protector god is the place of origin of some of the most important words in the biblical vocabulary. The Hebrew word *zedek*, or *zedakah*, is normally translated "righteousness," and the related word *zadik* "righteous one." The word's basic meaning, however, is indicated by its use in places where "righteousness" is clearly not an appropriate translation. Isaiah 41:2, for example, speaks of Cyrus the Persian in these words: "Who aroused one from the east whom *zedek* greets at his every step?" In that verse *zedek* is often translated "victory." Again, in Micah 6:5, Israel is directed to recall certain of the great events of the past in which Yahweh has stood by Israel "so that Yahweh's *zidkoth* (the plural of *zedakah*) may be known to you." Again, "righteousnesses" would not make good sense. The Revised Standard Version translates *zidkoth* with "saving acts," the New English Bible with "triumph."

The *sense* in which *zedek* or a closely related word is used in such passages, plus the fact that *zedek* and its cognates are so heavily used in literature connected with laments and thanksgivings, leads to the conclusion that the original meaning of *zedek* may have been connected with the action of a protector god toward a devotee who called upon that god. *Zedek*, or *zedakah*, was what took place when the desperate cry of a human being was heard and responded to by the god to whom the cry had been directed. *Zedek* did, therefore, denote a "saving act," a "triumph" or a "victory" for the god, a "vindication" of both the devotee whose faith had been justified and the god whose reputation as a deliverer had been sustained. *Zadik* denoted the one who had been saved, the one in whom the god's victory or triumph had been manifest, the one who had been vindicated by *zedek*. "Righteousness" and "righteous" came to be the sense of the word only when people began to think that delivery was connected with what the delivered one deserved on the basis of the record. At root, though, righteousness in the Bible is not something achieved by human beings. It is the gracious response of God to human need. What qualifies a person to be designated *zadik* is not what that person has accomplished, but the gracious initiative of God.[8]

Like the hymn, the thanksgiving is rooted in the culture and theology of the ancient Near East. In that theology which located all the significant action in the world of the gods, the great cosmic sovereign whose victory over chaos was celebrated in the hymn was not approached by the mass of common folk. The particular access of common people to the divine realm was through that member of the heavenly assembly who was specifically related to one's family or clan or locale. When someone was ill or unjustly treated or childless or in need of some kind, it was to one's own "personal god"[9] that lament was made. Then, when deliverance had taken place, it was to one's own particular god that *todah*, thanksgiving, was offered. That thanksgiving was concrete witness to how caring and how capable of putting care into effective action the god was. *Todah* covered what, to us, are several separate and distinct things. It did, in the first place, denote what we mean when we use the word "thanksgiving." It did so, however, by connecting the abstraction "thanksgiving" with concrete forms of words and concrete cultic actions. *Todah* denoted the type, the genre, of song of praise that form critics have designated a thanksgiving, the formal characteristics of which have been described above. Furthermore, *todah* also designated the cultic action, the specific kind of sacrificial offering, which was the context in which a *todah* song was sung. In ancient Israel it was not possible to say or think "thanksgiving" without its having those quite concrete connotations.

The *todah* sacrifice was different from the *'olah*, the whole burnt offering or holocaust which was the cultic context of the hymn. In a thanksgiving sacrifice only certain specified parts of the sacrificial animal, not the whole of it, were burned and offered up to the god. Certain other parts of the animal were assigned to the priests of the sanctuary as payment for their services. More significantly, provision was also made for a meal at which the family and friends of the one giving thanks, those who had cause to share in joy that the deliverance had taken place, were invited to share in the offering of *todah*. That is what lies in the background of Psalm 30:4:

> *Sing a song for Yahweh, fellow devotees of his,*
> *Do* todah *as a witness to Yahweh's holiness.*

That is also what is being referred to in Amos 4:5, where the prophet castigates Israel for worshipping in such a way as to impress human beings but not in the spirit that is pleasing to God. The verse can be rendered, "Make your *todah* meals tasty; send out engraved invitations to your freewill sacrifices! Yes, that is what *you* take delight in, O children of Israel!" The content of what the prophet says is disapproving of the spirit in which it is being done, but it indicates the way in which others were invited to join in the *todah* song and sacrifice.

The above reconstructions indicate the way in which the formal differences between hymns and thanksgivings are rooted in two different kinds of liturgical actions offered to two different kinds of gods in celebration of two different kinds of deliverance. The hymn, and the cultic action which was in all probability its setting, had to do with the cosmic sovereign, the great divine chief of the heavenly assembly and with that god's recurrent defeat of chaos and death on a cosmic scale. The closest the human community could come to praising such a god was to send a sacrifice completely up to the divine realm to be consumed there by other than human beings, and to call on those other than human beings who populated the heavens to sing the praises of the cosmic sovereign. The best that the human community could do was to use verb forms that described the character of the cosmic sovereign as reflected in nature's annual cycle, direct observation of those actions—using verb forms indicating direct observation—not being possible for human beings.

The thanksgiving and the cultic action which was likely to be its setting, on the other hand, had to do with the personal god of a specific human being, with the way such a god had, on a particular occasion and in a particular set of actions, rescued that human being from a threat to existence itself. That segment of the human community who knew the giver of thanks and the deliverance that had occurred were invited to share the sacrifice offered with the offerer and with the god, and to be the chorus that praised that god with *todah*. And that human chorus used verb forms describing the action of the god that they themselves had observed in rendering their praise.

Confusion and a Caveat

The situation in the Psalter in its present form in the Bible is not, however, as neat as a quick reading of the previous section of this chapter might lead one to believe. Psalm 29 *is* a quite pure example of the hymn and its formal characteristics. Psalm 30 *is* a quite pure example of a thanksgiving, all the formal characteristics being there also. But the occurrence of such pure examples of the two forms in the psalms is rare. More often than not the characteristics of the two forms are mixed together in one, single psalm of praise.

Psalm 33, for example, is usually listed in studies of the Psalter as a thanksgiving. It does celebrate the way Yahweh protects and delivers those who trust in and wait on Yahweh. It clearly praises Yahweh as a "personal god." Nevertheless, it displays many of the characteristics of hymns: it begins with plural imperatives; there are instances of verb forms normally supposed to be found in hymns; and, particularly in its first eleven verses, it celebrates those creative actions in which chaos is held in check and an orderly universe becomes capable of supporting life, the actions more normally celebrated in hymns. Again, Psalm 135 is, in its outline, in the form of a hymn. Yet, those to whom the introductory imperatives are addressed are clearly not inhabitants of the heavenly realm. They are human beings. The same thing is true of the conclusion in Psalm 135:19–21. Moreover, the form of the verbs in the body of Psalm 135 is that supposed to be normal for thanksgivings. The reason is clearly that the content of this psalm is Israel's deliverance in the realm of human history, not actions taking place somewhere beyond the boundaries of this world. And the same kind of thing is true of Psalm 136. The *form* of its first three verses—the imperative—is clearly that of a hymn, but the verb used is "give thanks." Furthermore, just as in Psalm 135, the introductory imperatives are addressed to human rather than divine beings. The body of Psalm 136, in verses 4–9, does take up the subject matter of hymns, and begins by employing the verb form typical of the hymn. The verb form soon switches, however, to that recitative mode typical of thanksgivings, and the subject matter shifts to how God delivered Israel from distress on the human, historical scene.

Examples could be multiplied. Those given above, however, should be sufficient to illustrate what is, admittedly, a fact. It is the case that, in the forms in which Israel's psalms of praise exist in the Psalter as we have received it, the form critical characteristics of hymns and thanksgivings are definitely intertwined in the same, individual psalms. Furthermore, that is the case more often than it is not the case.

That is the basis on which Claus Westermann challenged the existence of two forms of psalms of praise. His *caveat* was set forth in *The Praise of God in the Psalms,* one of the most significant studies of the psalms published in recent years.[10] Westermann traced in great detail the extent to which the form critical characteristics of hymns and thanksgivings are mixed together in the psalms. This was his conclusion:

> . . . There exists between hymn and song of thanksgiving really *no* difference of type, or category, and the song of

> thanks, of the individual and of the people, is really another type of hymn. The result is, then, that in the Psalter there are two dominant categories, the hymn (including the psalm of thanks) and the lament.[11]

Westermann did go on to recognize that the hymn—for him now encompassing what other form critics separated into hymn and thanksgiving—had both its "declarative" and its "descriptive" aspects. He thus recognized to some extent what his predecessors had pointed out about the difference between the verb forms of hymns and the verb forms of thanksgivings.[12] He was, however, insistent that, in Israel's psalms of praise, we are dealing with one, basic type. Westermann was making a point which, given the quality of his scholarship, had to be taken seriously. He issued a challenge to form critical orthodoxy that was not to be taken lightly. It was, actually, in the pondering and testing of that challenge that the line of argument pursued in this book began to come into being.

Hymn and Thanksgiving Mixed: the Transformation of a Myth

As our own discussion has shown, Westermann is quite correct about the present situation of the psalms of praise in the Psalter. On sheerly literary grounds alone, however, it is clear that support exists for the classic form critical discernment of two types of psalms of praise. First, there are instances in which individual psalms do conform exclusively to the set of characteristics posited for one or the other of the two types. That is true of the two psalms examined earlier in this chapter. Psalm 29 exhibits only the form "hymn," while Psalm 30 exhibits only the form "thanksgiving." Second, Westermann himself recognizes that there is something to the separation of psalms of praise into two categories when he has to say that some of his "hymns" display a "declarative" style, while the style of others is "descriptive."

Treating literature like the psalms, however, as if it were exclusively a literary phenomenon will never unlock everything embodied in that literature.[13] The psalms of the Hebrew Bible were not produced by poets who sat down to create poems after the fashion of modern poets. The origin of the biblical psalms lies, rather, in the cultic—the liturgical—life of a community of faith. To ask just who wrote a certain psalm at what time is to ask a question that means something, and that could, theoretically, be answered. It is, though, to ask a question that will only scratch the surface of what a given psalm really is and is all about. In the same kind of way that students of liturgy trace the *form* of collects or eucharistic prayers back through the history of its emergence and development and modification in the worship of the Church in order to uncover the various layers of meaning contained in the form, so must the *forms* of the psalms in the context of the life and experience and worship of the people of Israel be traced in order to get at the various layers of meaning contained in them.

To say that Thomas Cranmer wrote a certain collect on such and such a date, or that he wrote the prayer of consecration in the Prayer Book of 1549 on such and such a date, is only to scratch the surface of what his collect or eucharistic prayer really is. Or to say that, because collects or eucharistic prayers do not conform in a mechanical way to a common outline that is never varied and never contains variations, there is no *form* present in them is to overlook a fundamental reality. Collects and eucharistic prayers exist only because of and in relation to and in the context of the liturgical life of a real human community. They emerge from that life. They are not "composed" according to some outline followed by "authors." That is why speaking exclusively of "the psalmists" and never taking account of the living, historical community out of whose life of worship and praise the psalms came is not only to miss the point; it is to close off the possibility of understanding the psalms at the deepest level. It is to overlook both the forms and structures that enable communities to function communally and the living, fluid way that such forms and structures shift in response to the moods and issues present in historical, human communities.

That is why pointing out on the basis of the deposit left at one stage of the history underlying the Psalter that the supposed forms underlying hymns and thanksgivings are mixed together, and then to conclude on the basis of that observation that we are really dealing with one form and not two is to overlook many important things. If it is demonstrable, and the discussion above has gone a good way in showing that it is, that hymns and thanksgivings seem to have been associated with two different kinds of cultic occasions, and if there are reasons to conclude on purely literary grounds alone that two types do exist, then it would seem to be closing off the discussion too abruptly to conclude that there really is no difference between hymn and thanksgiving. There would seem to be warrant for going on from the, admittedly quite accurate, observation that the two types of songs of praise are mixed to the question of why they are mixed, and how, in the life of the community in whose cult they figured, they came to be mixed. It is our contention that likely answers to those questions can be found if the psalms are examined in the context of the culture from which they came and in the context of the cultic life that was their setting. It is also our contention that the answer to the question of how and why hymns and thanksgivings came to be mixed has very important theological consequences.

To get at the way in which hymns and thanksgivings, in the view of the present author, came to be mixed in Israel's psalms, it is necessary to take a closer look at the world view and the theology underlying the hymn form. The ethos of the hymn has been described above. It involved a view of life in which the realm that really mattered was the heavenly realm in which the divine beings dwelt. It embodied the conviction that what transpired in the human realm was only a reflection of what happened among the divine beings, outside the time and space in which human decisions and human actions took place. The sacrifice appropriate to what was celebrated in the hymn was a sacrifice sent up to the divine realm, not really participated in by the human beings who offered it. The hymn itself was not direct praise of the cosmic sovereign by the human community. It was only an exhortation by the human community to the divine community to praise the cosmic sovereign.

The presuppositions underlying all that are made quite explicit near the conclusion of the *Enuma elish*, the Mesopotamian form of the cosmic myth about the struggle between order and chaos that underlies the cultic activity which is the setting of the hymn. That myth holds that the earth which is the setting of human life came into being almost as an epilogue to the crucial drama, only as a sign and symbol that the god of order had, in fact, defeated the god of chaos. Moreover, once the earth was there needing care and cultivation, it was deemed beneath the dignity of even the meanest god to have to deal with earthly dirt and mud. It was, therefore, decided that human beings should be created solely to do the menial tasks necessary to keep the earth in order—for that and nothing more. Thus, human decisions and human actions were really of no significance. The decisions and actions that mattered took place in the divine realm. The stories that were significant enough to be recited were stories of what transpired in the divine realm, for the human story—history—had no significance. The literature originating in that culture in which human beings figured in any important way was of two kinds only. First, there was tragic literature in which human attempts to rise to the divine realm that really mattered always failed and were mourned. Second, there were genealogies of royal dynasties, the purpose of which was to show that the one ruling over human society was qualified to do so by descent from, or ancestral authorization by, the head of the divine society above, not by any human worth.[14]

The social and political structures of ancient Near Eastern culture reflected that view of things. The center of the earth for any specific people was the high place on which their temple and palace stood—one word served for both those buildings in Hebrew and the other Semitic languages. It was the complex of buildings in which, through the continual offerings of the cult that was the context of the hymn as well as through the person of the divinely designated king, the earthly, human community maintained the contact with the heavenly realm which alone gave life any meaning. Indeed, that complex of buildings was an earthly reproduction of the great, cosmic temple-palace in which the divine, cosmic sovereign was enthroned in the midst of the divine assembly and where the decisions affecting the destinies of the universe were taken.

From the temple-palace complex at the highest place in the kingdom, the place nearest to heaven, the order and security ensured by the cosmic sovereign flowed out into the city within whose walls people were safe under the protection of the king, the viceregent of the cosmic sovereign. Likewise, order and security flowed outward from the city to the city's cultivated and protected territories in which the king's plows and police held chaos in check. Out beyond those territories—*sadeh*, "field," is the Hebrew term—was the area not provided with order and security, overgrown and wild and desolate, or barren and arid and devoid of life, out of which came enemies and marauders and conquerors from other cities who insisted that there were other cosmic sovereigns. This wild area lying beyond the control of the forces of order as conceived in ancient Near Eastern culture is denoted in Hebrew as *midbar*. The word seems basically to mean "what is out behind what we can see." Given the character of the uncontrolled area around the land where Israel settled, the word is normally translated "desert." Had the terrain been different, the word might have had to be translated "wilderness" (as it sometimes is) or "jungle" or "ice fields," for its fundamental meaning is found in the view of the cosmos and human society prevailing in the ancient Near East and underlying the hymn, the view in which order is the more diluted the farther one goes from the temple-palace of the cosmic sovereign or the human king.[15]

There were, however, peoples in the ancient Near East who lived outside that culture and that society, or on their fringes, for whom *midbar* was home. From the point of view of those inhabiting the city-kingdoms they were outside the cosmos, without status in terms of the cosmic order. In Mesopotamia they were called Amorites, which seems to mean "westerners" and is connected with the fact that the *midbar* from a Mesopotamian point of view is the great Arabian desert which lies to the west of the Tigris-Euphrates basin.[16] In the Palestinian area such peoples were called *Habiru*, or *'Apiru*, in correspondence between Egyptian officials in that area and their superiors in the homeland, correspondence dating from approximately the time of Israel's settlement of Palestine.[17] "Amorite" and "Habiru" do not seem to be ethnic or generic terms, and those to whom they were applied may have been of various ethnic origins. The terms applied to a kind, a *class* of people the definition of whom was basically that they were outsiders to the city-kingdom culture and society of the ancient Near East.

From time to time such peoples would enter ancient Near Eastern society. They might do so by being captured and enslaved, thus becoming the bottom human layer of a pyramid-like social structure with slaves at its base and the divinely designated king at its apex. They might do so also by conquering a city-kingdom and taking it over and installing their own leading clan as the ruling dynasty. When the latter happened, the standard result seems to have been the taking on of the social setup, the world view, the culture, the cosmic mythology and cult that prevailed in the city-kingdoms of the area. From the point of view of the people of the time, the god of the new dynasty, who had probably formerly been the god of a seminomadic clan on the fringes of society, had turned out to be the cosmic sovereign who ensured order and life in the universe. So, cult and hymn singing would continue on those occasions when the victory of order over chaos was celebrated—annually, monthly, daily—but the cosmic sovereign would now be called by a new name, which name would be inserted into the hymns in place of the one formerly there. That that did indeed happen is confirmed by the existence of versions of the *Enuma elish* in which the original hero's name was replaced by the name of the Assyrian god Ashur after the Assyrians came to dominate the area, as well as versions in which Ashur's name is replaced by that of the neo-Babylonian god Marduk when the neo-Babylonian empire supplanted the hegemony of Assyria. There is further confirmation in literature from the Palestinian area, the Ugaritic epics, in which the younger Baal Aliyan appears to be supplanting the older El as the cosmic sovereign.[18] Since what happened in this world, on the human, historical scene had no real meaning or significance of its own, what happened when one dynasty supplanted another must only have reflected what occurred in the divine realm. Thus, what we call history—an account of the events that brought about the replacement of one dynasty by another—was not written at all. We can only attempt to reconstruct history by reading between the lines of the myth.

Israel originated as one of those "Amorite," "Habiru" type of peoples, indeed probably as several of them,[19] who existed outside the social-political-cultural order of the ancient Near East. While there has been much scholarly discussion of the issue, there can be no real doubt that "Hebrew," the term used in the Bible by non–Israelites to designate Israelites, is etymologically connected with the term *Habiru* or *'Apiru.*[20] Furthermore, just like others of those peoples, Israel finally took over one of the city-kingdoms and provided from Israelite ranks the dynasty which came to rule it. Jerusalem was that city-kingdom, and David began the dynasty that ruled it. Israel's experience, however, was such, and the historical route by which Israel came onto the stage of ancient Near Eastern society such, that Israel did not follow the course followed by so many peoples like Israel. Israel did not simply take over—or enter right into—the cult and the cosmic mythology which were the setting in which the hymn was the normative song of praise for the ruler of the universe. The character and the *modus operandi* of Yahweh, the God of Israel, were such that the transition could not be made in the same way that it had been elsewhere.

The experience that produced Israel did involve Habiru-like origins. It involved entering into ancient Near Eastern society in the first place under duress, as slaves in Egypt. The experience that Israel remembered as having resulted in its existence was an experience analogous to the one celebrated in the *todah* cult, a deliverance of the kind requiring a song of thanksgiving rather than a hymn. Israel had been unjustly oppressed in Egypt, and had cried out in a lament to its "personal god." Yahweh, its "personal god" had heard their cry, had intervened on Israel's behalf, had acted in the way that divine protectors did in order to merit *todah* songs and sacrifices. Furthermore, in doing so Yahweh had had to take on the Egyptian gods who were supposed to ensure cosmic order, making that act of deliverance more than a smaller, private kind of thing. Yahweh performed an act of deliverance in which the pyramid–shaped order of which the cosmic myth and cult were the justification was overturned. Israel was a band of Habiru who had come to the conviction that order prevailed in the cosmos not by becoming a ruling dynasty that saw the meaning of things as lying primarily in the annual, monthly, daily round of nature. Israel was a band of Habiru who came to the conclusion that order prevailed in the universe by having experienced, as slaves at the bottom of the social pyramid, the action of a personal, saving God whose power was such that it must be the ultimate, final power. Yahweh turned out to be the cosmic sovereign, but not in the usual way celebrated in the cosmic myth and the hymn. Yahweh turned out to be the cosmic God by engaging in a rescue of his devotees from oppression that had cosmic overtones.[21]

Thus, for Israel the nature of the God who ruled the cosmos was such that thanksgiving, *todah*, was the appropriate mode of offering praise to that God. The character of God and the way God worked made the kind of cultic praise that was the setting of the hymn inappropriate. The ruler of the cosmos had turned out not to be the kind of deity whose actions were only indirectly reflected in the round of nature, praise of whom could only be offered indirectly by the human community in verb forms that originated out of reflected actions rather than directly observed and experienced actions. The ruler of the cosmos had turned out to be a deity who chose to be involved and active in the events constituting the life and history of a people, whose actions were directly a part of a people's remembered heritage, praise of whom demanded the recitation in finite verb forms of how Israel had been delivered from slavery and oppression in a remembered course of events. Thanksgiving, *todah*, was demanded as the appropriate praise of the ruler of the cosmos, for *Yahweh* had turned out to be that ruler.

The ways in which human beings think and express themselves are, however, deeply affected by the forms and customs of the cultures in which they live. Though geniuses and prophets and great artists break loose and create new things,[22] it is still the case that what they create will be better understood and appreciated if it is seen against the background of the culture that produced them and of the forms in which that culture expressed itself. So it was with Israel. In spite of the fact that Israel's experience of the nature of Yahweh and of Yahweh's actions demanded thanksgiving as praise, Yahweh *was* being praised as the ruler of the cosmos. The form of song—and sacrifice and cult—in which the culture of which Israel was a part praised a cosmic ruler was the hymn. It is not, therefore, surprising that Israelites might begin to sing *todah* to Yahweh, but, as the singing proceeded, quite unconsciously lapse into modes of expression rooted in the hymn. On the other hand, Israelites might set out to hail Yahweh as the ruler of the cosmos using the hymn form appropriate to doing that, but, given the character and *modus operandi* of Yahweh, quite unconsciously lapse into words and phrases and forms associated with thanksgivings.

What Westermann so emphatically pointed out is, therefore, quite true. The characteristics of hymns and the characteristics of thanksgivings are indeed mixed together in Israel's songs of praise. That is not, however, simply because it was so from the beginning. It came about as a people, thoroughly immersed in the forms and modes of expression of the culture of which they were part, just as any people always is, sought to praise the One they believed to be ruler of the cosmos. It came about as the forms of the culture were used to praise Yahweh as cosmic ruler, but were also strained and transformed and mixed together because of the nature of the One being praised. It came about because in the experience and faith of Israel the divine ruler of the cosmos turned out to be the personal, saving God of a particular people. The forms are indeed there, lying in the background as they always do when human beings express themselves. The forms are, however, mixed together because of what Israel is seeking to express through the forms.

It is significant that Israel's experience and the nature of Yahweh seem to have resulted in another transformation of the forms present in ancient Near Eastern culture. In that culture the thanksgiving—as well as the lament, response to which on the part of the personal god led to thanksgiving—were invariably couched in the first person singular. The lamenter and the giver of thanks was an "I." That is because the set of cultic actions that was the setting of laments and thanksgivings was essentially private. They had to do with the needs and aspirations and deliverances of individual human beings, not with the overarching cosmic issues. When they did have to do with matters of corporate, public concern—as in cultic dramatizations of that battle between order and chaos out of which the universe had come—it was probably the case that they were done by the king as the divinely designated representative of the human community. That "I" laments and thanksgivings were used in both ways—by individuals on their own behalf and by the king on behalf of the whole people in a corporate cult—have led form critics to abandon Gunkel's original classification of them as "laments and thanksgivings of the individual." They are now more usually referred to simply as "I" laments and "I" thanksgivings, as recognition that they could serve a corporate as well as an individual purpose.

Against that background it is striking to note that—in the literature discovered to date—Israel is the only people of the ancient Near East to produce "we" laments and thanksgivings. That is probably due to what resulted in thanksgivings and hymns being mixed, the praise of a God whose character was such that the forms had to be altered and revised to be appropriate. On the one hand, when a form that had been employed in essentially individual, private cultic actions turned out to be the form appropriate for praising the cosmic ruler, the individual "I" just inevitably gave way to a corporate "we." On the other hand, when the link between the divine and human realms turned out to be the life and history of a people rather than a royal personage, "I" also inevitably gave way to "we." Thus, in Israel, a people's experience and Yahweh's nature resulted in the universalization of a private form, in the democratization of a royal form.

What we see happening in both the mixing of thanksgiving with hymn and the move from "I" to "we" is not the result of some conscious, arbitrary, theoretical decision. What we see is the need to conform other forms and ways of expression to *todah* as a norm because of a people's experience of the nature of God. We see *todah* emerging as a norm, a standard, as the idiom of a culture is used by a people to offer praise to a God whose character was manifest in the rescue from oppression of a band of slaves.

Hymn and Thanksgiving: The Mix out of Which Israel Did Theology

A personal, saving God had, in the experience of Israel, become the cosmic, order-bringing God. Yet, because of the character of that God as perceived from the beginning of those saving works through which Israel had become involved with that God, the cultural forms used for supplication and praise underwent change. The process leading to the mixture and transformation described above involved tension and disagreement and conflict. More than one attitude toward the employment of the cultural forms of the ancient Near East can be discerned in the Old Testament. From the perspective of our discussion up to this point, we can appreciate the different emphases and points of view preserved in the Old Testament not only as a result of Israel's formulation of a theology seeking to be true to the *todah* norm but also to make it clear in the culture's terms that Yahweh was the universal God. The process is analogous to what any community of faith goes through as it seeks to understand itself and explain itself to others in the terms of the culture in which it exists.

When the Old Testament narrative has come to the early chapters of the book II Samuel, and David has established his reign in Jerusalem, a Canaanite city-kingdom has become the cultic and political headquarters of the Israelite tribal league. A hymn sanctuary has become the home of the sacred ark of a people for whom *todah* is normative. That set of facts establishes a tension that runs all through Israel's history.[23] We can, on the one hand, see indications in the Old Testament that some Israelites, once Israel found itself at the center of a typical ancient Near Eastern city-kingdom, simply followed a theological method used by other successful Amorite or Habiru peoples again and again. They simply took the songs that had been sung in praise of Baal in the Canaanite culture into which Israel came, and replaced Baal's name with Yahweh's. Psalm 29, which we examined in some detail earlier in this chapter as an example of a hymn, is also a classic example of this method of doing theology.[24]

Psalm 29 pictures Yahweh as a typical ancient Near Eastern cosmic deity presiding in the assembly of the gods. It calls upon those gods to hail Yahweh as sovereign. It goes on, in its body, to picture Yahweh as manifesting power in thunder and lightning and rain and earth's fertility.[25] In a word, it applies to Yahweh all the imagery applied to Aliyan Baal in the Ugaritic literature.[26] What lies behind it is nature as experienced in the area of Syria and Palestine. The summer there is a time of drought in which plants dry up and life seems to give way to death. The Ugaritic epics account for that by telling how Mot, the god of death and infertility, captures Baal, the god of life and fertility, and renders him powerless—maybe even dead.[27] Then the epic goes on to recount how, through the intervention of his sister/consort Anath, Baal is rescued and brought back to life to ride over the earth in power in the thunder clouds. Clearly the imagery has to do with the end of the summer drought and the coming again of life and fertility with the arrival of the fall rains. That imagery is in every line of the body of Psalm 29, and the psalm is thoroughly Canaanite in both its form and its content. What has happened is that Yahweh's name has been substituted for Baal's in what was originally a Canaanite hymn. What is happening theologically is that someone in Israel is insisting that Yahweh and not Baal is the cosmic ruler by making use of a form which served a specific purpose in the culture, and not just by some abstract, theoretical statement.[28] The medium is the message.

That kind of theological statement about Yahweh has, however, completely abandoned the *todah* norm. It may have been dramatically asserted that Yahweh is the cosmic ruler, but there is no mention of any of the uniqueness of Yahweh's character and way of acting. That is why there are indications in the Old Testament that some Israelites would have nothing whatever to do with the hymnic imagery, and refused to make any use at all of the forms that would claim cosmic sovereignty for Yahweh. To do so, in their view, would be to compromise the very nature of Israel's faith, to turn Yahweh into another Baal. It is a point of view that finds expression in one of Israel's songs which did not find its way into the Psalter, but is preserved in the book of Deuteronomy. This song is known as "The Song of Moses," and its form is that of a call to covenant accountability.[29] Here are two of its verses, rendered in such a way as to make clear what they are saying in terms of the present discussion:

When the Cosmic Ruler created the various nations,
Divided up the human community,
That Ruler fixed the number of different peoples
So that it corresponded to the number of divine beings.
Yahweh's portion is Yahweh's *people,*
Jacob Yahweh's *alloted share.*

(DT. 32:8–9)

In spite of innumerable attempts to get around it beginning in the Hebrew text itself, what these verses are saying is very clear.[30] They are not at all concerned to assert that Yahweh is the cosmic ruler. Indeed, the plain sense of the text is that another god is the cosmic ruler and that Yahweh is one of those divine beings to whom a people was assigned by the cosmic ruler. Theological priority in these verses is put on asserting that Yahweh is Israel's God and that Israel is Yahweh's people. The uniqueness of that relationship is what is emphasized. The *todah* norm is being applied so rigorously that there is no attempt whatever to claim universal sovereignty for Yahweh. It is very likely that this kind of theological statement originated in opposition to, or was preserved from the more ancient past and continued to be used in opposition to, the kind of appropriation of cultural forms and the kind of theological statement found in Psalm 29.[31]

Such a sheerly reactionary application of the *todah* norm is, however, finally theologically intolerable. For the fundamental theological question, then as well as now, has to do with what—or who—is finally in control of all things. If the god we worship is not really finally sovereign, then our worship, however much it may mean to us and however much satisfaction we may derive from it, is finally meaningless. Those who appropriated Psalm 29 understood this and were not willing to acclaim Yahweh as merely a personal, private god. They insisted that it was Yahweh and not Baal who was ultimately in charge of the universe. Those who reacted to that and stuck to what the Song of Moses was saying, however, saw an equally important issue: that the nature of Yahweh and Yahweh's *modus operandi* as experienced and remembered in Israel were such that the *todah* norm had always to be applied if the nature of Yahweh was not to be misunderstood.

Those two examples illustrate the tension in the life of ancient Israel from which the witness preserved in the Old Testament came into being. Neither of the two examples, however, is typical of what we normally find in the Old Testament. What happened more typically, as the people, whose very existence was due to an act of deliverance demanding *todah*, sought to give adequate expression to the extent of Yahweh's dominion over the cosmos, was the mixing and transformation of the cultural forms available. The kind of inclusion in the same song of both hymnic and thanksgiving elements that we have already noted in Psalms 33, 135, and 136 is more common than either a Psalm 29 or a statement such as the one found in Deuteronomy 32:8–9. It was in the application of the *todah* norm to the use of cultural ways of acclaiming Yahweh as cosmic ruler, and in the songs and other statements that resulted from them, that Israel's creative development of a theology took place. It was also in the development of an understanding of *todah* as normative for the corporate life of a people and not just as an expression of the relationship of individuals to their private gods—in the shift from "I" to "we" in laments and thanksgivings—that Israel's creative development of a theology took place.

All that, as we see by putting ourselves back into the situation out of which the Old Testament came, did not arise in the first place out of writing divorced from acting things out cultically or from intellectual activity unconnected with life and liturgy. The hymn as a cultural way of stating that Yahweh was indeed the cosmic ruler existed precisely as a song sung in a cultic celebration, not as a piece of poetic literature in a library. The thanksgiving as the norm by which the adequacy or inadequacy of any statement about the nature and activity of Yahweh was judged existed only as part of the total reality denoted by the word *todah*. It existed only as part of a liturgical-cultic-sacrificial reality that was lived in, not just thought about, by those who gave us the Old Testament.

What it comes to is that that to which ultimate appeal was made when the adequacy of statements about God was at issue was not a doctrinal confession of faith, not an agreed upon collection of sacred writings, not a conceptual dogmatic proposition. It was a liturgical, cultic action entered into corporately by a people. It was a liturgical action formed and transformed by the nature of Israel's experience of God. It was a liturgical action, participation in which and acquaintance with which formed and transformed Israel's theological statements. ''Theology as thanksgiving'' is the theme of this book. What that means, arising out of what *todah* was in ancient Israel, is that the norm for doing theology was located in the liturgical life of the people of God.

2
Theology as Thanksgiving: The Israelite Epics

THE transformation described in the previous chapter, in which thanksgiving, *todah*, rather than the hymn and its cult became for ancient Israel the normative praise of God, produced both anthropological and theological consequences of great importance. The anthropology and the theology resulting from that transformation were not only formative of the biblical view of human nature and of God. They were also very influential in the formation of the world view and attitudes of western civilization. The appropriation and transformation of cultural forms by ancient Israel which is focussed in the mixing of the hymn form and the thanksgiving form was the matrix out of which, first, significant theological constructs emerged. It was, second, the matrix out of which the great theological epics that form the Torah and the Former Prophets of the Hebrew Bible (Genesis—II Kings) as well as the narrative complex that is Chronicles, Ezra, and Nehemiah come into being over the centuries of ancient Israel's history. The present chapter is, therefore, an exploration of the theological and anthropological consequences of the application of the *todah* norm to the forms and concepts of ancient Near Eastern culture, and then of the results of that application in the narrative epics of the Old Testament.

The Attribution of Significance to Humanity

One of the consequences of the thanksgiving rather than the hymn becoming the normative mode of praise of the cosmic ruler was the raising of human beings and the human community to a significance they had not previously thought themselves to have. The previous chapter described the way in which the world view and the theology and the anthropology of the hymn assign minimal significance to human beings and to the human enterprise. The decisions and actions that really mattered were, for ancient Near Eastern culture, those that took place in the realm of the gods. What the human community participated in in this world and its history was only reflective of divine decisions and actions. The only ultimate significance of the human community lay in its having been created to perform the menial tasks involved in the care and cultivation of the earth.[1] In the cultic worship that was the setting of the hymn, therefore, human beings participated only indirectly. The sacrifice they offered was sent in its entirety up to the divine realm. They did not really partake of it. The song sung in praise of the cosmic ruler was not one in which the human community directly lauded that god. It was one in which the human community called upon the lesser gods, the ones human beings cried out to in their less than really significant needs, to give to the cosmic ruler the praise that was fitting. Indeed, the lack of any significant direct role by human beings in the praise of the god who really mattered was both reflective of and productive of the ultimate insignificance of humanity and the human enterprise in the ancient Near East. This illustrates one of the basic convictions underlying this book. Liturgical activity is formative of theology as well as of a culture's assessment of the meaning of human life and history.

When, however, the nature of God and of the way God had acted to bring order out of chaos made the thanksgiving, the *todah* cult, the appropriate mode of praise for the cosmic ruler, the role of the human community in the cult came to be quite a different one. That was true in the first place because of what made *todah* appropriate as praise of the cosmic ruler, namely the manifestation of ultimate power and authority in the events of human life and history rather than in extra-worldly and extra-historical events. Moreover, in the second place, that was true because of the very nature of the *todah* cult. *Todah* involved a song in which the one delivered gave thanks to the god who had done the delivering, and it involved a sacrifice in which the one giving thanks and those who had cause to give thanks with that one participated together with the god in enjoying the meat of the animal that had been sacrificed. Where imperative plurals do occur in psalms of thanksgiving—as they do in Psalm 30:4—they are not addressed to divine beings, exhorting them to do the praising. They are addressed to the human family and friends of the giver of thanks, bidding them to participate in the singing of praise to the god as well as to share with the giver of thanks and the god in the sacrificial meal. In other words, in the *todah* cult the human role is significant and direct in relation to the god involved.

Both the events celebrated in *todah* and the form and content of the *todah* liturgy, therefore, assign to human beings and the human community a significance not imparted to them in the predominant cosmic mythology and cult of ancient Near Eastern culture. A human community for which *todah* came to be the norm for worship of the One ultimately in charge of things inevitably began to think different theological thoughts and to form different estimates of the meaning of its own humanity. Those new theological constructs and those new estimates of the worth of humanity are clearly to be seen in the Old Testament.

What we have just been discussing may very well be one of the central influences in the movement of Israel toward monotheism.[2] If the ultimate One has chosen to manifest divine power and authority in the human, historical realm and thus impart significance to the story in which human beings are involved, that plethora of divine beings with which cosmic mythology populated the heavens is not as necessary as it was. Furthermore, if *todah* is the cultic norm and the human community itself directly renders praise to the ultimate One, then the liturgical justification for the existence of the choir of heavenly beings begins to be undermined. It is very likely that realities such as these, rather than any conscious and logically thought out philosophy, led to the monotheism that finally emerged in ancient Israel. Once again, what happened was the result of the interplay between the forms of the culture in which Israel lived and the character and *modus operandi* of the One Israel's experience led it to believe was the cosmic ruler.

An example of this, in which theological monotheism is averred in imagery thoroughly a part of ancient Near Eastern culture, is found in Psalm 82. The form of this psalm seems to be that of a prophetic oracle in which someone reports on what, in an inspired state, was seen and heard when the gods convened in the heavenly temple-palace.[3]

God has taken the chair in the divine assembly,
In the midst of the gods is insisting that right be done:
"How long will you act unjustly,
Making the wicked happy?
Do what is right for the weak and orphaned;
The humble and needy vindicate;
Rescue the weak and poor;
From the power of the wicked snatch them."
(Thus God muses:)
"They (the gods) have no knowledge or ability to discern right from wrong. It is as if they are wandering around in the dark. That is why the earth's very foundations are threatened by chaos."
(So, God addresses the gods:)
"I said originally, 'Gods are what you shall be,[4]
Children of the Cosmic Ruler every one.'
But now (I say), 'Like mortals you shall die,
Like any battle leader you shall fall!'"

(Ps. 82:1–7)

In this psalm Yahweh is pictured, in the fashion of the ancient Near East, as presiding over the assembly of gods in the heavenly realm. The imagery, however, is used to say something quite remarkable, quite different from what it usually expresses. Yahweh begins the address to the divine beings by reminding them of what the responsibilities of a god are. That definition of those responsibilities is quite clearly based on what is celebrated in the *todah* cult. It is the business of a god to work *zedek* on behalf of those who are in need. Here is an explicit statement that the One who is the cosmic ruler is One whose definition of divinity centers on what Israel had experienced in being rescued from bondage in Egypt. Here is a definition of the nature of divinity that justifies *todah* as appropriate praise of the cosmic ruler.

The gods of the divine assembly, however, operate on other principles. They aspire—as the different heroes of the various versions of the *Enuma elish* demonstrate—to become cosmic rulers of the type praised in the cult with which hymns are associated. The gods are out to exalt themselves, not to be deliverers. They want, so to speak, to "make it" by gaining promotion from heroes of *todah* cults to cosmic sovereignty which is praised in the hymnic cult. That, as the psalm puts it, is why the universe is in such shaky condition. Thus the psalm asserts that the true cosmic ruler, Yahweh, has sentenced the gods to death. What is being said here in mythopoeic imagery, that in fact originated in the hymnic cult, is that the character of the One who really is ultimate is such that the gods with which ancient Near Eastern mythology populated the heavenly realm are superfluous, not really needed. Furthermore what is being said is that, insofar as there is any reality to those gods, it is subversive of the good and gracious purposes of the real cosmic ruler for whom *todah* was the meet form of praise. Monotheism is being born in this song, but not out of abstract, logical, philosophical reasoning. Monotheism is coming into being out of the remembered historical experience of a people, out of the kind of liturgical life in which the saving God who participated in that historical experience is praised. Monotheism is to a large degree in the Bible rooted in everything that is contained in the word *todah*, thanksgiving.

Furthermore, the reverse side of the demotion of the gods is the promotion of human beings in terms of a significant role in the universe. Both the action of God in human history that made *todah* the most appropriate praise of the ultimate One and the role played by the human community in *todah* magnified the significance of the human community and the human enterprise. The counterpart in the Old Testament of the theological statement being made in Psalm 82 is the anthropological statement made in the Bible's first chapter:

> God said, "Let us create a race of human beings in our image so that they can share in what we do, and so that they can have authority over the creatures that swim in the sea and the creatures that fly in the heavens and the creatures that dwell on the earth, even over the snakes that crawl around on the earth." So God did create the human race: in the image of the divine beings did God create humanity, created it to be both male and female. And God blessed them, saying, "Be fruitful and multiply, and provide the earth with a population. Bring the earth under your control, and exercise authority over the creatures of the sea and the creatures of the sky, as well as over everything that lives and moves on the earth itself."[5]
>
> (GEN. 1:16–28)

Though the writer of Genesis 1 may not have had Psalm 82 specifically in mind, the two passages together are saying an astounding thing in quite a specific way. They are asserting that Yahweh, the God of Israel, has done away with the divine beings that figured so prominently in the world view of the ancient Near East, and that Yahweh has chosen to assign to human beings the significant role occupied by divine beings in ancient Near Eastern mythology. Against the background of the culture which was the context in which it was written, the doctrine of the "image of God" in humanity set forth in Genesis 1 has to be understood in terms of role and function, not in terms of "being" in some abstract sense. That dominion over creation exercised by the cosmic ruler through the various gods in the view of the ancient Near East has now been assigned to human beings. That is the sense in which humanity bears the likeness of the divine. The real ruler of the cosmos has taken away from the gods the role that was originally theirs, and has cast human beings in that role.

The roots of that understanding of the nature of humanity and the human enterprise lie, as does Israel's theology, in an understanding of God's character and God's activity that makes *todah*, thanksgiving, the appropriate form for praising God. They lie in an understanding of reality rising out of concrete, human, historical experience, not out of what is observed in nature's cycle being interpreted as the reflection of events that transpire outside the world in which human beings live and the history in which they participate. The roots of that understanding of humanity and of the human enterprise lie in the *todah* cult in which the human community is the body which offers directly to the saving God the praise that God's saving activity prompts. Moreover, that understanding makes it necessary for the recital of Israel's own history to figure centrally in its liturgy and its theology. It requires anthropology and theology, as well as cult, to be *todah*, thanksgiving.

Covenant Understanding of Divine Sovereignty

Closely connected with the theology and the understanding of the significance of humanity described above is Israel's covenant understanding of the nature of God's sovereignty over the world and of the nature of the relationship between God and Israel as a people. Israel's faith required that there be found another explanation of God's role and of the way God and the human race were related to one another than was present in the myth and cult that gave rise to the hymn. The character of the One who turned out, on the basis of Israel's historical experience, really to be in charge of the universe was such that the predominant theological images of the ancient Near East just would not do.

Communities of faith must always articulate their faith in words and concepts and images available to them in the cultures in which they exist. Human language and human thought forms are the only things available to human beings to use in understanding and communicating their faith in God.[6] The theological enterprise, for Israel in the ancient Near Eastern world as for the Christian Church in the first centuries of its existence, does not consist of putting into writing dogmas that come directly down from heaven with no real relationship to human language or thought. The theological enterprise always involves the struggle of a human community of faith, believing in and seeking the guidance of God in that struggle, to find in the cultural heritage wherein it stands the thoughts and concepts and words and images which do the most justice to what faith demands be expressed about the nature of God and the nature of the relationship between God and the human community.

Ancient Israel clearly perceived in the concept of covenant the expression which did justice to what Israel had discerned to be the nature of God and of God's sovereignty, as well as to the nature of the relationship between God and the people God had chosen to replace that heavenly court with which the cosmic sovereigns of that place and time were usually believed to be surrounded. Furthermore, modern study of the culture of the ancient Near East as the background of the Bible has revealed the way in which, in taking up covenant as the concept that should normatively describe the character of God's authority and of God's relationship to human beings, Israel made creative use of a concept present in Israel's cultural world, a concept apparently not used elsewhere in a theological way.[7]

The covenant formularies in the Old Testament follow a certain pattern. That pattern is present in its classical form in the decalogue (Ex. 20:1ff., Dt. 5:6ff.). First, God is identified by name: "I am Yahweh your god." Second, there is an historical preface which provides the background of the covenant stipulations ("words" is the Hebrew term): "who brought you up out of the land of Egypt." Third, the covenant stipulations themselves are set forth—the "thou shalts" and the "thou shalt nots." The stipulations really boil down to two things: only Yahweh is to be recognized in life as well as worship as God, as sovereign; and the people of the covenant are to conduct themselves in relation to the human community as if only Yahweh is sovereign, never presuming to exploit another human being in any way. That pattern has been shown by scholars to have been taken over from treaties made by ancient Near Eastern rulers—most notably Hittite rulers who were present in Palestine not long before Israel's appearance there—with kings and peoples over whom those rulers were sovereign. Such treaties began with the naming of the ruler in question, continued with an historical preface in which it was narrated how the subjects owed their very existence to the graciousness of the ruler in not destroying them in his conquest of the territory over which he was sovereign, and then went on to a set of stipulations. However detailed and elaborate the stipulations might be, what they all came down to was the requirement that the ruler in question, and that ruler alone, be recognized as sovereign, and that the internal and external affairs of the people in question be conducted as if only that ruler were sovereign.

Thus, while in one sense it is anachronistic to say so because of the way in which the ancient world never separated what we call the sacred and the secular, Israel really chose what was in its world essentially a political form in order to give expression to the nature of God's sovereignty and of the relationship between the sovereign God and Israel itself. Israel chose a political form for the purpose, and rejected as normative that explanation of the character of the divine sovereignty which centered in the realm of nature and found expression in the myth and cult out of which the hymn form took its origin. That was one strong reason why, in Israel, the hymn form came to be modified by the admixture of *todah* elements. A divine sovereignty which was essentially political required a recitative, historical mode of praise. The consequences of Israel's choice of such a form were, however, much more than liturgical.

Israel's choice of the covenant form to characterize the nature of the relationship between God and the human community provides one of the most striking examples of a principle enunciated at the very beginning of this book: that the medium, the form, used to say something can very often convey a more significant message than the content itself. Indeed, the form appropriated by Israel to express the way in which God was believed to be sovereign and related to Israel said something so basic and fundamental that the relationship was absolutely unique, irrespective of the particular content that might be found in this or that particular instance of the use of the form. What the form, just by being used, stated was that Yahweh was more like a ruler in the historical, political realm in which the human community really lives than like the kind of god who had to be talked about in the cosmic mythology of the *Enuma elish* or the Ugaritic epics. What the form, just by being used, stated was that the relationship between Yahweh and Israel was more like the relationship between a ruler and the people governed by that ruler here in the historical, political realm than like the kind of relationship between gods and human beings which was only indirectly reflected in nature and symbolized in the myths and cults that were based on nature's cycles.

The consequences of the fundamental place of the covenant form in Israel's theology and self-understanding were tremendous. For one thing, Yahweh as a God was not the symbol of something that lay behind what was narrated about Yahweh and that was finally more real than Yahweh was. Yahweh was not a symbol, but, to use biblical terminology, Yahweh was "the *living* God." Yahweh could not be, finally, "demythologized" so that the human mind could finally grasp—as the human mind was supposed to do when ancient Near Eastern cosmic mythology gave way to philosophy—what Yahweh "stood for." All the concepts used to say things about Yahweh *could* be demythologized: even the covenant concept itself; indeed, even the concept "god" as the best category into which human minds could fit Yahweh. *Yahweh*, however, ultimately transcended all the concepts. Yahweh, the living God, was finally the reality being dealt with—in the same way that one's friend or parent or spouse, a living being, is finally the reality being dealt with in a human relationship and transcends all the categories such as lover, male, female, white, black, and so on.

For another thing, it was impossible for the people for whom the covenant form was the normative mode of understanding their relationship to God ever to recognize any human, historical ruler or structure as finally sovereign over them. Only God, given what the covenant form itself implies, regardless of the specific content the form might convey at any particular time or place, is sovereign. That, and not mere political differences or royal immoralities, is the reason for the tension and conflict that existed between Israelite kings and the prophets who were constantly calling the kings to covenant accountability.[8] That is the basis on which the exilic prophets, members of an on the whole quite insignificant people, presumed to announce that the great Cyrus was the servant of Yahweh, whose real historical destiny and significance was to be the means by which Israel's God reestablished the temple cult in Jerusalem.[9]

That was the reason that the heirs of ancient Israel's covenant understanding of God and God's rule—Jews and Christians—got into trouble in the Roman empire. The Romans, religious heirs to a large extent of ancient Near Eastern cosmic mythology, saw the heirs of ancient Israel's faith as atheists, not devotees of any *proper* god at all.[10] Furthermore, while it was possible for the Romans to tolerate that, what could *not* be tolerated was the claim of the Jewish and Christian heirs of the faith of ancient Israel to be subjects of the *real* emperor. There was the real issue: the claim of Yahweh's exclusive sovereignty implied in the covenant understanding of the relationship between God and God's people, not the emperor's divinity.[11]

The appropriation of the covenant form by Israel had, therefore, far-reaching consequences, consequences which continue to have their effect theologically, socially, politically in western civilization itself—and not just in synagogue and Church—down to this very day.[12] One final consequence of that appropriation, and one which is directly connected with what is being described in this book, was the reinforcement of *todah*, recitative thanksgiving, as the appropriate form of praise of Yahweh. Basic and central to the covenant understanding of God and God's relation to the human community was what was represented by the function of the historical preface in the covenant form. The very basis of the covenant relationship between a sovereign and a subject people lay in the series of events narrated in the covenant's preface. They substantiated God's claim to be associated with Israel as sovereign. More profoundly, they were the real basis of any theological statements, for, since Yahweh was the living God and not the symbol of some abstract truth, theology had to be done by recounting the course of events in which Yahweh had been involved and not by producing abstractions of which Yahweh was symbolic. The process was analogous to the way in which, in order finally to convey the reality of *who* a living someone is, we have to tell that person's story and not engage in racial or sexual or social or psychological or statistical abstractions. Israel's God was, in other words, the kind of God kept in touch with in the *todah* cult, as God's story involving Israel's deliverance was thankfully recited and as sacrifice was offered to God but also partaken of by that human community with which God had chosen to be involved. Thus it was that the theology of which Israel's God was the subject had to be based on *todah*, recitative thanksgiving. The norm, the standard, the canon for the adequacy of theology in ancient Israel was located in the course of events in which a people had found itself involved with God. Theology could not be done without reference to the participation by theologians in the *todah* cult, which was the place where the stuff of the only adequate basis for theology continued to live.

Narrative Recital as the Basis of Theology

The result of that fundamental characteristic of ancient Israel's life described above was that Israel consistently did theology through interpretative recital of its own history. Narration of the course of events in which faith discerned God present in the life and history of a people was the *form* theology took in ancient Israel.[13] It all began, apparently, very far back, long before the major narrative strands of the Old Testament came into being. Careful examination of the Old Testament narratives reveals the existence, in larger and later literary contexts, of what appear to be very ancient summaries of the story of God's involvement with Israel in the events of history. Gerhard von Rad called those summaries *credos*.[14] One such summary, made famous by von Rad's use of it as a basic example of the kind of *credo* in Israel's tradition that led to larger narrative recitals, is found in Deuteronomy:

> I am descended from a nomadic nobody who, part of a very small company, migrated to Egypt, and lived there long

> enough to become a people impressive in number and strength. The Egyptians, though, treated us badly, humiliated us, cruelly enslaved us and oppressed us. So, we cried out to Yahweh the God of our ancestors for help, and we were heard, and the humiliation and hardship and distress we were suffering were noted. And Yahweh freed us from Egypt's oppression with a mighty hand and an outstretched arm, with deeds that struck terror into the hearts of their beholders, with clear indications that a more than human power was at work. Thus it was that Yahweh guided us to this place, and made us a present of this land, a land the like of which we never expected to have.
>
> (Dt. 26:5–9)

Deuteronomy understands this little *credo* to be what is recited by an Israelite at a sacred place in bringing the first fruits of the harvest as an offering to Israel's God. The point is that such an offering is accompanied by thankful recital, by what is in essence *todah*. Many such passages are embedded in the Old Testament. A longer *credo* is, for example, found in Joshua 24:2–13. Its narrative setting is the entry into the land of Canaan of Israel under the leadership of Moses' successor, Joshua. Having entered the promised land, Israel engages in a solemn renewal of the vows by which they are bound to Yahweh in the covenant relationship. The recital that constitutes the *credo* clearly serves the purpose of the historical preface on which the covenant itself is based. Other examples of the same kind of thing are found in the Psalter, particularly in such psalms as 78, 105, and 106, designated by Gunkel as "legends"—that is, as recitals of Israel's story. These all seem to reflect the way in which, on important occasions, Israel interpreted the theological significance of its life by reciting its story according to a set pattern and in an interpretative way.

Von Rad's important contribution was the identification, through the examination of the passages just cited, of the form which underlies that great narrative complex running, in English versions of the Old Testament, from Genesis through II Kings—a narrative which is repeated in another and shorter form in I and II Chronicles, Ezra, and Nehemiah.[15] What seems to have happened at certain discernible points of social and political and cultural transition in the history of ancient Israel is that Israel's theology and anthropology—what Israel believed about God and the significance of the human enterprise—were rethought, reinterpreted, and restated. All this seems to have been done consistently in a narrative, epic way, the basis or outline or form of what was done being that outline and form which is there in those shorter and more ancient *credos* described above. It is probably evident by now, given the numerous times we have had occasion to point it out, that the cultic roots of the process undoubtedly lay in *todah*.

In fact, it seems to have started back in the earliest period of Israel's existence in Palestine, back in the period before David and the monarchy, back when Israel was only beginning to be conscious of itself as a people gathered out of various clan and tribal backgrounds by Yahweh's intervention in history. There seems to have taken place back then, probably in the shaping of an oral epic rather than in the writing of "literature" in the later sense of the word,[16] a narrative relating the traditions of the various elements that made up Israel to one another as well as to the fundamental narrative outline present in the early *credos*. The result of that process was the formation of what Martin Noth called the *Grundlage*, the basic, traditional outline on which all subsequent recitals of Israel's story depended.[17] What seems to have happened was that a confederation of tribes, the common background of each being Habiru in various ways, found itself increasingly in control of Palestine, increasingly replacing the Canaanite city-kingdoms as the significant power in the area. The theological significance of what was happening was not, on the whole, treated by seeking to insert Yahweh's name into the cosmic myth. Quite to the contrary, the theological significance of what was happening was stated by relating the backgrounds of the various tribes and clans that history had brought into the particular Habiru amalgamation that was Israel to that central *todah* recital of how Yahweh had brought a people to life out of the death that was oppression in Egypt. The *Grundlage* took shape as an Israelite theology emerged from various experiences being given thankful expression in the *todah* cult.

A crucial turning point in Israel's life came when, the Israelite tribal confederation having been destroyed by the Philistines, David resurrected Israel as an ancient Near Eastern power with its center in Jerusalem, the origins of which were thoroughly Canaanite in character. On the one hand, the people of Yahweh now provided the dynasty through which order was maintained on the earth, and Yahweh had turned out to be the cosmic sovereign who had designated that dynasty as the ensurer of divine order. On the other hand, however, Israel continued to remember how the ark, the symbol of Yahweh's presence, had come to rest in Jerusalem's holy place as a result of a series of historical events that centered on war with the Philistines.[18] All the issues focussed in the tension between the two points of view represented by Psalm 29 and Deuteronomy 32 came to the fore. When a people which had identified itself and understood its God over against the culture of the ancient Near East found itself in power at one of the centers of that culture, controlling one of its city-kingdoms, the question of what it all meant theologically and anthropologically inevitably arose. We have already seen how one answer was simply that Yahweh had turned out to be what Baal had been thought to be, and how another answer was that the only terms on which Yahweh could be understood at all were those used in the old, simpler, premonarchical days. We have seen how one answer was that Israel was the people whose God had turned out to be cosmic sovereign because Israel was the people from whom that God chose a royal dynasty, and how another answer was that Israel must have nothing at all to do with the civilization and culture of the ancient Near East, least of all with royal dynasties.

It was out of that set of tensions that the great Yahwist epic (the J document) came into existence.[19] The Yahwist is aware of what a heady and exciting thing it is for Israel to find itself at the center of a city-kingdom and for Yahweh to have turned out to be the sovereign who rules over the whole universe. The Yahwist is clearly enthusiastic about all that, and celebrates it. The Yahwist is also, however, unwilling to settle for the overly simple theological position of those who would just insert Yahweh's name into Baal's songs and cult. The Yahwist is aware of the uniqueness of Yahweh's character and of Israel's understanding of itself. The center and basis of the Yahwist epic was, therefore, that historical experience narrated at its briefest in the little *credo* in Deuteronomy 26, the account of how Israel originated as a people in connection with Yahweh's intervention to rescue slaves from Egyptian oppression. Neither, though, is the Yahwist willing to settle for that other overly simple theological position which insisted that Israel must continue just as it had, as if its existence had not been affected at all by the subsequent course of events that put the ark in Jerusalem and David on his throne.

What the Yahwist does is to take seriously the perspective present at the time at which the epic came into being. That perspective includes the concern of Canaanite cosmic-mythological faith with nature and the struggle in nature between chaos and order. It includes a consciousness of varied traditions about the origins of the clans and tribes and villages and places that are now parts of the amalgam that is Israel and the Davidic kingdom. It includes the course of events that led from Israel's origins in rescue from Egypt and the establishment of the covenant between Yahweh and Israel to Israel's occupation and conquest of

Canaan and the eventual establishment of the Davidic kingdom. From that perspective the Yahwist perceives Yahweh's character and purpose to be just as good and gracious as ever, but to involve a dominion infinitely more vast than had been dreamed in earlier days or than was being conceived of in the present by more narrow visioned and reactionary devotees of Yahweh. The Yahwist insists that it is Yahweh, not Baal or someone else, who is in fact responsible for the order in the universe that makes life possible, as well as for the origin of the human race. Yahweh's purpose for the world and for humanity is filled with promise and good, and that purpose has worked itself out through the people and events remembered in the traditions of the various elements of the Davidic kingdom. That good purpose was most clearly manifest in the time of Moses, when oppressive enslavement was supplanted by a chance for freedom and new life. The promise continued to be operative as Israel was guided through the desert and then experienced bad times at the hands of the Canaanites and the Philistines, but the goodness of Yahweh's purpose and the fulfillment of Yahweh's promise are now clear in the position Israel occupies in control of a land under the kingship of David. Thus, the Yahwist takes a theological position that is affirmative of what is there in the Davidic monarchy, but that does so without simply making Yahweh another Baal. The Yahwist takes a theological position that has at its center the older Israelite faith, but that does not close its eyes to present issues and realities.

Moreover, the Yahwist presents this impressive theological set of affirmations in a narrative running from the world's beginnings to the time of David, in the form of an epic.[20] Theological reflection takes place as the history that led to the point at which the Yahwist stood is recounted from the perspective of a faith, in an interpretative way. It is out of the ethos and experience of *todah* that the Yahwist epic is formulated. Its form, and therefore its content as well, is able to incorporate all sorts of things that had entered into Israel's heritage from Canaanite culture without becoming simply another product of that culture. The reason for that is that the source of the Yahwist's identity is the *todah* cult of Yahweh and not the cosmic-mythological cult of Baal.

Only a generation or so, however, after the establishment of that Davidic era which the Yahwist saw as the fulfillment of God's promises from the beginning, the kingdom split in two. The reason for the split was the continuing tension between those who were affirmative of what had happened under David and those who insisted that Israel could not be Israel and participate in any way in Canaanite culture. Tensions present even at the beginning of David's reign, and which erupted in the revolts of Absalom and Sheba while David was still alive, came to a head at the death of Solomon.[21] The ten tribes whose territories lay to the north of Jerusalem and whose traditions were most rooted in what was peculiarly Israelite broke away from the Davidic kingdom, designating themselves, significantly, as "Israel." Israel was by this time, however, too much established as the power controlling the area to function without structures through which government could be carried out, and the only such structures known in the culture were monarchical. So it was that "Israel" too became a kingdom. The resistance to kingship and all that it implied, however, was still there and, as a result, for a century and a half no dynasty established itself in the northern kingdom. Throughout that period the story of the northern kingdom was repeatedly one in which the successor to a deceased king was assassinated and a fresh ruler assumed power. Finally, in the middle of the ninth century B.C., a general named Omri decided that stability was necessary and that the only viable basis for stability was a monarchy erected on the model of Canaanite kingdoms. Omri's son and heir Ahab, therefore, married the Canaanite princess Jezebel, thereby establishing working relations with the Canaanites, and Samaria was built as a city to replace for the northern kingdom what Jerusalem had come to mean under David and Solomon.

All that, however, produced a violent anti-Canaanite-culture, pro-Yahweh-and-Israel revolution led in succession by two figures paralleling Moses and Joshua of old, namely Elijah and Elisha. The result of that revolution was the establishment of the dynasty of Jehu, under which the northern kingdom committed itself to strict loyalty to Yahweh and to the old Israelite traditions. When the revolution had run its course and its results were reality, Israel, or at least one significant segment of Israel, found itself at a new and crucial point in its life. Apparently at that point a new and fresh theological assessment of the nature of God and of the meaning of Israel's existence was made in that stratum of the Old Testament narrative designated the Elohist (or the E document) by Old Testament scholars.[22] Just as the Yahwist had dealt with what the theological significance of the emergence of the Davidic monarchy might be, so the Elohist dealt with the theological significance of the Israel that existed as a result of that intervention of Yahweh into the life of the northern kingdom through Elijah and Elisha.

As might be expected, the theological views of the Elohist were very different from those of the Yahwist. A product of the prophetic revolution against the Canaanizing policies of Omri and Ahab, the Elohist was much more strictly Yahwistic and Israelite than the Yahwist. For the Elohist, the beginning of anything significant at all was connected with the beginning of the existence of Israel as God's people. The Elohist epic, therefore, has nothing to say about the creation of the world, thus avoiding the contamination of its theology with anything at all borrowed from Canaanite culture.[23] The Elohist begins directly with God's call to Abraham, the Elohist version of that call being found at Genesis 15:1ff. The Elohist conceives of that call as having come in the set phrase in which prophets like Elijah and Elisha labelled their pronouncements as having originated directly with God as had the covenant stipulations pronounced by Moses: "Now the word of Yahweh came . . ." Thus, from the beginning, the Elohist sees Israel as living under the word of God, "word" being the Hebrew word for the stipulations of the covenant. The Elohist emphasizes the centrality of Moses and the deliverance from Egypt and the sealing of the covenant not only by giving much more space in its narrative to those things than had the Yahwist, but also by holding that it was not until Moses that God's specific name, Yahweh, was revealed. The Elohist emphasizes Samuel rather than Saul or David, is negative about the Davidic monarchy and positive about the secession of "Israel" from it, and seems to reach its climactic conclusion in the extended accounts of the careers of Elijah and Elisha in which errant Israel was finally called back from Canaanite hypostasy to loyalty to Yahweh.[24]

Thus, the Elohist reacts strongly against what the Yahwist had affirmed, adopts a view of Yahweh's nature and purposes that is very different from that of the Yahwist, sees the meaning of Israel's existence in quite different terms from those in which the Yahwist sees them. Yet the Elohist and the Yahwist have very much in common. They obviously recognize the same things as making Israel uniquely what it is. They are both concerned to bear witness that Yahweh is the One whose sovereignty and whose purposes give things their meaning. They both take Israel as Yahweh's people, and therefore Israel's life and history, to be central to the meaning of things. They both participate in that Israelite faith in which a human community has been given the significance and assigned the role which elsewhere belong to divine beings. Finally and centrally, they both do theology by constructing an interpretative narrative. Different as they are in the content of their theologies, *todah* is the place where their common method originated, for it is the *todah* cult that has formed the fundamental outlook of both.

A third crucial point in Israel's theological history came two centuries or more after the Elohist, near the end of the seventh century B.C. The historical setting was one in which the Assyrians had invaded Palestine, had destroyed the northern kingdom of Israel and also devastated most of the territory of the southern, Davidic kingdom of Judah, and had laid siege to Jerusalem itself—only finally to withdraw for reasons of their own. The setting was one following the reigns of several kings who had been subjects, and even backers, of the Assyrians, and in which King Josiah had finally asserted the independence of what was left of the kingdom of Judah. That assertion took the form of a thorough reformation of theological and cultic life, and led what was left of Israel after the Assyrian invasion to a dramatic recommitment, under Josiah, to the Mosaic covenant.[25]

In that setting the theological significance of the existence of Israel was once again treated in what is called by Old Testament scholars the Deuteronomic History of Israel.[26] The deuteronomic historians pondered particularly the tragic history that had run from the death of Solomon to the Assyrian conquest and domination of the land that had lasted right up to the time of Josiah. Their theological position was much more like that of the Elohist than that of the Yahwist. The God of Israel and the people of Israel were their exclusive focus. They had really no interest at all in the cosmos as a whole or in the other peoples around them in the world, except as those peoples were enemies of Yahweh and Yahweh's purposes. Yet their exclusiveness was tempered by their awe at the tender love of Yahweh for Israel.

The Deuteronomists, began, therefore, straightaway with Moses and God's calling of Israel into existence through Moses, not with Israel's ancient ancestors. They began their history with that account of what Moses was about and what Moses taught that is the book of Deuteronomy, and that is why they are called the deuteronomic historians. They seem to have made use of various pieces of narrative that had come out of the long life of Israel in putting their history together, and probably even used material covering the period after Moses that had been put together by the Yahwist and the Elohist. As they recounted what had transpired after Moses, they were single-mindedly concerned with one set of issues. Their focus was on the absolute covenant claim of Yahweh on Israel and Israel's response to that claim. That claim and that claim alone was what gave life meaning, whether Israel was obedient to the claim or disobedient. The recital of Israel's history given by the Deuteronomists was a catalogue of how loyalty to the covenant had consistently brought blessing and how violation of the covenant had brought disaster, and they traced that through the era of Joshua and the period of the judges, through the time of Samuel and Saul and David into the two monarchies and up to the time of Josiah.

The thesis of the Deuteronomists was that the real succession by which Israel's history was held together was not royal but prophetic. They held that the continuity in terms of which Israel's history had to be understood lay in the succession of prophets, beginning with Moses, through whom God's covenant demands had been voiced, and that only David and one or two other kings had ever been loyal to the covenant at all. It was precisely the disobedience of the kings to the prophets and the demands of the covenant that had brought about the splitting up of David's kingdom and the Assyrian invasions and all the disasters that had befallen Israel. They saw Josiah as the one who had finally seen the point, had even got the point out of their own basic book when it was found in the temple, who was the descendant of David and the disciple of Moses under whom a chastened remnant of Israel could now be what Israel had been meant to be from the beginning. Just as the Elohist, therefore, had probably concluded with the account of Elijah and Elisha, the Deuteronomists concluded with the account of the great reformation of Josiah and his great Passover ceremony of affirmation of the Mosaic covenant which is found in II Kings 22:1—23:25.

The Deuteronomists had very soon, however, to revise their work and produce a second edition.[27] Not much more than two decades after Josiah's reformation the Babylonians filled up the vacuum of power left by the Assyrian withdrawal from the Palestinian area. As they moved to do so, Pharoah Necho of Egypt marched northward through Palestine to encounter them, and, when Josiah went out to inform Necho of his new policy of independence, Necho killed him. Events then went from bad to worse, and the glorious promise present in Josiah and his reformation collapsed. Events led rapidly to the exile of the political and cultic leaders of Israel to Babylon and to the situation which obtains as the final version of the Deuteronomic History concludes at the end of II Kings. While the Deuteronomists had to revise what they had done in order to take those things into account, the broad outline of their work and their basic thesis remained the same as always. It was just that it had turned out that the disloyalty of Israel and Israel's kings to the covenant with Yahweh had really been so great that not even the faithfulness and the reforming zeal of Josiah were capable of averting the judgment that the accumulated sins of Israel had made inevitable. Minimal revisions by the Deuteronomists, therefore, resulted in the final form of their work embracing what in fact happened after the time of Josiah.

Once again, in the work of the Deuteronomists a theological interpretation of the life and history of Israel has taken place. That interpretation embodies a theology very different from the theology of the Yahwist. It is a theology more like that of the Elohist, though different in perspective at many points. The Deuteronomic History does, however, have in common with both the Yahwist and the Elohist what the Yahwist and the Elohist have in common with one another, namely a method of doing theology. That method, for all three, is the recounting of Israel's history in an interpretative way. *Todah* clearly lies in the background still.

The same kind of thing happened again in the exilic and postexilic period as that strand in the biblical narrative designated by scholars as the Priestly Code (or the P document) held that the meaning of Israel's existence lay in its being neither a nation nor a kingdom but the cultic congregation called into being by the one, true God to worship that God properly.[28] The Priestly Code interpreted the history of the universe itself, as well as the history of Israel, in terms of various elements in Israel's cultic observance. Creation, in which the week arranges itself into seven days, finds its meaning in the sabbath. The covenant with Noah after the primeval deluge was the basis of the dietary laws. The covenant made with Abraham, as God began to bring the people of God into existence, was the basis of the institution of circumcision. Finally, the content of the covenant between God and Israel of which Moses was the mediator was, for the Priestly Code, the provisions of the sacrificial cult through which it was the vocation of Israel to be, on the human scene, a continual witness to the existence and sovereignty of the one, true God.

The Priestly Code is much more a handbook of procedures for those responsible for the cult than anything else. Yet it explains and justifies those procedures, and gives them a theological rationale, by reciting Israel's history in its own interpretative way from the beginning of things to the covenant with Moses. The Priestly Code is very different from the Yahwist in its theology, ignoring social and political structures completely, and concentrating exclusively on sheerly religious concerns. It is very different from the Elohist in its incorporation into its specifications for the cult many things that are undoubtedly Canaanite in origin. It is different from the Deuteronomic History in its complete lack of interest in anything that transpired in Israel after Moses. Nevertheless, the Priestly Code conforms to what has been true of all the strands preceding it in the process leading to the formation of the Old Testament narrative. What it has to say theologically is said in narrative form. Different as its approach and its theological content may be from those of its predecessors, *todah* remains the ethos out of which it arises.

The process by which all the strands we have mentioned here, J and E and D and P, came in various stages to be combined into the narrative that presently runs from the beginning of Genesis through the ending of II Kings is too complicated to trace here, and attempts to reconstruct it require a great deal of speculation.[29] The interesting thing is how those responsible for it felt no compunction whatever about weaving into one fabric a series of documents differing greatly in content and theological perspective. The abstract content of theology was obviously not the issue. The fundamental thing, and this is our thesis, was the recitative mode of doing theology which all the strands, as well as the combination of them into one, have in common. Indeed, it was as if it was necessary to continue the process in which Israel's theology was done by narration, to keep all the results of that process in relation to one another. The basis of theology in Israel was *todah*, thankful recital of the course of events through which Israel believed itself to have been involved with and related to Yahweh. Thus, the norm, the standard, that made very different things compatible with one another was not abstract, theological content. It was their roots, different as their abstract content might be, in the common experience of the *todah* cult. That was the basis on which the great, complicated narrative of Genesis—II Kings came into being over the course of centuries as Israel pondered and witnessed to its life as God's people.

Furthermore, the tradition continued even after the principal narrative complex of Israel's Bible had taken shape. Although it comes in the Hebrew Bible in that concluding section called the Writings, after Genesis—II Kings and the books of the prophets, the smaller narrative complex formed by I and II Chronicles, Ezra, and Nehemiah follows directly upon Genesis—II Kings in English translations of the Old Testament.[30] That complex came into being in the postexilic period. It is yet another retelling of Israel's story.[31] The Chronicler—that being the name given by scholars to the writer of this work—has a theology built on aspects of what the great prophets had been saying about Israel's national pretensions through the years leading to Israel's collapse and exile, but principally on the view of Israel held in the Priestly Code. For the Chronicler's epic, all history from the beginning led to the reestablishment of the temple cult in Jerusalem at the end of the exilic period in which Nehemiah and Ezra figured significantly. History up to David is summarized in genealogies. The significance of David and the monarchy in Chronicles lies solely in their being the agents that made the establishment of the temple cult possible. The northern kingdom is entirely ignored, and kings after David—even Josiah who is so much a hero to the Deuteronomists—are uniformly faulted for taking the monarchy to be an end in itself and not merely the protector and patron of the temple cult. Finally, the collapse of the monarchy at the hands of the Babylonians is taken to have happened so that Israel could cease being a nation and exist only as the cultic community whose vocation it is to render proper worship to the one, true God. Cyrus the Persian and his successors have replaced the Davidic monarchy as the protectors and patrons of the temple cult. Thus, the worship offered to God day by day in the postexilic temple is what the long life of Israel was finally really all about.

The view of the Chronicler is quite different from the views of the epics which, combined, form the great complex that is Genesis—II Kings. Neither the universalism of

J and P that relates Israel to the whole of world history nor the intense passion for covenant righteousness that characterizes E and D is present. Furthermore, the Chronicler concentrates solely on that Jewish community that centers around the temple in Jerusalem, and ignores all those Jews of the postexilic period living in Mesopotamia and Egypt and around the Mediterranean, ignores all those places where the richness of what was to be the Judaism that survived the destruction of the temple was coming into being. Yet, in spite of the difference in content and even of the shallowness of content, the Chronicler stands in a definitely discernible tradition. Theology is still being done by reciting Israel's history in an interpretative way. *Todah* is still the basis of theology, both as the form utilized and as the cult, participation in which gives the theologian an identity and a point of view.

In all these strata which, together, finally form the Law and the Former Prophets—as well as a significant part of the Writings—the theological consequences of the replacement of hymnic praise by *todah* as the most fitting and normative mode of praise of the One who turned out to be the cosmic ruler are working themselves out. The God whose purposes and actions give the cosmos its meaning, having chosen to be involved and active in the course of events that is the human enterprise, rather than in events transpiring in some suprahistorical and prehistorical realm, it is the human, historical story that has to be dealt with to get at the meaning of things. That God having chosen a human congregation rather than a divine assembly to be the choir that sings the divine praises, human beings and human actions and human decisions assume a significance that requires their being taken seriously in the doing of theology. The theological consequences of the replacement of hymnic praise by *todah* continued to be present in the Yahwist, the Elohist, the Deuteronomists, the writers of the Priestly Code, and the Chronicler—as well as in the redactors who put the various epics together—not because all of them continued through a long history to hold some common, conceptual, intellectual, doctrinal position. The theological consequences worked their way out through very different ages of history, and in very different views of God and Israel and the world, as the common ground on which the various theological interpreters stood continued to be Israel's *todah* cult. *Todah* in that sense was the norm, the standard, the canon in relation to which widely differing Israelite theologians worked.

Todah's Final Transformation of Hymnic Mythology

It was in the conscious theologizing that took place as the great epics came into being and were put together into a vast whole that what had begun as Israel's experience made it inevitable that *todah* elements be mixed into hymns and hymnic elements be mixed into thanksgiving songs reached a significant conclusion. The cosmic mythology of the ancient Near East, which was the ethos out of which hymns originated, provided a coherent and complete interpretation of what the cosmos was all about. It constituted a myth: a statement of what "the story on things" really was.[32] What had happened when the theologizing of that succession of Israelite theologians whose work was informed by *todah* was finished was that a new myth had come into being, a new "story on the meaning of things," and the myth of ancient Near Eastern culture had been deposed as *the* myth and utilized only as part of a myth of quite a different kind. In this concluding section of the present chapter that observation will be given concrete content through an examination of three things. Two of them have to do with the use of cosmic mythology in the Yahwist and the Priestly Code, and one has to do with an issue in modern biblical theology.[33]

We begin with an examination of *the creation story from the Priestly Code* found in Genesis 1:1—2:4a.[34] It has long been observed that this narrative bears some kind of relation to the *Enuma elish*, the Mesopotamian version of the myth accounting for the existence of the universe by telling of the primeval battle between the forces of order and the forces of chaos. It has also long been pointed out how, in many particulars, the biblical version is significantly different from the *Enuma elish*. *Tohu*—chaos, the goddess Tiamat in the Mesopotamian myth—has been demythologized, is a some*thing,* not a some*one*. That is because, for the Priestly Code which stood at the conclusion of that dynamic movement toward monotheism discussed above, there was only *one* God, not an assembly of many gods. The heavenly bodies, sun and moon and stars, are not living beings in the Priestly Code, are not gods as they are in Mesopotamian mythology. They too are demythologized, and find their meaning only in relation to the human, historical enterprise. They exist to give light and to provide a means by which the human community may know when the seasons come around, when years begin and end, when the various festivals should be celebrated. These are only examples, and other significant internal differences between Genesis 1 and what is, in some way, its prototype could be catalogued.

The specific internal differences do not, however, constitute the most interesting and significant difference between Genesis 1 and the *Enuma elish*. Indeed, the character of the specific internal differences arises out of what is more significant, and the thing that is more significant falls, once again, into "the-medium-is-the-message" category. The most important thing is that what was, for the ancient Near East, *the* myth has now become simply the first part of, the opening chapter of, another kind of myth that goes on from there. The *Enuma elish* was, for the Mesopotamians, *the* story on things, just as the Ugaritic myths about Baal were for the Canaanites and the Egyptian cosmic myths were for the ancient Egyptians. What the *Enuma elish* recounted had to do with the real issue faced by the human community annually, monthly, daily, the issue that arose continually out of that struggle between the inhabitants of the divine realm and was mirrored in nature's cycle. That was *the* issue, the reality in which the human community lived and upon which the human community was totally dependent. The story on that was the only story that really mattered.

Israel's *todah* myth, however, located the real issue elsewhere. The real issue for Israel lay in that historical course of events in which and through which God had chosen to be revealed to and involved with a human community. The real issue lay in that covenant relationship that obtained between Yahweh and Yahweh's people as a result of the series of historical events recounted in the historical preface to the stipulations of the covenant. It was because of their consciousness of where their relationship with Yahweh caused the real issue to be located that both the Elohist and the Deuteronomist would have nothing to do with a creation story, but began their epics straightaway with the dealings of God with Israel.[35] They did not want *todah* theology to be contaminated in any way by being connected, even with major alterations, with ancient Near Eastern cosmic mythology.

The Priestly Code does see the issue about which E and D are concerned. But it was also, as was the Yahwist before it, concerned to make it clear that the *todah* demanding God with whom Israel found itself involved was the real sovereign of the universe, was the real source of nature's existence as well as history's existence. What the Priestly Code did, therefore, was to take what had been *the* myth and make it the beginning of, the first chapter of, a *todah* myth that sets forth the story on what things are finally all about by, beginning with its roots in the origins of the human race, reciting that history in which and through which God has been associated with Israel. In doing so the

Priestly Code, whatever may be true of specific matters of content *within* the narrative, had, just by the way it used the *Enuma elish*, given expression to a quite new and different view of God and the human community and the world, a view arising out of and continually informed and nourished by the *todah* cult.

Furthermore, the Yahwist had already done the same thing centuries earlier. The beginning of the Yahwist epic is that second of the biblical accounts of the origins of things found in Genesis 2:4b—3:24. That narrative probably also originated somewhere in the mythological lore of the ancient Near East, but the discovery of just where has so far eluded us.[36] It is a myth dealing not so much with the physical origins of the universe, although it does begin by recounting God's "making" of earth and heaven. It is more concerned with the story of the tragedy and alienation that seem to plague human life, and it is explicit in its expression of the ancient Near Eastern conviction that human beings are excluded from the realm that really matters, that human decisions and actions are rooted in meaninglessness, that human life consists of only toil and pain and death. The Yahwist, however, takes that myth which excludes meaning from human history and makes it the first statement in a recital of how God, by calling a people and being involved with them in history is at work to replace chaos with order and meaninglessness with meaning by acting toward humanity as a personal, saving God.

In both the Priestly Code and the Yahwist the inclusion of *the* ancient Near Eastern myth as just a part of another kind of myth had far-reaching consequences. Nature is demythologized, its various elements robbed of their divine significance and turned into things to be investigated and used by human beings.[37] Nature ceases to be *the* issue, and becomes the setting of the *real* enterprise. The issue for humanity ceases to be human finitude and mortality, the issues that arise when nature is seen as the only reality there is. The issue becomes being right with and obedient to the God who calls mortal men and women to play significant roles in history. Finally, when the cosmic myth has ceased to be *the* myth and has become simply the account of how nature came into being at the beginning, when it has become the start of another kind of story that goes along through a course of events, then an end is logically implied. Furthermore, that end, given the implications of Israel's *todah* myth, is not simply a return to some unchanging beginning. It is the result and fulfillment of, and something the character of which is influenced by, the history that leads to it. What P and J did with the cosmic myth was in a very real sense responsible for biblical eschatology, for the biblical faith that the events of history are given significance by their relation to the final outcome of the whole enterprise under the sovereignty of the God who has chosen to be involved in it.

The flood story in J and P is a second place where it is possible to see the ancient Near Eastern cosmic myth being supplanted by the *todah* myth.[38] As was the case with the creation stories, that account of Noah and the great deluge found in J and P is obviously connected with a tradition preserved in the lore of many human communities. In particular, it is related in some kind of way to a Mesopotamian narrative known as the Gilgamesh Epic.[39]

In the Gilgamesh Epic the flood story is only one element in a larger whole, and the larger whole has to be sketched in order to gain some understanding of the significance of the flood story. The epic has to do with how the human being Gilgamesh sets out to find the secret of how to shed humanity and become divine so that life will have some meaning. His search finally leads to Utnapishtim, a human being who has, in fact, achieved that which is Gilgamesh's goal. It is in the course of Utnapishtim's explanation of how he became divine that the flood story occurs. Once upon a time, Utnapishtim explains, the gods, distressed and disgusted with the human race, decided to destroy it by sending a great flood upon the earth. One of the goddesses, however, was piqued at some of her divine companions, and warned Utnapishtim in a dream of what was to happen. It was not that she was concerned for him, but only that she wished to get back at the gods with whom she was angry by thwarting what they were about and giving them cause for embarrassment. So, Utnapishtim built an ark, rode the flood out, and was, in fact, still around when the flood was over, knowing something of the smallness and fickleness that characterized the gods. So that he could not relate that information to other human beings—myths never being logical about such questions as where other human beings were going to be found after the flood anyhow—it was decided that Utnapishtim should be made divine, a part of the community of the gods.

Utnapishtim then tells Gilgamesh how divinity is to be gained. He must take the long journey back to earth, find a certain plant, and eat it. Gilgamesh, then, does make the long journey back to this world, finally finds the transforming plant, and proceeds to take a bath in a well so as to be clean before consuming it. While he is bathing, however, a serpent comes along, steals the plant, and leaves Gilgamesh just as he was when it all began, human and mortal and helpless and insignificant.

Obviously connected with the Gilgamesh Epic in some way through common cultural roots, the biblical story of the flood is very different in typically biblical ways. As in the creation story there is, for one thing, only one God, not a plethora of them. That God is not fickle, does not ordain the life-destroying deluge just because of some arbitrary whim. The flood is ordained for an understandable reason, namely that the persistent evil and violence by which human life has come to be characterized threatens to ruin the goodness of God's creation. In other words, the implied issue for human beings is not mortality, but obedience to the will of the God whose will it is precisely that human life should be a good and significant thing. Furthermore, God's decision is taken in such a way as not only to exclude fickle arbitrariness but also to be characterized by justice. Because one human being, Noah, is righteous, he and his family are spared.

The chief and most striking differences between the two stories are to be seen, however, in what follows upon them. When the Gilgamesh Epic is finished, nothing at all has changed. The gods are still the same fickle, arbitrary, amoral beings they always were. Human beings are still condemned to a meaningless, insignificant, mortal existence. That mortal existence is still at the mercy of divine whims. There is no assurance at all that a meaningless deluge will not once again take place. In the Bible what follows upon the flood story is significantly different. When the flood is finished, humanity in the persons of Noah and his family is indeed still there, subject to the same human passions and sinful tendencies that caused God to ordain the flood in the first place. God is still there too, good and gracious and righteous and just, full of care for the creation. It is, therefore, as if God is struck by the necessity to make a policy decision. Should the human race, full of promise and potential and creativity rising out of God's will that it should share in the divine activity, but also willful and lacking in wisdom and capable of great evil and violence, be allowed to multiply and continue? In that case there might very well be cause for a flood fairly often, and there might also be cause for the human race to come to participate in those tragic fears that find expression in the Gilgamesh Epic. Or, should some of what God had invested in the human race originally be taken away? Should human beings be deprived of some of the initiative and independence and creativity that always carried in them the possibility of evil and violence? Should humanity be rendered less than human so that the order and peace and beauty of God's natural creation might continue unmarred forever? It is as if God had to decide whether priority should be put on the divine commitment to humanity and the human enterprise, in which case some adjustment might have to be made in the divine standards for the quality of the universe, or whether priority should be put on the original standards God had for the quality of the universe, in which case God's original commitment to humanity and the human enterprise might have to undergo some adjustment.

The Bible is quite clear that God decided for the first alternative, to put priority on the divine commitment to humanity and the human enterprise. The Yahwist puts it this way:

> So Yahweh's decision was this: "Never again will I curse the ground because of the human race, however evil an inclination may be there in human nature beginning right from youth. I will never again destroy everything that lives as I have just done. No, while the earth lasts, planting time and harvest time, cold and heat, summer and winter, day and night, none of them shall ever fail to come around."
>
> (GEN. 8:21–22)

The Priestly Code goes into even greater detail, making the covenant with Noah—which, Israel not yet specifically having come into being, is really a covenant with the whole human race—one of the key points in its theology. The P account of the covenant with Noah after the flood is found in Genesis 9. God's accommodation of the original divine standards for creation to the realities inherent in human nature is presented even more dramatically there than in the Yahwist. God's original wish, implicit in what P had said in Genesis 1, had been that violence never be done to any living creature in the universe, that blood never be shed in any way or for any purpose whatsoever. Now, however, God takes account of what must be involved in putting priority on commitment to the human race rather than to maintenance of the original divine standards for creation by establishing the original and basic dietary law: "Every creature that lives and moves may be killed as food for you. I make them yours for food just as I once did all the plants. When, though, you eat the flesh, you must not eat the life that is in it, that is, its blood." (Gen. 9:3–4) The custom of draining the blood out of meat so that the meat is rendered *kosher* (ritually clean), a custom that continues in Judaism down to this day, is interpreted by the Priestly Code as a reminder to human beings of the extent to which God has been willing to compromise in order to stand by the divine commitment to human beings and the human enterprise.[40] Furthermore the depth of that commitment is bespoken when God goes on to insist that a price will have to be paid any time that *human* blood is shed.

Furthermore, God as well as human beings is provided with a reminder of the commitment that has been made: "This is the sign of the covenant which I have established between myself and you, as well as between myself and every living thing that surrounds you, the covenant which shall be in effect as long as generations go on: my bow have I hung in the clouds; it is the sign of the covenant between me and the earth." (Gen. 9:12) To God and the human community alike, the rainbows that occur along with rain exist as reminders that the solemn covenant promise of God is that the rains shall never again turn into the deluge that came in the time of Noah. Or, to interpret the imagery another way, the bow seen hanging in the clouds whenever rain becomes a reminder of the primeval deluge is the destructive, divine war bow, hung purposely by God out of the divine reach so that the divine wrath might never again result in the destruction of life on the earth.[41]

Seen against the background of the culture in which Israel lived, what is being said by the Yahwist and the Priestly Code in their accounts of the covenant with Noah is that the issue that is crucially central to ancient Near Eastern cosmological religion is passé. That religion was fundamentally concerned with whether or not the round of nature would continue, with whether—in the Mesopotamian form of that religion—the spring floods would in fact become another deluge by which life on the earth would be blotted out. Its whole cult centered on supplication that that would not happen, on the recital of and the acting out of the events in the divine realm that had prevented its happening, in calling upon the inhabitants of the divine realm to hail as chief one of their number who had held it off once again. That was what ancient Near Eastern cosmological religion was all about. What Israel is saying in the Yahwist and the Priestly Code is that all that is really irrelevant. It is, they are asserting, concerned with issues that have been settled by the God who is really in charge. It has become a part of past history for which thanks can be given in that recitative form of the verb employed in *todah*. The God who really is in charge has now located the issues in the history that goes on from there, is present to deliver and to judge and to be praised in the course of events that goes on from there. Once again the view of God and the human race and the cosmos that gives rise to *todah* has made use of something that originated in the mythology that is the ethos of hymnic praise, but has radically transformed what is used.

Finally, those two things, the use made in Israel's epic recitals of the cosmic myth and the use made of the flood story, lead to *an issue in contemporary biblical theology*. In Israel the cosmic myth is transformed into a creation story that leads into the recital of the history of the people of God. In the same way, the flood story is used to call the human community away from that concern for the survival of the cosmos and the life in it that characterized ancient Near Eastern religion to a concern for the course of events which continues on the basis of God's promise that the cosmos will survive. The various strands in Israel's recitative, epic scriptures, as well as the finished epic in which those strands have been included, represent Israel's consistent doing of theology through an interpretative recounting of its own history. A theology of the Old Testament cannot, therefore, be a reduction of that interpretative narrative to some abstraction that represents what its theological meaning finally is. A theology of the Old Testament can only be a setting forth of the interpretative recital of the various witnesses whose *todah* make up the Old Testament. To put it another way, the outcome of Old Testament theology cannot, given the nature of what is being dealt with, be the discovery of the abstract concept which is finally the content of divine revelation. All we really have is Israel's concrete, *todah* witness to its faith that God was involved with a people in the events *todah* thankfully recites.[42] We must finally understand, if we are to understand the Old Testament at all, that contact with God is made as a people lives a *todah* life, not as the finally true, abstract dogma is apprehended by the human mind.

All that is as intolerable to modern minds, conditioned to assume that reality finally lies in the abstract truths they can derive from life and history and the witness of faith, as Israel's *todah* myth was to people of the ancient Near East who could not believe at all that the highest God, the ruler of the cosmos, could possibly be inseparably and completely involved in the life of a human, historical people.[43] That is, however, the way it is in the Bible. There is no higher truth or deeper revelation than Israel's recital of its own history out of its own, human, culturally conditioned faith. We are, so to speak, stuck with that in spite of our purer theological pretensions. Furthermore, God is stuck with it too, is at the mercy of Israel's—and the Church's—interpretative witness to the divine involvement in its life. If there is any abstract truth that will capture what is being said in the biblical witness, it is just precisely that being stuck with the imperfect, historically conditioned witness of a human community to its faith that God is involved in the events of its life in history is all right with God. For the God to whom the Bible witnesses is One who is perceived—from the covenant with Noah to the Christological hymn quoted by Paul in Philippians 2:5–11—as putting priority on involvement with a human, historical community rather than on protection of the divine purity. That is why the humblest participant in the *todah* cult is more closely in touch with God than is the pretender to high, theological wisdom. That is the way Israel's great, epic, *todah* theologians would insist things finally are.

3
The Vision of the Prophets: A New Israel

In the previous chapter we have seen how, among the epic theologies emerging from Israel's *todah* faith, the Deuteronomists' and the Chronicler's works in particular had to deal with the demise of the kingdom that had begun with David's rise and the occupation of Jerusalem. The interpreters *par excellence* of the traumatic era that culminated in destruction and exile were the great prophets for whom that series of Old Testament books, beginning with Isaiah and concluding with Malachi, were named.[1] This chapter has to do with the contribution of those prophets to that *todah*, thanksgiving theology which is central to and normative for the Bible, Old Testament and New. For present purposes three things about the canonical prophets are important, and they will be discussed in this chapter.[2] First, the canonical prophets continued Israel's *todah* tradition, insisting that the terrible and destructive events through which they lived still constituted a course of history in which God was revealed to and involved with a human community. Second, in their interpretation of their era they picked up an element in Israel's ancient and original self-understanding, namely its conception of itself as a transtribal league, a nonethnic people of God, and they claimed that the events through which Israel was being destroyed and exiled were leading to the realization on a universal scale of what that self-understanding was all about. Third, in a chaotic and traumatic era in which Israel could discern no course of events that made sense as a basis of *todah* recital, the lives and work of the prophets themselves came for Israel to be the story of what things really meant.

The Prophets' Continuation of the Todah Tradition

The canonical prophets appear in that period of about two centuries (750–550 B.C.) in which the appearance and expansion of the Assyrian and then the neo-Babylonian and then the Persian empires in the ancient Near Eastern area heralded a new era of history.[3] Israel's territory was located in that strip of arable land running around the western and northern and eastern borders of the Arabian Desert that James Henry Breasted dubbed the "fertile crescent."[4] The strong powers in that area were usually located in Egypt at one end of the crescent, or in Mesopotamia at the other. For a period of five centuries running from about 1250 B.C. to 750 B.C., however, no great power was dominant there. It was then that Israel, along with a number of other peoples, gained independence as a kingdom and lived through the history we have touched on in the last chapter's discussion of Israel's historical epics. That vacuum of power in the fertile crescent which, from a sheerly political point of view, had made Israel's existence as a nation possible began, however, to come to an end when the Assyrians started to expand their territory in the middle of the eighth century. As a result of the Assyrian expansion, the northern kingdom fell in the last quarter of that century, and its people, in accord with an Assyrian policy calculated to keep the empire free from local insurrections, were mixed into the other peoples the Assyrians had conquered.[5] In the latter part of the seventh century the neo-Babylonian empire succeeded the Assyrians as the dominant power, and its expansion resulted in the fall of Jerusalem in 587 B.C. and the exile to Babylon of the members of the Davidic dynasty and other political and religious leaders.[6] Finally, Cyrus, who had formed an empire in Persia to the east of the fertile crescent, moved into the area early in the latter half of the sixth century, reversed a lot of the policies and situations that had arisen under Assyrian and Babylonian rule, and made it possible for exiled Israelites to go home and reestablish Yahweh's cult in Jerusalem, if not their political kingdom. It was through that tumultuous era that the great Israelite prophets claimed history still to be the place where Israel's God's sovereignty was manifest.[7]

Prophetism in Israel seems to owe its origins to two things, one intimately connected with Israel's own peculiar covenant self-understanding and cult, the other something that existed in ancient Near Eastern culture, particularly in royal courts, and with which Israel probably came into contact when David took over Jerusalem and its traditions. We have already had occasion to show how the Deuteronomists organize Israel's history around a succession of prophetic leaders, of whom Moses was the beginning and the prototype. Among these figures were Joshua, the judges, Samuel and Nathan in the books of Samuel, and then a series of figures beginning with Nathan and Ahijah in the books of the Kings. They are pictured as those who keep Israel and Israel's kings mindful of the covenant relationship between Yahweh and Israel which began with Moses. The origin of these prophets, and the forms employed by them in prophesying, probably lies in the cult in which, from time to time, the covenant relationship between Yahweh and Israel was reaffirmed. Scholars have conjectured that Moses was the prototype of a "covenant mediator" whose function it was to convene Israel as the covenant people of God, and to speak for God in setting the covenant before Israel as Moses had classically done in the decalogue at Mount Sinai.[8] The classic description of how a person became a prophet of this kind was simply, "The word of Yahweh came to me," or, "Yahweh's word was put into my mouth."[9]

It should be noted that the nature of Israel's faith was such that this office was not one in which the covenant formularies from the past were simply repeated on new occasions. Israel's faith did not understand God's activity in the events of history as having only happened in the past, as once-and-for-all revelation. Israel's faith affirmed the continuing involvement of God in its own history as a people. It was, therefore, part of the ministry of the inspired, prophetic covenant mediator to claim, from time to time, more recent events for the covenant's historical preface or, better, for God to do that through the covenant mediator. It was also part of the function of the person called to this office to explicate just what the classic covenant stipulations might mean and imply in new times and situations.[10] Israel's covenant faith was, by nature, something that had to be related to, indeed was inevitably related to, the events and situations of successive eras of history. That was because it was rooted in the conviction that Israel's God was sovereign in and through events of history. As a result, the office of covenant mediator was inherently prophetic. Thus it is not surprising that, from time to time, someone who claimed to be called to that office made of it a more than cultic thing, and related the covenant and Yahweh's sovereignty specifically and painfully and controversially to present events.[11]

Another way of understanding the prophetic office seems to arise out of a function performed by individuals who claimed to have been, in dream and vision, admitted to the deliberations of that divine assembly which ancient Near Eastern culture believed to be the place where the deliberations determining the destinies of the world and its inhabitants were taken. Letters from a kingdom called Mari, located in upper Mesopotamia, take such individuals for granted, and indicate that their function was to keep the king informed of what transpired in the world of the gods. In particular it was their responsibility to inform the king of what the gods might require by way of additions to and refurbishment of their temples.[12] Israel probably came into contact with these predecessors to the classical prophets when it was exposed to the culture of the ancient Near East in its Canaanite form in the traditions and customs of Jerusalem. It is interesting to note that, in spite of his taking David to task morally after the adultery and murder that brought Bathsheba to David as his wife, the most extensive oracles delivered by the prophet Nathan, who appears only after David has taken Jerusalem, have to do with the establishment of the royal dynasty and the building of a temple.[13] That this office in ancient Near Eastern culture was taken into Israel as one method through which Yahweh was believed to communicate with Yahweh's people provides another example of the way in which Israel utilized the concepts and institutions of the culture in which it lived in order to understand and articulate its faith. It is easy to see how, when the head of the divine assembly had come to be understood as involved in the events of history, this office and function could come to serve as a means by which events were interpreted in the light of Yahweh's sovereignty and purpose. The description of how a person had become a prophet of this type recounted how that person had been present in the heavenly assembly, hearing and seeing what transpired there as divine decisions were taken.[14]

Both of these offices were part of Israel's heritage, the one probably dating far back into the life of the tribal confederation that had preceded the Davidic monarchy, the other dating from the earliest days of Israel's life in the city-kingdom of Jerusalem. Through the centuries they had undoubtedly each played a significant role in Israel's life, its cultic life in particular. Though they were offices occupied by those chosen and called by God and not through inheritance or training—charismatic offices in the broadest sense of the word—there must have been many times when their occupants functioned pretty routinely as transmitters of tradition. At other times, though, as in an Elijah or a Micaiah ben Imlah, the offices seem to have come to life in relation to particularly crucial events, to have been not merely cultic but "for real."[15] It was during the two centuries of expansion and conquest by the great empires to the east of Israel's territory, the two centuries that brought Israel's existence as a nation to an end, that these offices—both of which came in tradition to be understood as one, as "prophet"—flourished as the principal means through which the *todah* tradition was applied to the events through which Israel was living.

One example of how this took place is found in Micah 6:1–8, the concluding verse of which is one of the most famous in the Old Testament. The prophecies of Micah originated in Judah in the period in which the Assyrian invasion of Palestine and conquest of the northern kingdom opened the era of destruction which was the setting of the careers of the great prophets. The form of the particular prophetic pronouncement found in Micah 6:1–8 is connected with the covenant cult and with the functioning of the covenant mediator whose prototype was Moses. One of the elements in those ancient Near Eastern treaties which were the origin of Israel's covenant forms is a calling of all the inhabitants of the universe to witness the agreement being made between the sovereign and the people subject to the sovereign. The witnesses would include the heavens and the mountains and the hills and all the features of the earth. Another element in those treaties is provision for their being recalled regularly and for the subject people to be called to account under the terms of the treaty.[16] One of the functions of the covenant mediator in Israel, therefore, was to serve as the one who recalled to Israel the provisions of the covenant with God and as the one who called Israel to account under the covenant stipulations. Indeed, one of the forms identified by scholars in the prophetic literature is the *rib* ("controversy" or "accusatory pronouncement") in which Israel is called to account by being accused of the ways in which it has violated the covenant provisions.[17]

It is precisely this form which is employed by Micah as Israel fearfully awaits the outcome of the invasion of its territory by the forces of Assyria. In the same kind of way that our own, contemporary, built-in, form-critical apparatus automatically tells us that a book we pick up is a novel and not a biography, or that a television program we tune in on is a newscast and not a drama, so Micah's hearers would have understood from the first words of Micah 6:1–8 that a covenant mediator was calling God's covenant people to account:

> *Arise* [*O Israel*], *argue your case to the mountains,*
> *Let the hills hear your plea.*
> *O mountains, listen to* Yahweh's *case,*
> *You too, everlasting foundations of the earth.*
> *For Yahweh does have a case against* (rib) *the people of Yahweh,*
> *Must hold Israel accountable.*
>
> (Mic. 6:1–2)

Both the form and the content of the beginning of the prophetic pronouncement would have signalled what was happening, would have had deep meaning in the consciousness of the Israelite hearers.[18]

The beginning of the pronouncement is followed in verses 3–5 by Yahweh's statement of just what Israel is being accused of, and then, in verses 6–7, by Israel's defense. Finally, the famous verse 8 is the prophet's statement of what is to be learned from the exchange. Here is Yahweh's accusation, filled with allusions to Israel's past and clearly implying that what Israel is really guilty of is a fundamental misunderstanding of the *todah* faith:

My people, what have I done to you?
How have I wearied you? Answer me!
Why, I rescued you from the land of Egypt,
From oppression as slaves ransomed you,
Provided guides for you in Moses and Aaron and Miriam.
My people, just remember!
What a plot was laid by Balak, the Moabite king,
And what an answer for him came from Balaam ben Beor!
[*What a triumphant crossing it was*][19]
From Shittim [*in Trans-Jordan*] *to Gilgal* [*on this side*].
[*Yes, my people, just remember*][20]
In order to understand Yahweh's ways of acting.
(Mic. 6:3–5)

This prophetic accusation, as is typical of such pronouncements, has about it a mysterious, allusive quality that made it hard to comprehend in its own time, but even harder centuries later in a different cultural setting. Our discussion in preceding chapters of this book, however, and particularly the discussion in chapter 1, has laid the groundwork for grasping the significance of what is being said here. Yahweh begins the accusation by a self-identification rooted in the content of the covenant preface, rooted in *todah* recital. Yahweh is the one who above all rescued Israel from enslavement in Egypt. Then that is driven home in so thorough a way as to imply anger and accusation. What began in the rescue from Egypt continued through the era of Israel's roaming in the desert (that is what the allusion to Balak and Balaam is about) and through the entrance of Israel into its own land (that is what the allusion to Shittim and Gilgal is about). What is being said is that Yahweh's *modus operandi* which first became clear in the exodus from Egypt has continued consistently in the subsequent history of Yahweh's involvement with Israel.

Finally, the vocabulary of the concluding sentence of God's accusation is rich with words that come directly from the *todah* cult in which Yahweh's deliverances are celebrated. This is true in particular of the word for "remember" and of the Hebrew word rendered above as "ways of acting." Above all else, the *todah* cult is a cult of remembering, of calling to mind, of living again events which have occurred where the human community could see and experience and appropriate them as its own. The *todah* cult does not involve the symbolizing of things which are not remembered but only intuited, as was the cult based on the mythology of the ancient Near East. Further, remembered, eventful things such as are catalogued in Yahweh's accusation are the only basis on which there can be any real understanding (the word for "understanding" implies the kind of intimate knowledge of another that is there in sexual intercourse) of Yahweh's "ways of acting." The word underlying the latter phrase is the plural of that word so central to the *todah* cult discussed in the first chapter of this book, *zedek* or *zedakah*. It is the latter, the feminine form, which is used in Micah 6:5, but either form denotes the deliverance in which the personal, saving god praised in the *todah* cult is known by and related to that god's devotee. Thus, what Micah's accusation is saying is that Israel is looking for Yahweh elsewhere than the classic place where Yahweh is typically manifest and involved with Israel, namely in the course of events that form Israel's life in history.

That this is, in fact, the point of the accusation becomes clear when the prophet continues the sarcastic pronouncement by setting forth the words of Israel's response:

With what shall I come into Yahweh's presence?
How can I adequately honor the most high God?

Shall I come into God's presence with whole burnt offerings,
With the choicest yearling calves?
Will Yahweh be satisfied with thousands of rams,
With ten thousand rivers of oil?
Shall I offer even my own first-born for my rebellion,
My children for the sin I have committed?

(MIC. 6:6–7)

There is heavy irony in the defense the prophet puts into the mouth of Israel. What is being said is that Israel does not really understand at all, has ceased really to be intimately acquainted with Yahweh. Its response to God's accusation asks "How much do you want?" in terms indicating that Israel's understanding of God and God's requirements has ceased to be distinctively Israelite and has become just like that of Israel's neighbors in the ancient Near East. The kinds of sacrifices mentioned (whole burnt offering, *'olah*) and the designation of Yahweh as God most high assume that Yahweh is the kind of god praised in the cult that is the setting of the hymn as the normative song of praise. There is even indication that Israel has come to think of Yahweh as arbitrary, fickle, incapable of being understood with regard to what is required to Yahweh's devotees. Ancient Near Eastern gods were like that, and some prayers addressed to them were pathetic pleas that they not leave their devotees in the dark as to their will and ways.[21] Micah's indictment of Israel is saying that Israel has completely forgotten the *todah* cult and its theological significance, has completely forgotten who Yahweh is and what Yahweh's nature is. The consequences of that in the present moment of Israel's history, in which the Assyrian invaders are at hand, are then spelled out in the climax of the passage, the famous verse, Micah 6:8:

You have been shown, you mortal creatures, what is good!
What are Yahweh's requirements of you?

Just these: to do what is just,
to love steadfast loyalty to the covenant,
and humbly to go along with what your God ordains.

In stating what Yahweh requires of Israel, the prophet begins by using two words rich with traditional meaning in the context of Israel's covenant understanding of its relationship with God. *Mishpat* is traditionally translated "justice," but its meaning must be understood in more than a legalistic sense. The verb from which it comes, *shaphat,* can mean "to judge," but when it is used, for example, with "widows and orphans" or "the poor and oppressed" as its objects it has to do with more than a legal process. It means to "do what is right" by those who are in need, to have the kind of regard for human beings and their needs that was manifest as part of the character of God when Israel was rescued from oppression in Egypt. *Chesed,* the second key word in the statement of Yahweh's requirements for Israel, has traditionally been translated as "mercy" in this verse: "to love mercy." Its basic meaning, however, is "loving loyalty." That is why the Revised Standard Version of the Bible almost always translates it as "steadfast love." In Israel it is part of the covenant vocabulary. *Chesed* is that loving loyalty to covenant commitment that is manifest on God's part in the events recited in *todah* and which is required also of Israel as the other party to the covenant.

Thus, in those first two parts of the prophet's statement of God's requirements for Israel, the people of God are being called away from their understanding of Yahweh as a god like Baal or Ashur or Marduk, away from cultic praise of Yahweh in terms and actions associated with gods like those, away from ancient Near Eastern cosmic mythology and hymnic praise. They are being called back to that covenant relationship with Yahweh which invests human decisions and actions in history with dignity and importance, back to that service of God which includes other human beings and what is right for them as well as one's own lovingly loyal allegiance, back to a theology and a cult in which the human community does not look to the heavens for what alone is significant and does not praise God with totally consumed sacrifices of which it itself does not partake. Israel is being called back to the covenant and to the *todah* cult. That is the framework for the final climax. For, having used two traditional words, words that the hearers would have recognized as venerable in spite of the hearers' apostasy, the prophetic pronouncement pins down what covenant loyalty and a *todah* understanding of reality should involve *now*, in the historical present which involves Assyrian destruction of the northern kingdom and Assyrian presence on the soil ruled by the Davidic monarchy, by bringing into parallelism with the two traditional words a word which not only has no previous theological significance but which occurs only at this place in biblical Hebrew. Micah may very well have done this in order to dramatize and emphasize the point he was making.

The word in question is *hazne'a.* It is a *hapax legomenon,* a word, that is, which occurs only this one time. We have to search for its meaning in languages cognate to biblical Hebrew, and that meaning may be the traditional "humbly" or something more like "wisely." The most important thing about it, though, is its use in opening this final and climactic statement of the prophetic pronouncement of which it is a part, the way the introduction of a "secular" word following the two traditional words that have preceded would have jolted the original hearers. It leads into the phrase that follows: "to walk with your God," or, "to go along with your God," and modifies that phrase by making it mean either "Having abandoned your hymnic pretensions (i.e. humbly), go along with your God," or, "Having gained a proper understanding of the issues (i.e. wisely), go along with your God." In either case, what the prophet is presumably saying, in that poetic idiom always used by the prophets, is something like this: "Israel's God is not to be found far above the heavens, the recipient of whole burnt offerings. Israel's God is, as always, present in the events that are God's people's history. Our God is here now precisely in what we are going through as the expansion of the Assyrian empire involves us." That is why the translation above renders the final line "and humbly to go along with what your God ordains," for that is the sense in which the prophet says "humbly walk with your God." Micah is claiming *todah* significance for even the events that are leading to Israel's national downfall. He is doing so out of that understanding of the prophetic office that goes back to Moses' role as a covenant mediator.[22]

Isaiah does the same kind of thing out of an understanding of the prophetic office originating in that ancient Near Eastern belief that kings were the earthly viceregents of the cosmic ruler, an understanding involving the prophet's having been, in vision or dream, admitted to the deliberations of the assembly of the gods so that the decisions taken there could be communicated to the king.[23] That Isaiah understood his prophetic vocation that way is indicated by the account he gives of his call to be a prophet in Isaiah 6. Yahweh is seen as enthroned as the cosmic ruler with the heavenly court, "seraphim" seeming to represent an Israelite demythologizing of more polytheistic imagery, present in the throne room. A decision is being taken, a decision spelling invasion and destruction and disaster for Israel, and that decision must be announced. So, Isaiah's "Here am I, send me," represents the acceptance of the office of the messenger who announces divine decisions in human society. That that is the ethos out of which Isaiah understands his vocation as a prophet is also probably indicated by the fact that he so often addresses his prophetic pronouncements to the king and to the ruling classes in Jerusalem.[24]

Out of that understanding of the prophetic office, Isaiah speaks in the same time and situation as did Micah. Different though their theoretical understandings of the nature of the prophetic office and function might be, the messages of the two prophets are very much the same. For example, there is a set of pronouncements of Isaiah which closely parallel what is said in Micah 6:1–8. They are found in Isaiah 1:4–17, and they probably come from the time just after the Assyrians, having destroyed the northern kingdom and devastated most of the territory of Judah as well, first laid siege to Jerusalem and then unexplainedly lifted the siege and left.[25] Isaiah first pictures the situation which obtained in the land as a result of the Assyrian invasion in two different images, as how a person is left just barely alive after a terrible beating and as how lonely and desolate the shelter built at harvest time looks in a field where none of the life or joy of harvest remains:

How much more must you be wounded,
Must you continue to avoid the truth?
The whole head is one wound,
The body full of infection,
From the soles of the feet to the top of the head
Not a sound spot is to be found.
There is nothing but bruises and welts and open wounds,
Undressed, unbandaged, untreated with healing oil.
(Is. 1:5–6)

Your land is desolate,
Your cities burned with fire;
Your soil is still your property,
But foreigners are devouring its fruits;
The desolation is like that at Sodom's destruction.
Only Zion is left,
Like a shelter in a vineyard,
Like a shed in a vegetable garden,
Yes, a city under guard.
(Is. 1:7–8)

The implied accusation against Israel, which for Isaiah is really the city-kingdom of Jerusalem,[26] is clearly that it is avoiding the truth about what has happened, not admitting that the Assyrians have really destroyed it, not acknowledging that the Davidic kingdom exists in name only, that the end has clearly come for what has been. In other words, Israel is not really taking seriously the historical reality in which it is presently living, has missed or avoided the significance of the course of events through which it is now passing. And what *is* Israel presently doing? Exactly the same thing for which Micah faulted Israel, even if Isaiah pictures it in different poetic imagery and with more angry irony:

Hear Yahweh's word, you rulers of Sodom,
Attend to the instruction of our God, you people of Gomorrah:
What do your countless sacrifices mean to me?
That is what Yahweh is saying.
I am fed up with whole burnt offerings of rams,
As well as of the fat of cattle.
The blood of bulls and sheep and goats
Is in no way what I want.
When you come into my presence
Whoever required that kind of thing of you,
You tramplers around in my courts?
Do not keep bringing useless offerings,
The stench of sacrifices repels me.
New moon and sabbath as set gathering times I can't take,
[Any more than] fasting and solemn assembly.[27]
Your new moons and days of obligation,
I hate with all my heart:
They are as a heavy load on my back,
Which I can no longer carry
When you spread out your hands in prayer,
I will turn my eyes from you;
Even if you increase the number of your prayers,
I will refuse to listen to them.

(Is. 1:10–15)

The description of what Israel is doing cultically, as well as the vocabulary employed in the description, clearly indicate that Israel's sacrifice and praise are being offered after the manner of ancient Near Eastern cults of the cosmic ruler. Israel has turned away from the stuff on which *todah* is based, from looking to the events of human life and history as the material out of which praise of God arises. Israel's attention has been turned to that divine realm where the culture around Israel located the real significance of things. Israel's sacrifices have come to be the kind in which the human community does not really participate but which are sent totally up to the divine realm. Yet Yahweh remains the one who has deposed those gods whose favor the kind of worship Israel is engaging in is calculated to woo. Yahweh continues to be the One who is present in and acting through the history in which human beings participate. Yahweh is there in those realities Israel is avoiding, not in that kind of cultic direction in which Israel is looking. So, Isaiah, still using the ancient Near Eastern imagery connected with belief in a heavenly court, delivers the message of Yahweh which states the truth about the present in which Israel finds itself:

Yes indeed! The Assyrian is the rod of my anger,[28]
The staff of my wrath is in his *hand.*
Against an apostate nation do I send him,
Over a people with whom I am furious do I give him authority
To despoil and to plunder in the most terrible way,
To trample them like mire in the street.

(Is. 10:5–6)

In those words Isaiah makes quite explicit what he, as did Micah, sees as the significance of the events through which Israel was passing in his time, events that were leading to national collapse and to exile.

Micah and Isaiah have been cited as examples of what is to be found in all the canonical prophets, and as examples representing the two traditional sources of prophecy in Israel. Numerous other examples could have been presented.

The point is that the prophets, through those two hundred years that saw the end of Israel's existence as a nation gradually brought about by the expansion of the great empires, continued that insistence to *todah*, thanksgiving, as normative that went way back into Israel's origins and that had been the basis on which the great Israelite epics did theology. The prophets insist that the *todah* cult is the origin and the norm for what Israel is called to be. Further, they insist that the purpose and the power of Israel's God are as present in the events bringing Israel's collapse as they were in the events which brought Israel into existence in the first place. In so far as those events spell doom, they are God's judgment on an Israel which has abandoned the norm implicitly present in the *todah* cult. That God's judgment is, however, present in the events that spell doom for Israel means that those events have significance, that they are a continuing basis for *todah*. Once again, in the prophets, we see the continuance of a tradition which grows out of a cult, as what is present in that cult, and not some abstract reasoning, is applied to present reality.

The Outcome of National Collapse: a Nonethnic Todah Community

The prophets, however, did not see judgment as the only meaning of the events of that era in which they lived and out of which came the demise of Israel as a nation. They saw a new Israel emerging from that era, an Israel that would embody all that God had had in mind for Israel from the beginning. They saw the events of their time, terrible as they were, leading to a future in which what Israel, as the people of God, had always really been all about could be reborn in a newer, universal way.

It needs to be emphasized that Israel, originally and by its very nature, was a transtribal, transethnic reality. It was not one tribe. It was a league of tribes.[29] What made an individual or a clan or a tribe part of Israel was not a common bloodline or common ethnic origin. What made Israel Israel was participation in its life and history through assent to the covenant between Yahweh and Israel, and participation in the *todah* cult by which Israel identified itself liturgically. That was the basis of the covenant insistence that identity and obligation as an Israelite came first, before tribal or family loyalties. That was also the basis on which membership in a tribal league, established by a deliverance accomplished by Yahweh in spite of the power of Egypt, guaranteed the worth of the different, particular human identities of those who constituted that league. Unlike Amorites and Habiru and other tribal peoples, Israelites did not lose their particular tribal and family heritages and identities by being absorbed into the culture dominated by the cosmic myth. The "people of God" was neither a trans-ethnic replacement for the ethnic identity one had by birth nor some new ethnic reality. It was a confederation within which, because of its having been convened by the absolute One, particular human identities could dwell together without the need to elevate their particularities to absoluteness and then either be threatened by or seek to conquer other particular brands of humanity.

Rooted in that new kind of phenomenon in human society that was named Israel, a basic contrast runs through the Old Testament and, indeed, through the Bible as a whole. It is, to use the Hebrew terms, the contrast between *goy* on the one hand and *'am* (people) or *kahal* or *'adath* (congregation, assembly) on the other hand.[30] *Goy* has come traditionally to be translated "Gentile" as contrasted with "Israelite." Insofar, however, as that translation implies a qualitative judgment on one who is not part of Israel, it misses the real meaning of *goy*. *Goy* basically denotes what a human being is in terms of that human being's natural, human identity. It has to do with race and nationality and even sex and class. It denotes what we are by nature. It is in that sense that it stands in contrast to "Israel." Israel is a confederation of assorted *goys* which is defined by initiatives and actions of God in historical events, not by the natural antecedents of its members.

That understanding of the nature of Israel, contrasted with what *goy* denotes, is, like so much else in the Old Testament, intimately connected with the *todah* cult and the *todah* understanding of reality. We saw in Chapter 1 how closely the cosmic mythology and the cult of the cosmic ruler in the ancient Near East were connected with the social and political structures in which they existed. In a very real sense the cosmic myth, in a form such as that found in the Mesopotamian *Enuma elish*, is a justification of nature. It is also, therefore, a justification of the natural identity of the people who recite it, who participate in the cult which is its setting, and who sing the hymn which is the normative form of praise in that cult. It is, in a word, a justification of the ethnicity, the *goy*ness of those who hear the cosmic myth and sing the hymn. In clear contrast, Israel is an amalgam of human natures, of ethnicities, of *goy*nesses. Israel owes its existence to events of history that have to be recited in *todah*, thanksgiving form rather than in a cosmic, mythological form. Thus, the *todah* norm and the *todah* cult are not only the result of Israel's experience. They are the result of Israel's very nature, of Israel's being the *'am Yahweh* (the people of Yahweh), the *kahal Yahweh* (the congregation of Yahweh), the *'adath ha'elohim* (the people of God). In view of the discussion in the first two chapters of this book, it is interesting to note that the last term is precisely the one used in Psalm 82 to denote the assembly of the gods. Israel, the people called into being by the action of God to perform the functions reserved for gods elsewhere in the ancient Near East, is not a *goy* even though Israel is made up of a variety of *goys*.

All of that is set forth in the Yahwist epic in a typically *todah*, narrative way in Genesis 11:1—12:3.[31] The passage begins with the story of the Tower of Babel (Gen. 11:1–9). Whatever questions may arise in connection with details in the story and with whether or how the story refers specifically to Babylon, what the story is about is very clear to anyone with any familiarity at all with ancient Near Eastern culture and society and with the cosmic mythology that justified that culture and society. The tower is clearly the structure through which the human community made contact with the heavenly community whose existence was the real basis of life and meaning in the cosmos. The building of such a structure, the temple-palace complex, was both literally and figuratively the central goal of ancient Near Eastern culture. Through its contact with the heavenly temple-palace, in the person of the king and in the actions of the cult and in the recital of the cosmic myth, the earthly temple-palace was the place where human society in the particular form—particular *goy*ness—in which it existed in a given place was given divine undergirding and justification and validation.

The building of such structures, however, never quite accomplished all that it was meant to accomplish. The perfection and security and meaning those structures were meant to provide for the human societies that built them were never quite realized. That is why the great tragedies in human literature from the Gilgamesh Epic on have, on the whole, spoken with more credibility and authenticity and power to sharers in the human lot than have theological or philosophical masterpieces. The Yahwist, therefore, picks up on that disillusionment which always resulted from the inability of such structures to fulfill what they promised, speaks powerfully of how such structures do not work, describes the way in which the best efforts of human beings to justify and protect their brand of humanity results only in scattering, in alienation and conflict and further separation of human beings from one another. Furthermore, the Yahwist lays the groundwork for what is to come by making it clear that the reason such structures do not work, do not fulfill what they promise, is that the God who really is in charge does not approve of them. The God who really is in charge has another plan in mind.[32]

The story of the Tower of Babel is really a sarcastic caricature of ancient Near Eastern culture and society and religion, and in some kind of way it has Babylon in mind, that great and prestigious and powerful center of that culture and society and religion. That should be borne in mind as one comes to the genealogy which follows the story of the Tower of Babel. The genealogy traces, with material from the Priestly Code now overlaying the Yahwist's original and simpler narrative, the ancestry of Abraham and Sarah, here still called Abram and Sarai (Gen. 11:10–32). The real reason for the genealogy is not interest in the antecedents of Abraham and Sarah, at least not in the Yahwist. The real reason for the genealogy is to demonstrate that those in whose lives the remote beginnings of Israel were located possessed by birth impeccable credentials from the point of view of ancient Near Eastern society, from the point of view of those who built Towers of Babel. Sarah and Abraham are introduced into the biblical narrative in the first place as *goys* whose *goy*ness was very distinguished indeed. By nature and by birth they were connected with one of the greatest centers of the culture which understood life in terms of cosmic mythology.

Thus do the story of the Tower of Babel and the genealogy which follows it provide the setting for what is said in Genesis 12:1–3, a setting that makes that passage a fundamental and central and astounding theological statement on the part of the Yahwist:

> Yahweh said to Abram:
> Leave your homeland and your genealogical roots and your immediate family. Leave them for the land which I will show you. I will make of you a truly great *goy*. I will make your fame great. You will be a blessing. I will bless those who bless you, and curse whomever curses you. And by the blessing that is in you will every human identity find blessing.[33]

Those whose credentials are impeccable by the standards of ancient Near Eastern society are called out of that society's attempt to justify *goy* identity into an historical future. Abraham and Sarah are called to leave the place in the physical cosmos that gives them their identity and through which their contact with the divine realm has been established. They are called to turn their backs on that traceable descent from their ancestors which connects them with the culture of the place. They are called to leave their immediate family (the Hebrew is "father's house") which mediates to them the ways and the traditions of the culture. It is precisely when they do leave all that, respond to the call of God to set out toward a promised historical future, take their identity not from what they are by nature but from God's call toward an unfolding course of events—it is precisely then that they become, for the Yahwist, the forebears of Israel, the prototypes of what it means to be an *'am,* a people, rather than a *goy*. In this passage the Yahwist makes a normative statement about the nature of Israel, and shows why Israel's very nature demands *todah,* not the hymnic praise of the cosmic cult, as the standard for theology as well as worship. It was when Abraham and Sarah moved away from the genealogical ties that bound them to that view of reality which was present in ancient Near Eastern mythology and cult and, in response to God's call, began to view reality as an unfolding history that the drama of salvation began. That drama, for the Yahwist, is of such a character that it can be described only by narrating a people's history. It must be witnessed to through *todah.*

To pick up once again something already introduced in the preceding chapter of this book in connection with our discussion of the creation story, the Bible's view of reality as enunciated in that extremely significant piece of theology set forth by the Yahwist in Genesis 11:1—12:3 is implicitly and inevitably eschatological.[34] What was implicit in the transformation of the cosmic myth into a creation story, into the opening part of a drama that goes on from there, now has to become explicit. The call to Abraham and Sarah is not the first point on a circle in which a cyclical drama goes around and around. It is the beginning of a pilgrimage that begins at one point and proceeds toward another, that is headed somewhere in God's purpose. That is why it was inevitable that visions of the *eschaton*, the final time, such as the one set forth both in Isaiah 2:2–4 and Micah 4:1–3 should arise in Israel:

> This is what shall be when the succession of days has reached the point toward which it is moving:
>
> *The mountain on which Yahweh's house is established*
> *Shall tower over the mountains and be higher than the hills.*
> *To it shall all the* goys *flow,*
> *Yes, every last people journey, saying,*
> *"Come, let us ascend Yahweh's mountain,*
> *Ascend to the house of Jacob's God,*
> *So that we may be instructed in the ways of that God,*
> *May walk in the paths laid out by that God."*
> *For from Zion shall go forth instruction* (torah),
> *And the word of Yahweh from Jerusalem.*
> *And Yahweh shall do what is right among the nations,*
> *Shall set things straight for every last people.*
> *They shall beat their swords into plowshares,*
> *And their swords into pruning hooks;*
> *One* goy *shall not raise a sword against another,*
> *And they shall never again study the strategies of war.*

When that passage is read against the background of the *'am* (people) versus *goy* contrast that is basic to the Old Testament, against the background of what is said by the Yahwist in Genesis 11:1—12:3, it is clearly no nationalist or imperialist vision. It is a vision in which all the earth's *goys* have finally become a universal Israel. It is a vision in which order has finally been brought out of chaos by a process the nature of which is such that it must be hailed by *todah*, not cosmic, hymnic praise. It is the description of an outcome of human history in which what Abraham's response to God's call represents in the view of the Yahwist, finally participated in by every last bit of humanity, has indeed become that in which every family of the earth has found blessing. It is an eschatology in which fulfillment is found in a universal realization of what Israel, that non-*goy* gathering of multifaceted humanity, was meant to be by God.

That understanding of Israel enunciated by the Yahwist in Genesis 11:1—12:3 accounts for the tension that existed all through Israel's national history beginning with Samuel and Saul. From the point of view of those for whom Samuel is the hero in the narrative of the first book bearing his name, Saul's assumption of a kinglike leadership over Israel in response to the Philistine threat represented the turning of Israel from a tribal confederation into a *goy*, the abandonment of what Israel was supposed to be in terms of the call of the God who had created it.[35] In spite of the popularity of David in his own time and of the exalted place he came to occupy in Israelite tradition, that tension was not absent during his reign over Israel. The appeal of Absalom to the people of Israel as he laid the groundwork for his revolt lay in his contrasting what Israel was really supposed to be with what it had become under David as a city-kingdom, and the rallying cry used by the rebel Sheba was, "We have no stake in David, no investment in the dynasty of the son of Jesse. Let's everyone of us return to our tents, O Israel."[36] It was fundamentally that tension that led to Jeroboam's revolt against Solomon and the founding of the northern kingdom.[37] Given that tension, it is significant that the northern kingdom called itself "Israel" and that, until the dynasty of Jehu committed itself to the ideals of Elijah and Elisha and their prophetic revolution, the north was not able to establish a stable dynasty. A dynasty was a *goy* institution.[38] It is that tension that explains the way in which, according to the deuteronomic historians, a succession of prophets stood over against the royal succession as the true source of continuity all through Israel's existence as a kingdom.[39]

So it was that when, roughly between 750 and 550 B.C. Israel's national existence was destroyed and Israel was caught up into the imperial histories of Assyria and then Babylonia and then Persia, the succession of canonical prophets saw as one central issue in what was happening that *'am* versus *goy* tension. In the events that the prophets interpreted as judgment on Israel by Yahweh as well as in the events that finally made a restoration possible, those prophets, coming out of varying traditions and holding different theological views, were united in seeing Israel's true nature as Israel as a central issue. What was taking place in the history into which Israel had been caught up was that Yahweh was destroying Israel as a *goy* so that Israel could become the people of God, that *'am* which God originally had in mind when Abraham and Sarah were first called. Furthermore, the absorption of Israel into that wider, even from the prophet's point of view, universal history that was represented by the great imperial powers spelled God's re-creation of Israel on a universal basis.

One of the earliest statements of this prophetic conviction is found in the prophet Hosea in the time in which the Assyrians were destroying the northern kingdom. Hosea is fiercely Israelite, passionate in his emphasis on the exclusive demand Yahweh's call makes on Israel, totally negative about world powers in general and about Israel's having taken on a *goy* identity in particular. He sees the doom that is befalling Israel, therefore, as doom for Israel's *goy* existence rather than for Yahweh's loving concern that had created an Israel in the first place. The chaos which is overtaking Israel is, for Hosea, only a return to the desert[40] where, as had been the case in the beginning of Israel's existence, Yahweh would woo and win and form a people, an *'am:*

[Yahweh says:]
So I *am the one who will woo her* (*i.e. Israel*),
Will go after her into the desert,
Will restore covenant meaning to her existence again . . .
And she will respond there as in the days of her youth,
As at the time of her rescue from Egypt.[41]
(Hos. 2:14–15)

Clearly Hosea envisages the re-creation of Israel in the image God had in mind in the first place, an Israel which will once again praise God with *todah,* not with the hymnic praise used by *goys*. That is very probably the meaning of the last two lines quoted above in light of the discussion so far.

The *'am* versus *goy* issue is also what underlies the dramatic narrative found in Isaiah 7. The background of that narrative apparently lies in the attempt of the kingdom of Damascus and the northern kingdom of Israel to organize themselves and their neighbors into an alliance that would resist the Assyrian incursion into the Syro-Palestinian area. Ahaz, king of the southern kingdom of Judah refused to participate in that alliance, and so in 734 B.C. Damascus and Israel seem either to have invaded or to have threatened to invade Judah in an attempt to force Ahaz to join them. That threat in the offing, Ahaz, in the narrative in Isaiah 7, is out making sure that the water supply of Jerusalem is secure against a siege. He is behaving as a responsible king and commander-in-chief, as a good *goy*. That is the point of what Isaiah has to say to him: "Take heed, be quiet, have no fear . . . If you will not *believe*, there will be no security" (Is. 7:4,9). But Ahaz refuses to see that consulting Yahweh as convenor of Israel has anything to do with the kind of situation that now threatens Israel's national (*goy*) security. That is the background against which Isaiah says that before a child already in its mother's womb and, indeed, about to be born attains maturity, the Syro-Israelite threat will have vanished and the Assyrian power being employed by Yahweh will have come into the area and unimaginable destruction have taken place. What Isaiah faults Ahaz for is Ahaz's total misunderstanding of what Israel really is, for taking Israel to be a *goy* rather than an '*am*, a worldly power rather than the people of God. That is why, for Isaiah, judgment and doom are coming. Given the way in which Israel has ceased to be Israel and has become merely another *goy*, judgment and doom are necessary before that vision of the future in Isaiah 2:2–4, at which we have already looked, can be realized. The Israel that has become a *goy* is being destroyed and swept up into the more universal history represented by the Assyrian empire so that the universal Israel pictured in Isaiah 2 can be brought into being by God.

The same thing is said in a striking way and in another set of images in Jeremiah 23:7–8:

> Behold days are coming, this is Yahweh's oracle, when it will no longer be said, "By the life of Yahweh who rescued the Israelites from the land of Egypt," but instead, "By the life of Yahweh who rescued and who gathered the successors to the house of Israel from the land of Zaphon and from every one of the countries in which they were scattered so that they could live on soil of their own."

It has been pointed out, and quite rightly, that an astounding and blasphemous thing is being said here.[42] The translation above has rendered the Hebrew words usually translated "As Yahweh lives" literally. "By the life of Yahweh" is the form of a solemn oath. The most solemn thing on which an Israelite could take an oath was that which lay at the heart of Israel's *todah*, the living God who had rescued Israel from oppression in Egypt. Now, at the beginning of the sixth century B.C., probably when Israel's deliverance from Egyptian oppression as the basis of an oath had persisted for more than half a millenium, the Babylonians are threatening Israel's very existence. Jeremiah not only insists that Yahweh's hand is in that, but goes so far as to insist that all of that is leading to the demise of an Israel that has become just another *goy*, so that Yahweh can gather out of the scattered human *goy*nesses present in the world a new and genuine Israel. So the form of the most solemn oath will no longer invoke what had been *the* norm of Yahweh's identification. It will involve a new act of redemption in which a new Israel will be rescued from the chaos of judgment and destruction,[43] gathered from all the countries. Once again, as had Hosea and Isaiah, an Israelite prophet is claiming that the destruction of Israel's national (*goy*) existence is the prelude to the creation of a new, more universal Israel which is what God meant Israel to be in the first place.

The same kind of thing is said in the canonical prophets again and again, and it reaches its height in the prophecies in the latter part of the book of Isaiah which come from Babylon in the time in which the taking over of the Babylonian empire by Cyrus the Persian made it possible for Israelites in exile to return to their homeland and reestablish the cult of Yahweh in Jerusalem.[44] Those prophecies are crystal clear in their interpretation of the era of imperial expansion that had led to Israel's national demise as an era that had led to the establishment of a new Israel that is what Yahweh had had in mind from the time of the call of Abraham and Sarah.

First, Second Isaiah is as explicitly clear as Jeremiah that the events that were formerly the content of Israel's *todah* have been superseded:

> [Yahweh says:]
> *The former things, lo they are over,*
> *And new things are what I am talking about.*
> (Is. 42:9)

Remember not the former things,
No, do not think about things from the past.
Look at me doing a new thing,
It now *pops like a bud, can't you recognize it?*
(Is. 43:18–19)

Second, that new thing in Second Isaiah nowhere involves Israel's being any longer a kingdom or a nation, any longer a *goy*. Equally as revolutionary as the assertion that the "former things" are being replaced by a "new thing" is the assertion in Second Isaiah that what the dynasty of David had represented in Israel has now been handed over to the non-Israelite Cyrus:

This is Yahweh's pronouncement to Yahweh's Messiah, to Cyrus,
Whose right hand I have strengthened
So that nations collapse before him,
So that kings are defenseless before him,
So that doors fall open before him,
And gates cannot keep him out . . .
(Is. 45:1)

Just as David had arisen from within Israel to make Israel's continuance possible when the Philistine invasion of Palestine had made Israel's convening to praise Yahweh impossible, so now Cyrus has, at the initiative of Yahweh, arisen from outside Israel to perform a parallel function in a new and different time. Cyrus is now the Messiah, the "anointed one." Israel itself can now really be Israel, no longer needs exist as a *goy*.

Rather, and this is the third significant thing in Second Isaiah, Israel is a new, non-national, non-*goy*, cultic community whose vocation it is to give to Yahweh the praise that Yahweh deserves:

[Yahweh says:]
I am saying to the north, Release them!
To the south, Hold none of them back!

Bring my sons from afar,
My daughters from the ends of the earth,
Yes, everyone who calls on my name,
Whom I created for my glory,
Whom I formed and prepared.
(Is. 43:6–7)

The last three lines are quite explicit about the forming of a nonethnic ("everyone") community which exists for the praise of God ("who calls on my name"). Moreover the passage is not isolated in Second Isaiah. The conclusion of some verses which have already been quoted makes it clear that the outcome of the new thing Yahweh is about as the Persian empire overcomes Babylon and makes it possible for Israel's exile to end is not a restoration of Israel's *goy* power but the creation anew of a people whose vocation it is to praise Yahweh:

Remember not the former things,
No, do not think about things from the past.
Look at me doing a new thing,
It now pops like a bud, can't you recognize it?
Here's what it is: I'm making a safe way through the desert,
Making rivers in the most barren places.
Honor will be done me by the wild beasts,
Primeval monsters as well as ostriches.
For I have placed water in the desert,
Rivers in the most barren place,
So that there might be drink for the people I have chosen.
This is the people I have put together for myself:
My praise is what is on their lips.
(Is. 43:18–21)

Furthermore, what that new, non-*goy*, specially formed people's praise is rooted in is made quite clear by another one of those observations of a situation in which "the medium is the message." A recurrent exhortation in the prophetic pronouncements in Second Isaiah is, "Fear not!"

(cf. 43:1,5; 44:2,8; etc.). This phrase is rooted in the cultic setting which is the location of *todah*. It is the pronouncement made by the priest, or cultic functionary of some kind, in response to the lament voiced by a suppliant. It is the form of the *Heilsorakel*, the oracle of reassurance.[45] It is assurance that the cry of the suppliant will be heard, has been heard, and that deliverance will come from the saving God. The reassurance bespoken in that kind of oracle and the deliverance it promises, which in the time of Second Isaiah is available in accord with Cyrus' policies to *all* who have been in exile and not just to those whose former nation was Israel,[46] is what qualifies one to be a part of the new Israel envisaged in Second Isaiah. The qualification for being part of the new Israel is not a *goy* qualification. It is being one who has reason to offer *todah*.

Thus it is that Second Isaiah focusses what is said in various ways and out of various prophetic traditions by those prophetic figures who, through the two centuries that swept Israel up into larger ancient Near Eastern history and destroyed Israel's national life, claimed the history through which they lived as taking place under the sovereignty of Yahweh in as complete a way as the history that brought Israel into being in the celebrated past. The series of events formerly recited in Israel's *todah* is being replaced by a new series of events which is recognizable on the basis of the past as the product of Yahweh's sovereign will, but which is new and definitely more universal than anything Israel had formerly known. The reason that has happened is that the Israel of the past had forgotten what Israel is by nature, had become a *goy*. The content of the new series of events is the rescue from *goy* existence of a new, nonnational, transethnic, non-*goy* Israel whose vocation it is to be the people who witness to the true God through doing *todah*, through giving thanks. That is the message through which the prophets stood in succession to those who framed Israel's great epics, through which they claimed a new era of history as the medium in and through which God had chosen to be known by and related to a human community.

It should be noted, as this section of our discussion comes to its conclusion, that the Chronicler (the writer of I and II Chronicles, Ezra, and Nehemiah), narrow as was that writer's vision, did grasp that point in one way. As we have already had occasion to note, the Chronicler wrote Israel's history as if Israel's vocation to be the nonnational community which rendered the proper worship to the one, true God had been there from the beginning. For the Chronicler, the only real function of Israel's monarchy had been to provide the setting and protection necessary for the performance of the cult. When, in the Chronicler's view, the monarchy had forgotten that, had become an end in itself, its function was transferred by God to Cyrus and Cyrus' successors.[47] The Chronicler, even if for understandable reasons in a time in which Israel had to fight for its identity and integrity, completely missed the universality of that vision of Israel which had been held by the canonical prophets, and hence was one of those most responsible for narrowing the meaning of *goy* to "Gentile" in the sense of "outsider." Yet, the Chronicler did grasp the nonnational, non-*goy* implications of the prophetic vision of a new Israel, even while failing to grasp all the facets of that vision. The Chronicler finally still stood in the *todah* tradition by interpreting the meaning of the restored, postexilic cult in a new recital of Israel's life in history. Thus it was that the prophets' witness was understood, even if imperfectly.

The Prophets Themselves as the Basis of Todah

The attempt of the Chronicler to find a continuation of the history of God's involvement with Israel in an historical course of events through the exile and into the postexilic reestablishment of the Jerusalem cult was not finally credible. Judaism had already begun to become the richer, more complex and variegated religion that survived the fall of the temple to the Romans in A.D. 70–135, and the majority of the Jewish people were not part of the Jerusalem community around the temple. The Chronicler's narrative was just not adequate as the story of the people of God. It is probably both the result of that and a symbol of that that the work of the Chronicler did not come to be woven into the great narrative that runs from Genesis through II Kings, the narrative into which the successive witness of the Yahwist and the Elohist and the Deuteronomists and the Priestly Code had come to be included, but came to be preserved only at the very end of the Writings, the very last section of the Hebrew Bible, as well as almost never to be read publicly in the Jewish community.[48] The trauma of what happened when events had arrived at those described at the end of II Kings was so great that Israel as a whole was not able to see a communal history going on from there as the bearer of God's revelation to and involvement with Israel. There was, in other words, no continuing communal basis for *todah*.

What the Israel of the exilic and postexilic period did, however, was to place right after the narrative complex that begins with Genesis and ends with II Kings the books of the prophets: Isaiah, Jeremiah, Ezekiel, and the Book of the Twelve.[49] It was as if, through a period in which the "former things" had indeed seemed to come to an end but in which the promised "new things" seemed to fail to come to fruition, the lives and work of the prophets were the only things that could be recounted in order to provide any meaning for what was happening. It was as if the occupants of an office which had heretofore been part and parcel of, and found its meaning in relation to, the continuum that was the history of the people of God now themselves became the bearers of the only saving history that could be discerned.[50] The *prophets* and the events of their lives, not the corporate people of God and the events of its history, became the only content there seemed to be for *todah*. That is apparently what led to the narratives *about* the prophets coming into being and then being included in the books, which are for the most part collections recording what the prophets *said*. There was interest in the autobiographical narratives in which the prophets explained how they had come to take up the office in the first place and in which they sought to validate their claim to be those who spoke for God. Those narratives come to be preserved not only for that original reason but also as *todah* recital of how through a terrible period God had at least been involved in human history in the calling of a Hosea or an Isaiah.[51] That interest also led to the development of narratives about the prophets, about how their words had been backed up by their lives, about what it had cost them to be faithful in delivering the message God had committed to them. Thus, even in the comparatively small book bearing the name of Amos, a book the obvious basic purpose of which is to record the sayings of the prophet, space is devoted to a brief narrative of how Amos got into trouble with the authorities for what he was saying, a story found in Amos 7:10–16.

In some instances the narratives in the prophetic books present a picture of the prophet and the prophet's message at variance with the picture of the prophet derived from his recorded words. In the same way, in the New Testament, the picture we get of Paul in the Acts of the Apostles is not exactly the same as the picture derived from Paul's own writings. Such may be the case with the short narrative in Hosea 3 in which the hints we now have in chapters 1 and 2 about the marriage and family of the prophet are not necessarily borne out. What may have happened is that both the marriage imagery Hosea uses to describe the relationship between God and Israel and the sheer passion of his pronouncements resulted in the rise of that kind of legendary embellishment that inevitably comes to be attached to the memories of great human beings.[52] That kind of thing is certainly true of the narratives about Isaiah which are preserved both in Isaiah 36–39 and in the Deuteronomic History in II Kings 18–20.[53] It is indeed true that Isaiah was a product of ancient Near Eastern culture as it was mediated to Israel through the traditions of the city–kingdom of Jerusalem which had a Canaanite history before it was taken over by David. It is true too that, using the imagery of cosmic mythology, Isaiah saw Jerusalem as the hub of Yahweh's sovereignty, as the place where Yahweh's rule over the whole earth would finally be manifest. It is also true, however, as we have seen in discussing Isaiah 1, that Isaiah insisted that Israel must accept the judgment Yahweh was bringing on Jerusalem through the Assyrians. Isaiah 22 seems to indicate real anger on Isaiah's part at a population which cheered as inevitable deliverance what Isaiah believed to be a mere pause in the Assyrian campaign. Nevertheless, the Isaiah pictured in the narrative, and this is true in one way in chapter 7 as well as of chapters 36–39, is a prophet who preaches the doctrine of the inviolability of Jerusalem as Yahweh's holy city.[54]

The exaggerations and even distortions of legends, however, arise precisely out of thankfulness for what the one being honored meant to the human community which remembered that one. Terrible as the prophet's pronouncements of doom had been for Israel to hear, it was still the case that those pronouncements were what finally gave some meaning to the events which spelled the end of Israel as it had been. Terrible as the destruction which overtook Israel was, if the prophets were correct in insisting that the destruction was the consequence of God's judgment, then the message of the prophets redeemed an otherwise meaningless era from meaninglessness. Furthermore, if the prophets suffered because of their faithfulness in the delivery of the message they believed God had committed to them at the hands of those who would not accept that message, then not only the content of their words but their lives themselves had been redemptive. Their suffering was, as it were, the vehicle through which the truth of their words had come to Israel. That is what led to the legends. They are really *todah* being recited on the basis of the only thing a stunned Israel could see as being worthy of *todah* in those centuries of devastation by Assyrians and Babylonians.

It was the prophet Jeremiah who, above all, was the subject of such narrative. One reason may be that Jeremiah seems to be the prophet into whose own inner struggles about what was happening we have the most insight. There is to be found in the book of Jeremiah a series of passages which have been called Jeremiah's "confessions." They make exquisite use of lament forms to picture what happens in the dialogue between God and a prophet who must be faithful to the prophetic vocation to find any fulfillment at all, but for whom the prophetic vocation involves the pronouncement of doom on everything that means anything at all to the prophet. If it is the case that tradition has attached a lot of lament material to Jeremiah, it is also very likely the case that there was something about Jeremiah as remembered by those around him that made that a fitting thing to do. There seems to have been that something about Jeremiah, and about the events through which his prophetic career took him, which made it abundantly clear what it cost to be a prophet.

That aspect of Jeremiah is what gave rise to the narrative about him that is found in chapters 26–45 of the book that bears his name, about forty percent of its contents. Those chapters do not form a coherent whole from beginning to end. They seem to represent the gathering together of different strands of tradition about Jeremiah's life and career.[55] What is uniformly emphasized, however, is what prompted one German scholar to entitle Jeremiah 26–45 "*die Leidensgeschichte Jeremias*," "the passion narrative of Jeremiah."[56] What the narrative shows is how, from the beginning to the end of his career, Jeremiah's pronouncement that the Babylonian invasion and conquest and the exile that followed must be accepted as God's judgment and as God's opening of the way to the gathering of a new and more universal Israel met with nothing but misunderstanding and rejection. It shows how Jeremiah, to whom his people's life and traditions and structures meant so much, found himself increasingly ostracized by Israel as a result of his call to be a prophet, which call had come precisely through those structures and out of those traditions. It shows how he suffered humiliation and imprisonment and physical torture for what he said in obedience to God, and how, finally, he was unwillingly dragged off to Egypt by some compatriots who were still seeking to avoid the reality Jeremiah had been insisting was there as a result of the sovereignty of Israel's God over history. The separate parts of the Jeremiah narrative and then the narrative as a whole are there because of the way in which the story of Jeremiah and his faithfulness and his suffering came to be, for some in Israel, the story that gave meaning to the time through which Jeremiah had lived. That story alone in that time was really *todah*, the kind of thankful recital that redeemed a terrible time from meaninglessness. It is in that sense that, at the end of the narrative, the life of Baruch, who may very well be one of those chiefly responsible for preserving the narrative, is described as a "prize of war" (Jer. 45:5). Out of all that had happened, Baruch, in whom the story that made sense of it all, the story of Jeremiah, was present in memory, was something of great value preserved out of great destruction.

That view of the significance of the prophets, the view that sees them in their words and their lives as the means by which an otherwise meaningless time is redeemed from meaninglessness, is probably what gave rise to the famous "songs of the suffering servant" in Isaiah 40–55.[57] The debate about whether the servant depicted in those songs is an individual in Israel or Israel itself as a corporate entity has been endless.[58] It may be that that question is not the one which will unlock the basic significance of those songs, for the nature of Israelite thought is that it does not make the neat distinctions between individual and corporate realities that we do.[59] It may be that there is a more significant thing to be said about those songs if we are to get at their basic meaning, and that thing may very well lie in that aspect of the ministry of the great prophets, manifest above all in Jeremiah, which gave rise to the narrative parts of the prophetic books. For, what those songs are saying can be summarized under three headings. First, the servant of God (whether individual or corporate), who is the epitome of everything God was trying to accomplish is the call to an Israel that began with Sarah and Abraham, is one in whom self never strikes out at others or becomes defensive in order to justify or protect what that self is (cf. Is. 42:1–3; 50:4–9). Second, that servant is one whose redemptive ministry God means to be for every part of the human community, not just for Israel in a narrowly *goy* sense (cf. Is. 49:1–6). Third, that servant is one whose utter, persevering obedience of God clear to the point of death becomes the means by which humanity (even kings!) is brought to its senses (cf. Is. 42:4; 52:13—53:12).

The vision in the "songs of the suffering servant" of what will bring about that eschatological *todah* in which humanity finally finds redemption is clearly based on what happened in the career of a Jeremiah as well as in the careers of others who shared Jeremiah's prophetic vocation. That vision came because of the way in which prophetic faithfulness and devotion, through those two centuries in which imperial expansion destroyed Israel's national existence, were the only basis on which Israel could find any reason for *todah*. That is why Israel, when the attempt of the Chronicler to find subject matter for *todah* after Jerusalem's exile had begun simply did not ring true, decided that the lives and words of the prophets were what belonged in the scriptural canon after the great epic, *todah* narratives. While exiled Israel waited on God, *todah* was still fitting as praise of God because of God's continued involvement in history in a terrible period. That involvement was through the calls and careers and faithfulness of God's servants the prophets.

4

Wisdom's Reinterpretation: Adaptation to Exile

As time went on for Israel after the traumatic series of experiences focussed in the fall of Jerusalem to the Babylonians in 587 B.C., the history which had for the great epics been the medium of God's revelation to and involvement with Israel receded further and further into the past. Furthermore, the new history promised in the pronouncements of the great prophets seemed increasingly to be delayed. It was as if any basis for Israel's identifying itself as the people of God by offering *todah* had ceased to exist. Only the *memory* of Israel as such a people remained. This is what led to the preservation of the records of what was remembered that came to be the Hebrew Bible. We have seen how the words and the narratives about the prophets' lives were preserved and cherished as indication that God had, through an era of unmitigated disaster, been at work to keep in touch with Israel. Also, the situation in which Israel found itself after 587 led to the preservation of those great *todah* interpretations of Israel's existence found in the Yahwist, the Elohist, and the Deuteronomic History, to their combination with one another into a larger and more comprehensive epic, and then, later on, to their final inclusion within the framework of the Priestly Code.[1] That situation also resulted in the collection and preservation of the psalms which, during the period of the exile, were probably brought together for the first time into one collection, and, like the Pentateuch, divided into five books.[2] In all this, Israel sought to remember who it was by preserving the heritage of the past.

The present, however, remained insignificant for a people who had seen life's meaning in terms of their relation with God in the course of events that was their history. How was God related to them now? Was God really related to them at all in the present? It was as if Israel, in terms of all that the word "Israel" really denoted, had ceased to exist. It was as if Israel was only a memory of the past and a hope for some unrealized future in the minds of separated, exiled Israelites torn loose from any history in which they could find an identity as Israel. It is that tragic spirit in a people whose identity had been bound up with history and *todah* that is what the word "exile" is all about. "Exile" is not, for Israel, simply a matter of geographical separation from a homeland, although that is one powerful meaning of exile. In a deeper sense, however, those who remained in the devastated homeland were also in exile. Exile is a state of the spirit, a state of being:

Beside Babylon's *rivers: to dwell there was to weep*
Because of our memory of Zion.
On the trees watered by them
We hung up our lyres.[3]
In such a place our captors wanted us to sing a song,
And our tormentors to make melody:
"Sing for us one of Yahweh's songs!"
Oh, how is it at all possible to sing Yahweh's song
On alien soil?

(Ps. 137:1–4)

It is clear that this "we" lament does have to do with exile to a place, with exile from Jerusalem and Yahweh's land.

But something deeper rings through the words. The normative kind of song sung to Yahweh is *todah*, and Israel finds itself in a place, using the word in a more than physical sense, at which there is no basis for singing *todah*. The medium of God's presence, the history that is celebrated in *todah*, is no longer there. That is the deep sense in which Israel found itself in exile.

It seems to have been in that situation that Wisdom came to be important theologically for Israel. It was as if, undoubtedly gradually and not as a result of some conscious decision, Wisdom came to replace Israel's history and the *todah* to which that history gave rise as the medium through which Israel believed God to be related to it. It should be emphasized that this did not take place as the result of some abstract, arbitrary decision on the part of some individual or some group in a position of theological authority. It came about as a result of the actual situation that obtained in the era of the exile. It came about as, once again, a people found the idiom through which the reality of God's presence with them and the meaning of that reality could be expressed in the cultural heritage in which they lived.

Wisdom in the Ancient Near East and in Israel

The phenomenon of Wisdom and of wise men and women was a part of the culture of the ancient Near East from Egypt at one end of the fertile crescent clear around to Mesopotamia at the other. Wisdom literature from all parts of that geographical and cultural area abounds.[4] That wisdom literature is one manifestation of the kind of practical, aphoristic, proverbial, pragmatic guidance for human life to be found in all human communities, even if it does have its own distinctive forms in the ancient Near East. Furthermore, Israel was acquainted with it, took it for granted, participated in it throughout its long history. Israel did so inevitably and naturally as a people that was part of the culture in which Wisdom figured.

To be "wise"—the word *hakam* in Hebrew is both the adjective "wise" and the noun for "wise person"—does not mean to possess large quantities of theoretical knowledge or to have a high I.Q. or to have an advanced education. The wise person may indeed possess those things, but Wisdom—the Hebrew word is *hokmah*—does not consist in them. To be wise is to have practical know-how, to be skillful, to be shrewd. The fingers that sew lovely things, or the hands that form beautiful shapes of wood or stone, or the ability of a ruler to keep peace in a community containing factions that rub one another the wrong way: these things are characterized as "wise." It is in this context that the genre central to oral and written literature connected with Wisdom is to be understood. That genre is a form of words (remember form criticism!) called in Hebrew a *mashal*. *Mashal* is most often translated "proverb," and its plural form, *meshalim*, is the Hebrew title for the biblical book of Proverbs. The meaning of the word is, however, wider than can be contained in one translation. *Mashal* may, given the particular form it takes, be variously translated, in addition to "proverb," by "riddle" or "parable" or "allegory" or "fable." The basic meaning has to do with a form of words in which some specific reality is verbalized, articulated, stated in such a way that the reality in question can be seen for what it really is and then dealt with. Indeed, although human beings are seldom conscious of the etymological background of words they use, it is interesting to note that the noun *mashal* seems etymologically to be connected with a verb that means "to control" or "to have dominion over." A *mashal* is a form of words which gives human beings control over a reality by articulating that reality so that it can be seen for what it is.

The "wise" in a more specific and technical sense were those who had the ability to formulate such sayings, who had committed to the storehouse of their memories many such sayings, who had the insight and the skill to match some specific reality with a *mashal* that put that reality into words. The "wise" were those who, out of the heritage of the Wisdom tradition, could come up with the *meshalim* that revealed to men and women what the nature of given situations really was so that men and women could be the masters of those situations and not their victims. When one is, precipitously and without any responsible consideration, about to invest heavily in some object that has struck a momentary fancy, the saying by someone, "A fool and a fool's money are soon parted" shows up the situation for what it really is, may bring the person in question back to reality, and avert a silly and even harmful action. That is what Wisdom and *meshalim* are all about.[5]

"Education" in the ancient Near East was connected with all this. It consisted in putting oneself under the tutelage of one of the "wise" in order to learn a stock of *meshalim* sufficient to cover the various realities and situations that arise in life and in order to learn the art of formulating and applying *meshalim* to realities and situations. A storehouse of *meshalim* readied one to act with that shrewdness which kept things on an even keel, averted disaster, kept life in order. Thus education, to a large degree, consisted in committing series of *meshalim* to memory and in committing lists of the various animal and floral and other phenomena of life to memory so that one was provided with the words that could make things recognizable for what they were. A stock of such words saved one from being ignorant and powerless in the face of life's realities, made one master of what one encountered. The lists of *meshalim* and natural phenomena were very often acrostics, each successive item beginning with the next letter of the alphabet in order. Such an obvious mnemonic device ensured retention in memory of all the items on the list in their proper order. It also came to have deeper significance. To know everything from *aleph* to *tau*, or from *alpha* to *omega* or from A to Z, was to have the whole list in mind and to be in control of things, to be *hakam*.

That kind of training took place in the court schools in which those who were to succeed to kingship or to assume roles of leadership in society were prepared for their responsibilities. In a culture where writing was not an end in itself but a means to ensure that essentially oral literature was repeated accurately, the "wise" were probably also those skilled in the art of writing, the scribes and record keepers, since they needed notes to make sure that their lists of *meshalim* were accurately repeated. The role played by the "wise" in the royal courts of the ancient Near East accounts for the way in which rulers were their sponsors, served as patrons of the Wisdom enterprise. Since Solomon was the king under whom ancient Near Eastern culture and all that went with it became a significant factor in Israel's life, it was undoubtedly in his time that formal, court schools of Wisdom also became part of Israel's life. That was why Solomon came to be remembered as the fount and patron of Wisdom in Israel, Israel's *hakam par excellence*.

In addition to the schools at the royal courts, life in families and among the people of villages and cities was a setting where all the participants in the culture learned and practiced the traditions of the Wisdom heritage. It was part of the cultural air breathed by the people of the ancient Near East. The gathering in the evening in the gateway of a town—the gateway being the only place in crowded, ancient towns where a group of any size could gather—would be where the activity of the day was reviewed, its meaning sought and then stated in a *mashal* or a series of *meshalim*.[6] The Hebrew word for such a gathering is *sod,* and the way in which it was the source of wisdom about life is indicated by the fact that *sod* has the meaning of both "council" and "counsel." How its imagery can be used in striking ways is illustrated by Amos 3:7. A prose sentence in the middle of a poetic passage, that verse may have originated as someone commented on Amos' insistence that prophecy must follow a word of God, someone who marvelled and rejoiced at how

God did not leave Israel in the dark but continued to send prophets to reveal the divine will and purpose. The verse is usually translated, "Surely the Lord God does nothing without revealing his secret to his servants the prophets." In more literal terms what it says is, "Surely Yahweh the Sovereign never does a thing (or, never brings a word into being) without opening up Yahweh's *sod* to those who serve Yahweh as prophets." The imagery would have been rich and colorful for the original hearers, picturing God's creation of realities as taking place in a way that was analogous to the human community's way of coming to an understanding of realities.

The formal literature of the Wisdom enterprise took two basic forms which almost always are associated with one another. First, there was the "instruction" of a given wise person, the collection of *meshalim*, proverbs, in which that person's teaching had been given. Second, there was the "tale," the account of the *hakam* way in which the wise person in question had always lived, very often in circumstances that tried wisdom very severely. The tale, in its way was also a *mashal*, a form of words in which wisdom was imparted and in which, above all, the point was made that the structure of life was such that wise behavior, as contrasted with foolishness, always finally led to an outcome that made sense. The tale was also an account which established, on the basis of the actual deportment of the person in question, the credentials which underlay the teaching. These two forms, the instruction and the tale, go together in the wisdom literature. Even if the teaching of a given wise person is not preceded by a tale of any length about that person, the *hakam* from whom a collection of *meshalim* comes is always at least named. The point seems to be that the adequacy of the teaching is established by the reputation of the teacher as being not just a formulator of teachings but wise in the living of life. On the other hand, tales about wise persons, even if the tale is unaccompanied by a set of instructions, inevitably allude to their teaching, to their *meshalim*. The point seems to be that the life of a *hakam* inevitably issues in teaching through which the wisdom, the *hokmah* that undergirds life is communicated to the human community.

The scattered presence in the Old Testament narrative of allusions and passages whose origins lie in Wisdom indicates the extent to which Wisdom and what came to be written down in the wisdom literature were just part of the atmosphere in which Israel lived. Saul, to take one example, having been designated leader of Israel by Samuel "got religion" in a way that was not consistent with his reputation. "Therefore a *mashal* came into being, 'Is Saul also among the prophets?' " (I Samuel 10:12). In that verse, as in other places, *mashals* are taken for granted, are just part of tradition. When the saga at the end of Genesis of which Joseph is the hero comes to its climax and the power of Egypt is in the hands of one who has every reason to want vengeance on his brothers, Joseph's "put down" to those who have acted foolishly rather than wisely are, "I am definitely not God. In what you did, you plotted evil against me. But God used it in a plot that led to good" (Gen. 50:19–20). That statement is a perfect embodiment of Wisdom's practical, pragmatic, empirical, take-what-life-deals-out shrewdness. Moreover, it is not surprising to find it in the mouth of Joseph, for the basic narrative form used in the Joseph saga in Genesis is, in fact, the *hakam* tale, the tale about the person who embodies Wisdom.[7] Once again, in a context originating with the Yahwist and the Elohist and the theological orientation based on *todah*, form criticism shows in a "medium-is-the-message" way how something there in the culture is taken up into Israel's literature. There are elements of Wisdom in the narrative of the birth of Moses, in the narrative of how Solomon came to be David's successor that is found in II Samuel 9–20 and I Kings 1–2, as well as in the books of the prophets.[8] We could go on and on, for there is ample evidence that Wisdom was just taken for granted as a part of the culture in which Israel lived.

There does not, however, seem to be any evidence that Wisdom was of any real theological significance in Israel before the period of the exile. Even the statement "the fear of Yahweh is the beginning of wisdom" which is so traditional and is found in so many places in the Old Testament is more like a *mashal* than a profound theological observation. It is in line with Joseph's statement to his brothers in Genesis 50:19–20. What that statement asserts is that the indispensible foundation on which the whole Wisdom enterprise is based is a recognition of the limitations of human strength and ingenuity. What is really being said is that the beginning of any real wisdom at all is acknowledgment of what God is and what human beings are not, and that is really a *mashal.*[9] What is there is really simple, wise, practical, shrewd advice. No real theological meaning or significance is attributed to Wisdom.

That is not to say that, by Wisdom's very nature as well as in the explicit content of some of the ancient Near Eastern literature originating in Wisdom, there were not some presuppositions about the nature of reality on the basis of which the Wisdom enterprise existed. Consciously or unconsciously Wisdom depended on the presupposition that the realities constituting the universe and the life that goes on in it are undergirded by an order that is consistent. That was not the abstract point from which the Wisdom enterprise set out to create *mashals*. Once, however, one began to think about it in a wise kind of way, it became apparent that the fact that a *mashal*, once formulated, was always applicable to the same kind of reality that had given rise to it in the first place did imply an order that made that possible. So it was that, in Egypt at least, that order came to have a name, *ma'at*. *Ma'at* is rendered "justice" in most translations, and there are many instances in which that rendering does make sense. What *ma'at* fundamentally names, however, is precisely that order undergirding reality which makes the Wisdom enterprise possible. Furthermore, given what happened later on in Israel, it is interesting to note that there are passages in Egyptian literature in which *ma'at* has been personified, is a some*one* and not merely a some*thing*.[10]

Nevertheless, even when the presuppositions underlying Wisdom and the wisdom literature of the ancient Near East have been pointed out, there is still no indication that preexilic Israel engaged in speculation about the significance of Wisdom in any theological way. Wisdom seems simply to have been accepted as a part of the culture, taken for granted, one of the things used by the human community in dealing with life. Israel's theology, the terms and concepts in which Israel consciously thought about God and the relationship between God and Israel, Israel's calculated consideration of the ultimate meaning of things, involved the way in which the Yahwist, the Elohist, and the Deuteronomists dealt with things. *Todah* and covenant were what were to the fore, and the recitative interpretation of history that both *todah* and covenant required, when preexilic Israel worked at its equivalent of theology.

Wisdom as a Theological Idiom[11]

When all that has been said, however, it is still quite clear that, probably subsequent to the formation of the Law and the Prophets as a body of literature in the form in which they still exist, sometime during the period of the exile, Israel did begin to be interested in a theological way in Wisdom and the wisdom literature. For one thing, books whose origins manifestly lie in the Wisdom ethos are present in the Writings, that third large section of the Hebrew Bible which follows the Law and the Prophets. Proverbs and Ecclesiastes and Job, different as they are from one another, are certainly correctly classified as wisdom literature by those who study and interpret the Old Testament. For another thing, the wisdom literature is represented proportionately even more in those writings present in the ancient Greek version of the Old Testament but not in the Hebrew Bible, those writings known since Jerome as the Apocrypha.[12] The Wisdom of Solomon and Ecclesiasticus are quite definitely examples of wisdom literature, and elements that are clearly manifestations of the Wisdom ethos are to be found in Tobit and Judith and Baruch, as well as in other writings in the Apocrypha. For yet another thing, Wisdom is not only what lies behind several of the psalms in the Psalter, but those psalms seem also to be located at such key places in the final structure of the Psalter as to indicate that Wisdom somehow was very significant to those who put Israel's sacral songs into the collection in which they have come down to us.[13] Finally, it is also the case that, in a number of the writings mentioned above, theological speculations and assertions about the nature of Wisdom are set forth. It is clear that, in the exilic and postexilic period, not only did Wisdom come to occupy a significant role in Israel's religious life and theological writings but also came to be considered by many a replacement of the events of history as the medium through which God was revealed to and involved with the human community.

What brought this about is most likely to be explained by that situation in which Israel found itself after the Babylonian conquest of Jerusalem and the beginning of the exile, the implications of which increasingly came to be realized by Israel as the years of exile went by. In spite of the promise present in the words of the prophets, it became clearer and clearer that the history that had been the medium of God's involvement with Israel had come to an end with the fall of Jerusalem in 587 B.C. With the passage of time that history became more and more a relic of the past, not the prototype of what was being experienced in the present. Furthermore, the resumption of such a relationship with God as had been promised by the prophets seemed increasingly illusive and unreal. God may, an exiled Israelite might have thought, have been present with my ancestors in their history, and *todah* may have been a beautifully appropriate way for them to praise God as well as a reasonable basis for their theology, but in what discernible way at all is God with us now? What is the medium through which God is related to us now? Is there any way through which God is related to us in our present exile? The lament of Psalm 137 rang truer as an answer to those questions than did the attempt of the Chronicler. For some exiled Israelites the only prayer that seemed to have an integrity at all was, "O Silence, Silence, Silence!"[14]

That seems to have been the situation in which Wisdom came to be no longer just a taken-for-granted part of the cultural milieu but something treasured and explored and praised, and then personified and taken to be the reality, replacing the course of historical events, through which God was involved with the human community. The exiled Israelite who raised the questions of the preceding paragraph might, in considering Wisdom, have had some further thoughts. If, that Israelite might have speculated, no discernible course of historical events is now the means of a relationship between God and myself, there is still that practical guidance for life present in the teachings of Wisdom which are part of our communal heritage from the past. Indeed, that Israelite might have said, as I look desparately for some way in which contact with God is available, maybe I can begin to take Wisdom seriously as my people have not taken it seriously in a theological way in the past. Wisdom just may be, indeed is, that means created and cherished by God as God's way of contact with human beings.

That kind of thinking in the Israel of the exilic and post-exilic period led finally, by a process parallel to the one by which the framers of the great epics had earlier worked toward the theological statement found in Genesis through II Kings, to the position occupied by Wisdom as a mediatrix between God and the human community in some of the later Old Testament writings and some of the writings of the Apocrypha. Although there is no way to be certain about the chronological order in which the writings we are about to examine came into being, and although we will use them in the order we do to *illustrate* the process by which Wisdom probably came to occupy the theological position it did, it is nevertheless possible to trace with some degree of certainty what seems to have happened.

Job 28 is a meditative piece of poetry which seems not necessarily to be an intrinsic part of the context in which it is now found.[15] It begins with a poetic celebration of human skill for its ability to unlock the riches and secrets of the earth:

Of course, there are mines for silver,
And places inhabited by the gold which human beings refine.
Iron is mined from dust,
And stones are turned into copper.
The miners do not let darkness stop them,
Follow a vein to its utmost end,
Seek ore in the deepest darkness.
They open shafts beneath unpopulated valleys,
Walkers on the surface are unaware they're down there
In a situation more precarious than normal for human beings.
The earth! Out of it grows bread,
But below its surface it is raked like a bed of coals.
Its stones conceal sapphires,
And gold dust is one element of which it is made up.
No bird of prey knows how to get to what we are describing,
No, the far seeing falcon cannot spot it.
The proud beasts have not trodden there,
No lion takes that route.
It is the human hand that strikes the granite,
That lays bare mountains' foundations,

That cuts mining shafts in the rocks
So that the human eye beholds a plethora of gems.
Human ingenuity dams the very sources of the streams,
So that the hidden riches of the earth come to light.
(Job 28:1–11)

Human curiosity and human ingenuity and human skill are indeed remarkable. They are impressive in what they can accomplish. The central question, however, has to do with Wisdom, and none of the impressive accomplishments of human beings in uncovering the riches of the earth has turned up Wisdom. The central question remains:

But Wisdom, where is Wisdom to be found?
Where is the hiding place of understanding?
Mortal human beings are not at all acquainted with the way to it,
Nor is it located in the realm in which they dwell.
(Job 28:12–13)

What is the origin of Wisdom? That is the question with which the poem is really concerned. Who, so to speak, controls the mining of that most precious of all resources?

The primeval depths say, "Not here!"
And the sea says, "Not here!"
Gold can never buy it,
Nor is there silver enough for its price.
Even Ophir's gold is valueless for this purpose,
As is precious onyx or sapphire.
Neither gold nor crystal can be compared to it at all,
Nor the finest gold filigree come near it in value.
Don't even mention coral or alabaster,
For a mere smidgin of Wisdom is worth more than any pearl.
Topaz from Ethiopia is no match for it at all.
Fine gold is valueless in comparison.
So Wisdom? Where does *Wisdom originate?*
Where is the hiding place of understanding?

Nothing alive on the earth can see it,
And it is hidden from the birds in the sky.
Even the most awe-inspiring mythological beings say,
"We've only heard the faintest hint of an answer."
(Job 28:14–22)

That poetically beautiful set of nonanswers to the crucial question sets the stage for the answer in which the writer of the poem has come to believe:

God *is the One who understands the way to Wisdom,*
The One acquainted with its hiding place.
Yes, God's glance takes in earth's farthest bounds,
God can see everything under the heavens.
When God assigned to the wind its power,
Decided on the volume of water,
When God set a limit on how much it could rain,
Determined how lightning and thunder should work,
Back then God saw Wisdom, could describe it in detail.
God established it, knew everything there was to know about it.
(Job 28:23–27)

In the same way that someone in Israel in the time of David probably substituted Yahweh's name for Baal's in Psalm 29 in order to assert in the theological idiom of the culture that Yahweh was the final cosmic authority, someone is also, in this poem, using a concept available in the culture to assert that Israel's God is in control of what ultimately matters. In the same way that the Priestly Code uses the myth of the cosmic struggle between order and chaos in Genesis 1 to make the statement that Israel's God is in final control of things, so the poet from whom Job 28 comes is stating, in a time in which Wisdom has come to be accepted as the principle which gives life and the universe their meaning, that the source of and authority over that principle is Israel's God. A new and different cultural idiom is being employed, or is on the way to being employed, in the doing of theology. A new and different way of understanding the nature of the relationship between God and human beings has been found in the cultural heritage. When, therefore, an old, traditional *mashal* is used by the poet at the conclusion of this exquisite passage, it has taken on meaning that it never had as a simple, pragmatic statement of human limitations. What is asserted theologically in the poem preceding it has made of the old *mashal* a crucially climactic theological statement:

> *So, God said to the human race, "Lo,* [*here is the answer:*]
> *The fear of Yahweh, in* that *is Wisdom present,*
> *In departing from evil,* there *will understanding be found."*
>
> (Job 28:28)

In Job 28 Wisdom is still really a principle, a some*thing*, and the translations of the passage into English recognize that.[16] In Job 28 Wisdom is clearly that important order which holds all things in the universe together, is the ultimate resource of the cosmos, fulfills the role attributed to *ma'at* in Egypt. Wisdom is that through which Yahweh exercises sovereignty over all things. All that is implied in the poem in Job 28, but not set forth in detail. Specific statements, other than the one made by including the traditional *mashal* as the conclusion of the poem, about the relationship of Wisdom to human beings are not made. Wisdom is an important principle, but not yet a some*one* in relationship to whom exiled human beings can come to feel at home in the cosmos.

It is in the first nine chapters of the book of Proverbs that Wisdom has, in the Old Testament itself, come to be personified as well as to replace explicitly an historical course of events as the medium through which God is related to the human race. Chapters 10 through 31 of the book of Proverbs consist of a series of collections of *mashals* which, in the usual fashion of wisdom literature, are validated by the tracing of their origins to traditionally wise human beings,

Solomon himself in the first place, and then the staff of King Hezekiah, Agur, and Lemuel. The origins of those collections probably go far back into Israel's history, back even as far as the time of Solomon.[17] That they were collected into the book which is now their context, however, was quite likely due to the particular interest in Wisdom and the heritage of the Wisdom tradition that came about in the exilic and postexilic period when Israel was so desparately in need of discerning some medium through which God was involved with Israel. Furthermore, the opening chapters of the book of Proverbs, Proverbs 1–9, seem to constitute an introduction to the collections of *mashals* which follow, an introduction which sets forth what the Israel of the exile, or significant numbers of Israelites in exile, had come to see as the theological significance of Wisdom. They provide evidence of a theology very different from the one which had given rise to the narrative complexes found in Genesis through II Kings and in Chronicles, Ezra, and Nehemiah, as well as from the theology underlying Isaiah and Jeremiah and Ezekiel and the Book of the Twelve.

The heart of the theology found in the introduction to the book of Proverbs is found in Proverbs 8:22–31 in which Wisdom is not spoken *of* as in Job 28, but in which Wisdom speaks for her*self*, is definitely a some*one*:[18]

Yahweh created me when the divine activity began,
Before Yahweh did anything else, at the very beginning.
In the most primeval time was I fashioned,
Even before the earth had its beginning.
When even the primeval depths did not yet exist was I born,
When there was as yet no source of water at all.
When as yet the mountains had not been shaped,
Before the hills were there was I born.
Yes, even before Yahweh formed earth
Or even the faintest speck of dust.
When Yahweh put the heavens into place I was there,
Yes, when a boundary was drawn around the primeval depths.

When Yahweh set the canopy of heaven overhead,
Set the springs of the primeval depths in place,
When Yahweh assigned to the sea an outer limit
So that its waters should not disobey the divine command,
Thus providing secure foundations for the earth—
Then was I right there with Yahweh like a little child,
Then was I Yahweh's delight from one of those days to another,
Reveling in Yahweh's presence at each one of Yahweh's accomplishments,
Reveling particularly in the habitable part of Yahweh's earth,
Taking my *delight in those human creatures.*

(PR. 8:22–31)

The imagery of that passage is connected with the imagery of the Mesopotamian *Enuma elish* utilized in the Priestly Code in Genesis 1. Creation in that imagery involved first of all the watery, primeval depths, *tehom* in Hebrew, the chaos monster *Tiamat* in the Mesopotamian version. Then it involved the formation of the earth itself and the heaven that stretched out over the earth. Above all, however, and finally, it involved holding the primeval depths, chaos, in check so that the earth would be safe and so that life on the earth could go on. That basic plot underlies the poem in Proverbs 8:22–31, but two significant things intrude into it. First, even before the primeval, watery depths had come into being, Wisdom had already been created by God as the first product of the divine creativity. Wisdom, a some*one* who can speak for herself, was the companion of God from the beginning. The translation given above has chosen to resolve an obscurity in the Hebrew text by having Wisdom describe herself as a little child back there in the days of creation, as a child in whom Yahweh takes great delight, for that imagery seems to be more consistent with what follows in the poem. Another possible translation, however, implies a significant role for Wisdom in the work of creation itself, characterizing her as a "master artisan."[19] Whichever alternative is chosen, Wisdom is conceived of as occupying a place of importance in the divine scheme of things from the beginning, and Wisdom, as the source of that order which underlies creation, is taken to be the creation and colleague of Israel's God.

Moreover, Wisdom having been introduced into the Mesopotamian picture of the origins of the earth as God's close companion, a second addition to that picture is made in the poem in Proverbs 8:22–31. It has to do with the relationship between Wisdom and creation, and it asserts that Wisdom exists in a special and, from Wisdom's point of view, pleasing relationship with the human community. To translate the climactic lines of the poem in a slightly different way from the way in which they were translated just above, Wisdom concludes her account of her origins in this way:

At creation was I at Yahweh's side as a little child,
And just as I am Yahweh's delight from day to day,
Reveling before Yahweh at each of Yahweh's accomplishments
And reveling particularly at the habitable portion of earth,
So my *delight is in those human creatures [who inhabit it.].*[20]

(Pr. 8:30–31)

Thus Wisdom, the first of Yahweh's creatures and that which assures order in the cosmos, is by choice and with pleasure in a particular relationship with human beings. What the purpose and function of that relationship is is stated in many different ways in the theological treatise on Wisdom found in Proverbs 1–9. Here is one example:

Does not Wisdom call out,
Understanding raise her voice?
At the top of the hill beside the path,
Or at the crossroads she stations herself;

Outside the gates at the city's entrance,
Or where one actually passes through the portals she cries out,
"To you, men and women, do I call,
Raise my voice to you human creatures."

(PR. 8:1–4)

Thus is it explicitly stated that Wisdom is the means through which divine communication comes to human beings. The content of that communication is clearly conceived of in terms that come from the Wisdom heritage of the culture of the ancient Near East. It has to do with prudence and noble things and truth and righteousness and understanding and instruction and knowledge and discretion. (Cf. Pr. 8:5ff.) It has to do with human behavior and action which are *hakam*. It sees all that, however, in a more exalted and theological way than had the earlier Wisdom enterprise which concentrated on pragmatic shrewdness in the handling of the content of life. Just as what precedes it in the poem in Job 28 changes "The fear of the Lord is the beginning of wisdom" from a pragmatic *mashal* into a theological principle, so the elevation of Wisdom to the position of God's mode of contact with the human race gives to the content of Wisdom's instruction theological significance that it had not had before. It is now more than shrewd advice, and its opposite is more than foolishness. Just as Wisdom calls the human community into ways that lead to God, so there is another—also a female being—who calls human beings into ways that lead to perdition. Clearly, given the way they provide a contrast to Wisdom, passages about that other woman such as those in Proverbs 7 are not simply exhortations to avoid consorting with harlots. They have to do with a reality in the universe, with which human beings have to deal, which is the opposite of what Wisdom represents as God's contact with human beings. Against that reality Wisdom arms human beings with the good teachings coming from the Wisdom tradition, with the kind of instruction that is found in the collections in Proverbs 10–31.[21]

All this brings us into quite a different theological world from the one which gave rise to the great Israelite epics and the books of Israel's great prophets. It brings us into a theological world in which *todah* is no longer either the theological norm or the norm by which the issues of human life are defined. Wisdom having replaced an historical course of events as the medium through which God is revealed to and involved with human beings, God has to be talked about by discussing the virtues which constitute a good and wise life rather than by recounting the events through which God's deliverance of devotees who cried out to God in their need took place. Wisdom having replaced a course of historical events as the medium through which a relationship between God and human beings exists, the praise of God consists of living a prudent and virtuous life rather than in the offering of *todah* recital and sacrifice. Wisdom, rather than a people's history, having become the medium through which a people believes itself to be related to God, that people's normative means of identifying itself as God's people is no longer participation in the *todah* cult but the study and meditation which will allow Wisdom to impart her instruction in the art of living. All that began to happen in Israel in the period of the exile, the synagogue—the *beth din* or house of learning—replacing the place of worship to such an extent that ultimately it made no difference at all to the character of Judaism when the Roman empire destroyed Jerusalem's temple. It should be emphasized that all that began to happen because of the situation in which Israel found itself in the exilic and postexilic era, and not because some theoretical, arbitrary decision was made that Wisdom theology should replace *todah* theology. It began to happen in an Israel in which history had ceased to be filled with God's actions and presence, in which Wisdom seemed to serve that abiding purpose of Israel's God to remain involved with the people of God.

Moreover, not only does the statement of the theological significance of Wisdom found in Proverbs 1–9 bring us into quite a different theological world from that of the Israelite narrative epics and the great prophets of Israel. It also brings us into a world in which there is no mention at all either of those epics or of those prophets. Aside from the names and allusions found in the titles to sections of the book in Proverbs 1:1, 10:1, and 25:1, Proverbs contains no references whatever to those sections of the Old Testament known as the Law and the Prophets, no mention of the history of Israel which is the very basis on which the Law and the Prophets do theology, no indication whatsoever of the historical context out of which the book of Proverbs originates. Had the theology of Proverbs 1–9 become the norm in Israel, we might never have heard at all of that narrative complex found in Genesis through II Kings or that collection of material connected with the great prophets contained in Isaiah, Jeremiah, Ezekiel, and the Book of the Twelve. Israel's theological shift could have gone so far as to have resulted in the loss of that tradition we have discussed in the previous chapters of this book, and indeed may have gone that far in some circles. It was undoubtedly the case during the exilic and postexilic period that many Israelites simply lost their identity as Israelites and were absorbed into the world and culture that surrounded them.

Wisdom Theology and Israel's Narrative Traditions

It is, however, apparent that the Wisdom interpretation of the nature of God and of God's relationship with the human community did also come to involve a use and a reinterpretation of Israel's historical traditions. That is seen, first, in allusions to and the use that is made of those traditions in literature that comes out of the Wisdom theology of exilic and postexilic times. The book Ecclesiasticus, or the Wisdom of Jesus ben Sirach, comes from the second century before the Christian era.[22] It is a product of the view expounded in Proverbs 1–9. It is basically a collection of sayings, of *mashals*, which instructs its readers how to live a good and successful life. The reason for the collection is the belief that the teachings of the Wisdom tradition are the means through which Wisdom imparts to human beings the truth that comes from God. Near the conclusion of the book, however, comes a section in which Israel's history is recounted in the form of a catalogue of the great heroes of its life as a people. That list, found in Ecclesiasticus 44:16—50:21, runs from primeval Enoch to Simon, a high priest contemporary with the writer of Ecclesiasticus.[23] Its ultimate origins lie in the *todah* tradition, both in its rendering of praise by a recital of events and in its continuance of that recital right up into the present in which it originates. The list, however, is set out for quite a different purpose from that which gave rise to and was central in the *todah* cult. What that purpose is is made quite clear in the opening verses of Ecclesiasticus' catalogue of heroes found in Ecclesiasticus 44:1–15:

> *Let us sing now the praises of the famous ones,*
> *The heroes of our nation's history.*
> *Through them the Lord's fame became known,*
> *The Lord's glory manifest generation by generation.*
> *Some ruled over kingdoms,*
> *Made themselves famous by their deeds.*
> *Others were* sage counsellors,
> *Whose speech was prophetically inspired.*
> *Some led the people by their* counsel,
> *By their* knowledge *of their nation's inherited* instruction,
> Taught *from their rich* wisdom.
>
> (ECCLUS. 44:1–4)

The emphasized words betray what the writer takes to be the real significance of the heroes lauded in the chapters that follow, and they are also accurate indicators of what is the predominant tone and content of what follows them. The tradition of the tale in wisdom literature is what underlies Ecclesiasticus 44—50, the lives of the famous heroes of the past being models of what living under the tutelage of Wisdom can mean.

The same thing is even more explicitly true of the Wisdom of Solomon, a writing which may well have come into being very shortly before the time of Jesus of Nazareth.[24] Chapters 10 through 19 of that book are a recital of the narrative contained in the Pentateuch. The tone and emphasis are readily seen in what is said about Adam and Noah and Abraham:

> Wisdom it was that guarded the progenitor of the human race when he alone existed. . . . Wisdom came to the rescue of the one good human being, teaching him how to sail his crude vessel. . . . It was Wisdom who selected one good man and kept him righteous in God's sight after the heathen nations who had joined together in wickedness were scattered in confusion. . . .
>
> (WIS. 10:1–5 *passim*)

The recital continues in that vein, giving, to cite another example, this interpretation of what the evil of Israel's Egyptian oppressors really was:

> Your people's enemies indeed deserved to have daylight taken away and to be imprisoned in darkness, for they had enslaved your children through whom the unquenchable light of the Torah (the basic meaning of the word is "instruction") was to be given to the world.
>
> (WIS. 18:4)

Here not only is it the case that the genre of the wisdom tale about the deportment of a wise person is the form in which Israel's history is recited. Here also is the explicit assertion that the significance of Israel and of Israel's saints lies in their having been the bearers of the presence of Wisdom in the world.

That the wisdom interpretation of the nature of God and of God's relationship with the human community came to involve a reinterpretation of Israel's historical traditions is seen also in the way the significance of the Law and the Prophets, Israel's scriptures, comes to be stated in the postexilic period. Ecclesiasticus 24 contains a beautiful poem in which, in the same way she does in Proverbs 8, Wisdom speaks of her origins and her relationship to God:

I am the utterance that comes from the mouth of the Most High,
I am the one who covers the earth like the primeval mist.
My original abode was in the highest heaven,
My throne set in a cloudy pillar.
I alone have circuited the vault of the heavens,
Have explored the deepest part of the abyss.
In the ocean's waves as well as in every part of the land,
Among every people and nation do I have property rights.
I searched all of them, looking for a place to establish my home,
For which territory should be my dwelling place.

(ECCLUS. 24:3–7)

As in Proverbs, Wisdom is the first creation of God, God's means of communication with the earth. She does not wish to live removed from the human community in heaven, so, having the right to settle anywhere in the universe, she tries to decide where she will settle in this world. Here is the answer:

So the Cosmic Creator commanded me,
My own Creator ordered where I was to dwell,
Saying, "Take up residence in Jacob,
Become involved in Israel's destiny."
Before time began God created me,
And I am immortal,
But in Israel's sanctuary I served God,
And came to be located in Zion.

God established me in God's favorite city,
Gave me authority in Jerusalem.
I came to be rooted in the people the Lord honored
By choosing them to be a peculiar possession.
(ECCLUS. 24:8–12)

As does the Wisdom of Solomon, this poem takes Israel's significance to lie in its being that place in the cosmos in which God has ordained Wisdom should dwell. That is what makes Israel's life and history important. Just as the story of a *hakam*, a wise person, sets forth the Wisdom that dwells in that person, so, given Wisdom's abode in the people Israel, Israel's corporate story becomes a revelation of the Wisdom through which God gives meaning and order to the universe. Moreover, that is also what gives significance to the book in which Israel's story is preserved. When the poem in which Wisdom speaks, from which we have quoted above, is finished, Wisdom at its conclusion having extended a moving invitation to all to partake of those blessings which are hers to give, the writer of Ecclesiasticus goes on in quite specific terms:

All this is the book of the covenant of the most high God,
The Torah which was given through Moses,
To be the heritage of the assemblies of Jacob.
(ECCLUS. 24:23)

A similar statement is made in the book of Baruch, named for the prophet Jeremiah's companion and scribe but probably dating from the early years of the Christian era:[25]

Has anyone gone up to heaven to find Wisdom and to bring her down from the clouds? Has anyone sailed the seas to find her, or purchased her for the richest gold? No one can know the route or ever learn the way that leads to her. Only the One who knows everything is acquainted with Wisdom. . . . This is our God with whom nothing or no one is to be compared. The way which indeed leads to knowledge was revealed by that God and given to God's servant Jacob, to

> God's beloved Israel. That is how Wisdom came to be available on earth, to be present with the human race. She is the book of the commandments of God, the Torah which remains in effect forever. . . . Happy are we, O Israel, for we know what pleases God.
>
> (BAR. 3:29–32; 3:35–4:1; 4:4)

That passage sounds very much as if its writer might have been acquainted with the poem acclaiming God as the source of Wisdom in Job 28. This passage, however, goes much further in its establishing of connections between God and Wisdom than did the earlier poem. Here, as in Ecclesiasticus 24, Wisdom is understood not only to be specifically present in Israel but also quite specifically present in that book in which Israel's story is preserved. Furthermore, what pleases God is not thanksgiving, *todah* praise, but living by the instructions given by Wisdom in that book, obeying the teachings of that book.[26]

What has happened when, in that process by which the Israel of exilic and postexilic times came to see Wisdom as the medium of God's involvement with human beings, we get to the assertions of Ecclesiasticus 24 and Baruch 3—4 is that, without their content having been changed at all, the Law and the Prophets have become a different kind of book. What had been the commitment to writing of the *todah* in which Israel witnessed to the presence of God in human history had now become something quite different. It was now the written repository of Wisdom. What had been *todah,* theology done by thankful and interpretative recital of Israel's story, has now become *torah*, a volume of sacred teaching. Whereas what had made a person part of Israel had been the experience of deliverance that resulted in one's joining with the people who offered *todah*, what now made one part of Israel was knowledge of the teaching imparted by Wisdom and recorded in Israel's sacred book.

Those developments led to the great enterprise of seeking to extract the Wisdom, the *torah*, there in the book. That enterprise began to take place in the exilic period, and flourished in the postexilic period and well into the Christian era. It was the enterprise which resulted, finally, in the existence of "normative," rabbinic Judaism.[27] The first step in that enterprise was the writing, by students and teachers of the sacred book, the rabbis,[28] of commentaries on the scriptures which set down the *torah*, the instruction, which Wisdom had placed in them. These commentaries were called *midrashim*, the singular of that word being *midrash*. Though it may not have come about by any conscious decision, it is interesting to note that the word used to denote such a commentary, *midrash*, is a noun related etymologically to the verb *darash*, the meaning of which is "to seek," A *midrash* is the result of that search for wise teaching the roots of which go back beyond postexilic Judaism to the Wisdom heritage of the ancient Near East. The justification for midrashic expansion on the texts of the scriptures themselves came to be that, in providing Israel with its basic deposit of truth, Moses had given not only the written Torah, but had also given oral teaching. That teaching, it was believed, had been handed down by a traceable succession of teachers through Israel's history. The *midrashim* were believed to be based on that teaching,[29] and originate in the concern of the Wisdom enterprise of the ancient Near East that teaching be certified by a connection with a truly wise teacher.

The connection of the rabbinic search for the *torah* embedded in the scriptures with ancient Near Eastern Wisdom is further manifest in the forms taken by the midrashic writings. In expounding the meaning they believed to have been found in the scriptural books, the rabbis produced *haggadoth*, the singular of which is *haggadah*, and *halakoth*, the singular of which is *halakah*. A *haggadah* is a narrative, a writing in which the origin and meaning of something is expounded in a story. Its etymological meaning has to do with narration, with story telling. The *midrashim* abound in narratives about the patriarchs and Moses and the other heroes of the past who figure in the Law and the Prophets, narratives which expand on and, for the framers of the *midrashim*, make clear the *torah* that is imbedded in the scriptures. *Halakah*, on the other hand, means "teaching." The noun is derived from the verb that means "to go" or "to walk," and denotes instruction derived from the Law and the Prophets about the direction human life should take. *Halakoth* are teachings about conduct derived from the scriptures. Once we have seen the way in which the enterprise of scriptural interpretation of which the *midrashim* are the products is rooted in ancient Near Eastern Wisdom, it is easy to see where the two literary forms utilized in the *midrashim* find their ultimate origins. *Haggadah* is the descendant of the wisdom tale which is both the demonstration of how the wise life of a teacher qualified that teacher as someone who should be heeded and itself a teaching device. *Halakah* is the rabbinic equivalent of the *mashal*, the form of words in which teaching on a subject is articulated and handed on.

As the enterprise we are describing continued down through the years and then the centuries, the teaching derived from the Law and the Prophets by the rabbis came to be codified according to subject. The multiplication of *midrashim*, as the search for the wisdom imbedded in the scriptures continued in each generation, must have made it more and more difficult to find everything that had been said on a given subject or a given question. A *midrash* was a commentary, and so its teaching took the form of comments on the text of a biblical book, following the order of that text. That meant that, when one wished to find all the *torah* on a given subject, one had to go through all the *midrashim* that had been produced. The difficulty of such a task once the midrashic literature had reached significant proportions, as well as a desire to sort out the *torah* that had gained fairly universal approval from that which was more the product of the search of individuals, led to the collection of the midrashic teaching into "tractates" by subject. The original collection of those tractates came to be called the *Mishnah*, the various sections of which treat, among others, subjects such as sacred festivals, ritual purity and uncleanness, regulations concerning agriculture, and the relations between men and women.[30] The tractates of the *Mishnah*—the etymological meaning of which has to do with repetition, that is with handing down teaching—in their treatment of a given subject trace what was taught about it by the various generations of teachers who had worked at extracting *torah* from the scriptures, naming each teacher in turn, and then usually conclude by stating which opinion on the subject, again naming the teacher who held that opinion, came to be generally accepted. Again, a characteristic of wisdom literature is retained in the rabbinic enterprise. That concern of the wisdom literature to name the wise person from whom a collection of *mashals* came in order to validate their value is carried over into the rabbinic literature in a concern to associate teachings with the rabbi with whom they originated. Indeed, one guarantee of the validity of *torah* in the Jewish tradition was a tracing of the great teachers by pairs back through the generations to Moses.[31]

The teachings collected into the *Mishnah* seem to go back far enough in the history of Judaism to be the basis of the continuation of the rabbinic enterprise in various areas in which Jewish communities were to be found. As the search for the *torah* implanted by Wisdom in Israel and in Israel's scriptures continued, the content of the *Mishnah* was expanded in writings called *gemara*. The *Mishnah* itself plus the expansions on its tractates called the *gemara* together constitute the *Talmud,* the root meaning of which is "teaching." That the enterprise was a living thing, taking different directions in different places, is indicated by the fact that both a Babylonian and a Palestinian *Talmud* exist.[32] Palestine, and Jerusalem in particular, was obviously an important center of Jewish scriptural study and teaching. A significant Jewish colony continued, however, in Babylon even after the rise of Cyrus and the Persian empire made the return of Jews to their homeland and the resumption of temple worship in Jerusalem possible. The *Mishnah*, the tractates of which undoubtedly contain the most ancient teaching, is the same in both the Babylonian *Talmud* and the Palestinian *Talmud*. The *gemara* of Palestine is, however, different from the *gemara* of Babylon. Furthermore, the process that resulted in differing *Talmuds* continued. Searching and teaching went on, and teachings which had not been included in the *Talmud* or that come into being after the *Talmud* had taken shape were preserved. The *Tosephta* is such a collection, dating from the early centuries of the Christian era, and teachers such as the famous Maimonides continued the rabbinic enterprise down into the middle ages and further.

The process we have been tracing here in briefest outline, which produced rabbinic Judaism,[33] in which the implications of ancient Near Eastern Wisdom's becoming the medium through which God is related to human beings were worked out in relation to Israel's historical traditions and Israel's scriptures, was not the only thing happening among the people descended from the Israel whose cultic and theological norm had been *todah*. The memory of the significance of *todah* never died out, and forms of it persisted. We have already seen how the Chronicler, using the *todah* mode of doing theology which had earlier been employed by the Yahwist and its successors, produced in postexilic times an epic that explained the meaning of the postexilic temple cult by reciting history. Something like that also happened when the Maccabean revolt of the second century B.C. brought Palestine under Jewish rule again for a time, and that historical era was celebrated in the apocryphal book I Maccabees.[34] *Todah* continued to play a part in the life of people at home, and the Passover *haggadah* is an example of that. It is also the element in the Jewish heritage which lies behind the *berakoth*, those recitative table blessings believed by Father Bouyer to figure so importantly in the background of the Christian Eucharist.[35] It was not possible to be in contact with the heritage of Judaism and not be touched by the pervasive presence of *todah*.

Furthermore, if *todah* continued to have its effect as part of the tradition through those centuries in which the rabbinic enterprise was based on the assumption that the medium of God's relationship with human beings was Wisdom, a lot of other things were happening in Judaism. The developments leading to the existence, at the beginning of the Christian era, of Sadducees and Pharisees and Essenes were taking place. Apocalyptic literature was being written, and the point of view underlying it was widely present in Jewish communities. Judaism was a richly varied phenomenon. The forms taken by the faith of Jews were many indeed. Persian and Hellenistic and Roman cultures continued to have their effects on how Jews understood and articulated their faith and their heritage. We must not commit the error of conceiving of the Judaism out of which Christianity emerged as a simple, monochrome, uniform thing.[36]

Nevertheless, what we have been describing in this chapter does seem to have been the ethos out of which the variations in Judaism emerged, the common background against which they all have to be understood. Different as they are, they seem to share in that shift away from viewing history as the medium of God's involvement with a human community to viewing Wisdom as the medium of that involvement. That is true of the Chronicler whose recital is really the aetiology of a book and a cult rather than of a living, historical present. It is true of the Sadducees who are the heirs of the Chronicler's point of view. It is manifestly true of the Pharisees both in their concern for the careful observance of the teachings of the scriptures and in their mystical reverence for the *torah* present in the scriptures.[37] It is true of apocalyptic literature and groups, such as the Essenes, whose concern is not really for the history in which human beings are involved as the place where God is present as it is for that coming, transhistorical realm where God will reign and the nature of which is revealed by Wisdom in the scriptures and to the wise. In spite of the impression that may result from a first glance, the apocalyptists are very different from the prophets.

An apocalypse like Daniel, for example, has much more in common in form and ethos and atmosphere with the wisdom literature than it does with the prophetic literature. Daniel and his companions are characterized as learned and skillful in all letters and wisdom, and Daniel as having *understanding* through visions and dreams (Dan. 1:17). Furthermore, the genre of the stories about Daniel and his friends in the first six chapters of the book is that of the wisdom tale, the account of how the pragmatically prudent behavior of the wise person is vindicated by the order underlying things. Significantly, in this case, the wisdom of the wise ones consists specifically in obedience to the teaching, the *torah*, of those scriptures believed to be Wisdom's abode. Then, following the tales about the wise person comes the teaching, here the *mashals* taking the form of visions. Daniel provides a beautiful example of how very different products of Judaism have been profoundly influenced by what has been discussed in this chapter.[38]

There is indeed great variety in the manifold particular things that can be identified in postexilic Israel. Underlying the variety, however, and deeply informing all the particular things is that common presupposition that wisdom, understanding, knowledge gained through study, teaching, *torah* is the means of contact with God. Underlying the variety is a commonly shared assumption that the basic meaning of Israel lies in its being the people in whose life and heritage and traditions and *book* God has placed the

Wisdom which is the source of understanding and knowledge and *torah*. That assumption is there even when specific consciousness of its origins in ancient Near Eastern Wisdom is not. It is the faith arising out of that assumption which distinguishes Judaism as a religion from Judaism's predecessor, the faith and point of view and religion of ancient, preexilic Israel. The latter was a richly variegated, polychrome phenomenon too, producing epics as different as the culture affirming Yahwist and the culture denying Elohist, prophets as different as Isaiah of the city-kingdom of Jerusalem and Jeremiah of the Mosaic covenant cult. Underlying the variety present in ancient, pre-exilic Israel, however, was the common presupposition that the course of events that had been and was and would be Israel's history as a people was the means of contact with God. Those two quite different basic presuppositions—the one that Wisdom is the medium of God's involvement with human beings, the other that history is that medium—are what divide Judaism from ancient Israelite faith in spite of the many differences to be found within each of those two faiths. *Torah* had replaced *todah* as normative. That has to be understood if the nature of first-century Judaism and the nature of the issues confronting the earliest Christian community as a part of first century Judaism are to be understood.

That having been said, two things need to be said at the conclusion of the discussion in this chapter. The first is really a repetition of what has been said already. The shift from *todah* to *torah* as the norm for understanding the nature of God and the nature of the relationship between God and human beings did not occur because of some ideological decision by a community or its leaders that it should be so, that a better idea had been discovered. It took place because, from Israel's point of view after the fall of Jerusalem to Babylonia in 587, a course of events which it was possible to view as the medium of God's relationship to human beings had ceased to exist. It took place as a people, conditioned by long centuries during which *todah* had been the norm for belief that the good and gracious God was involved with them, looked to its experience and heritage for a possible medium of God's continuing relationship with them in exile. In a way difficult to trace at this distance in time, but surely discernible, the search turned up Wisdom.

The second thing to be said in conclusion follows from the first. It is that the assertion, on the basis of what appears to be good evidence, that *torah* replaced *todah* as the norm for understanding the nature of God and the nature of God's relationship with human beings is descriptive and not a value judgment. That needs to be said because of the dreadful record of the Christian community in the long history of its relations with the Jewish community. Value judgments which fed anti-Semitism already began to be made in the New Testament, and such judgments have continued to feed anti-Semitism down through history. It is our contention that an understanding of how and why *todah* had been replaced by *torah* in post-exilic Judaism will help us to understand both the nature of Judaism and the issues the earliest Christians had to deal with within the context of Judaism. It is our contention that the *experience* of the earliest Christians, not some ideological decision, made *todah* once again an appropriate norm for the cult and for theology. That contention, however, need not involve a value judgment. It is descriptive. Moreover, that is quite in accord with what *todah* is. *Todah* is really thankful, recitative description of how God has chosen to redeem human life by being involved in human life. *Todah* is not value judgment on others.

5

Thanksgiving Reappropriated: The New Testament Canon

IT was into the postexilic Israel described in the preceding chapter that Jesus of Nazareth came. It was in that setting that the Christian Church emerged as a result of the teaching and life of Jesus, and it was in that setting that the earliest Church first had to define its faith and the significance of the message it proclaimed. In the same way that ancient Israel had to articulate the nature of the God in relationship to whom it found itself living, as well as the nature of the relationship itself, in terms available in the culture of which it was a part, so it was with the Christian Church. It was within Judaism, scattered as the Jewish community was about the Graeco-Roman world and affected as Judaism was by the culture of that world, that the Church first existed and first had to understand itself.[1] Thus, its self-understanding was inevitably closely tied up with the fundamental presuppositions of Judaism, with those basic assumptions underlying the differences which set various groups and emphases within Judaism over against one another. Significant light may be shed on various aspects of early Christianity by discovering specific links with those different groups and emphases, but the fundamental assumptions beneath all of them need to be understood if we are to gain some understanding of the fundamental issues involved in the early Church's interpretation of itself and its message. An appreciation of how *torah* had replaced *todah* as the norm of theological understanding in Judaism is indispensible to an understanding of the early Church's struggle to articulate accurately what it and its message were about.

That is not to say that the earliest generations of the Church were characterized by a uniformity of thought, by no differences of emphasis in theological and other matters. Indeed, it becomes increasingly clear that, even in the Church's earliest years, the interpretations of Jesus and the gospel and the Church itself differed widely. It was the thesis of a very important work, published originally in Germany in 1934 but delayed by World War II and its aftermath from appearing in English until 1971, that the imposition of the concept—not just the standard, but the concept itself—of orthodoxy on the earliest age of the Church's life and on materials coming from that age had resulted in inaccurate perceptions of the early Church and its theology and Christology. Walter Bauer's *Orthodoxy and Heresy in Earliest Christianity* makes it abundantly clear that there was, in early Christianity, no one, simple, main line of theological and Christological understanding to which variations were related in a simple way.[2] Bauer's book had significant influence through the seventies on work on the New Testament and the earliest Church. He emphasizes the very different brands of Christianity present in the opening century or so of the Christian era, and asserts that it was only later, when Paul's interpretation of the issues at stake gained ascendency, that the concepts of orthodoxy and heresy emerged, and were then imposed—retroactively as it were—upon the New Testament and other early writings in such a way as to obscure the variety that was really there.[3]

The results of such work are indeed compelling. Modern treatments of the early Church are still apt to give the impression that there was, on the one hand, that mainline Christianity which finds expression in the New Testament and, on the other hand, that distortion of Christianity known as "gnosticism."[4] Recent research, however, has shown the way in which, in the first two or three centuries, "mainline Christianity" was really the particular brand of Christianity which existed in the Aegean area of the Mediterranean world as a result of the work of Paul. The same research also shows how two other areas, each with its own different emphases in theology and Christology, can be identified. One of these is Syro-Palestine itself, the other is Egypt and the farther eastern Syrian area between which two centers there seems to have been significant contact.[5] Furthermore, that research points out ways in which the New Testament itself provides evidence of varieties of interpretation. The source common to both Matthew and Luke known as Q seems to have originated in the Egyptian–eastern Syrian ethos. Matthew and the epistle of James seem to have originated in Syro-Palestinian circles, as does the gospel of John in its own way. The Pauline epistles and the gospel of Mark seem to be the products of the Christianity of the Aegean area influenced by Paul. What has been said in this paragraph alludes in the briefest kind of way to a great deal of scholarly work, all of which indicates that orthodoxy and heresy are concepts which emerged only centuries later and which are simply not applicable to the material that originated in the earliest centuries of the life and history of the Church.

This book, and particularly what will be said in the present chapter, does not dispute that. That fact needs to be emphasized. Orthodoxy and heresy are indeed concepts quite foreign to the Judaism which was the matrix within which earliest Christianity existed and interpreted itself.

Indeed, they are concepts, at least in the form in which they have existed in the Church, foreign to Judaism down to the present day.[6] Nevertheless, it is an empirical fact and not just an "orthodox" judgment that we are indeed talking about a reality, even if we have tended to perceive it through later concepts of orthodoxy and heresy, when we talk about the "canon" of the New Testament. The Greek word *kanon* carries none of the connotations of "orthodoxy." It simply means "standard" or "norm." This book, and this present chapter in particular, have grown out of a search for what that *kanon*, by which the Church judged the adequacy of a given statement or a given writing as a witness to what God had wrought in the Church beginning with Jesus, really was. It is our contention that that *kanon* is not some intellectual, doctrinal, confessional, ideological, abstract, conceptual orthodoxy. It is, rather, that the *kanon* is provided in the liturgical action in which the Church identified itself under God as Church. We maintain that *todah*, thanksgiving in the full cultic sense we have described earlier is that *kanon*, the Greek word for *todah* employed by the Church being *eucharistia*. It was only later, when the Church's *thoughts* about itself came to take precedence over itself as a reality, that "orthodoxy/heresy" became the *kanon*. The roots of that shift in perception may themselves, strangely enough, lie in some of the things which the earliest Church, using a *todah* norm, dropped along the way as not congenial to its canon.

Paul and the Nature of Christianity

New Testament scholars are pretty well agreed that the earliest writings in the New Testament itself are the letters written by Paul to the churches which had come into being as a result of his travels as a witness to the Christian gospel. They bring us about as close as we can get to the earliest generation of the Christian Church. Already in those letters there is clear indication that a heated controversy is taking place over the significance of Jesus of Nazareth and the nature of Christianity and the Church.[7] It would be possible to get at the nature of that controversy by beginning at many places in the Pauline letters. We have chosen here to get at it by beginning with an examination of I Corinthians.

After an introduction and a statement of thanksgiving for the Church in Corinth (I Cor. 1:1–9), Paul, in characteristic fashion, turns directly and bluntly to what is on his mind. He is appalled at having received reports that the Christians in Corinth are splitting up into different factions on the basis of which teaching and which teacher is taken to be authoritative. Some insist that they are disciples of Paul, others that they are disciples of Apollos, others that they are disciples of Cephas, and still others—in the way that different groups of Christians down through the ages have sought to resolve differences of interpretation within the Church by equating their own position with that of the founder himself—that they are disciples of Christ. Paul insists that the issue is not which teaching or which teacher is authoritatively correct. He refuses to add another name to the list. Paul's insistence is that to frame the issue in the way that it is being framed by the Corinthian Christians is fundamentally to miss the point of what the issue really is. It is not, for Paul, a matter of which teaching, which interpretation, which doctrinal position is right (I Cor. 1:10–17). It is probably because of his concern to make that point as clearly as possible that Paul reminds the Corinthians that baptizing converts was almost no part of his work among them (I Cor. 1:14–17). Then, as now, being the minister of Christian baptism involved instruction of the candidates for baptism in the Christian faith, and what Paul is asserting is that the giving of instruction was no significant part of his ministry among the Corinthians. He is concerned to emphasize that neither in the content of his message nor in his actions did he give any indication whatsoever that Christianity is by nature a set of teachings. To engage in controversy based on the assumption that that is the nature of Christianity is not only to split the Church into factions, it is to misconceive the very nature of Christianity. Thus Paul is neither agreeing with any one party nor creating a new party in opposition to the ones already in existence. He is challenging the assumptions shared by everyone engaged in the controversy in Corinth, the assumptions that make the controversy possible in the first place.

Paul then goes on to expound what the fundamental nature of Christianity really is in his view by drawing a contrast between—and note the significance of this in light of the discussion in the preceding chapter of this book—*wisdom* and the *power of the cross* (I Cor. 1:17–25). The Greek word translated "power" is *dynamis*, the source of the English word "dynamic." Paul is insisting that wisdom does not provide the category which leads to an understanding of the nature of Christianity. The question "Which teacher and which teaching?" is, therefore, not the primary question. It is, indeed, an irrelevant question. What Christianity is really about is a dynamic introduced by God into human history beginning with the historical event of the crucifixion of Jesus of Nazareth (I Cor. 1:17–25).[8] That dynamic, according to Paul, is what has continued to underlie the historical events through which the Corinthians have been caught up into that history, beginning with Jesus, in which what the cross represents is basic (I Cor. 1:26—2:5), and resulting in the presence in the corporate, historical body which is the Church in Corinth of a Spirit which gives that body understanding of the gifts with which God has endowed it (I Cor. 2:6–13). Thus it is that Paul insists:

> Since we are speaking truths connected with the Spirit that is part of the dynamic released by God to those who form the body in which that Spirit dwells, what we are saying has not been learned from human wisdom, but from that Spirit.
> (I Cor. 2:13)[9]

An assessment of the total context would seem to indicate that the contrast drawn by Paul between human wisdom and the Spirit is not, fundamentally, a contrast between intellectual reasoning and some mystical method of apprehending reality. It is a contrast between conceiving of Christianity primarily as a set of abstract truths to be mastered, a corpus of teachings external to the community being taught, and looking at the concrete, historical phenomenon that is the Church and apprehending what it really is that gives it its existence and vitality. In a word, Paul seems to be insisting that *todah*, *eucharistia*, thankful, recitative celebration of the history in which the Church is living, is more appropriate as a norm for understanding what is afoot than is the *torah* approach which had been normative and which is presupposed by all parties to the dispute in Corinth which disturbs him so much. Furthermore, Paul asserts that that is so not because of the teaching advanced by some teacher, not as a decision reached by either a reasoning process or a conceptual revelation. He asserts that *todah*, *eucharistia*, is the more adequate norm for understanding what is afoot in the Church because of the initiative of God in making a course of events the medium through which a community of human beings finds itself related to God.

All that, it can be argued, provides a context in which the whole of I Corinthians can be better understood.[10] What Paul has set forth in chapters 1 and 2 about the nature of Christianity and the Church is continued through chapter 4, these opening chapters of the epistle concluding with Paul's moving statement of what it means to be an apostolic servant of Christ and the Church. The letter then continues with a long section, chapters 5 through 11, in which all kinds of very practical matters affecting the life of the Church are touched on. They range from questions of sexual behavior, to whether or not food sold in the market after having been offered to idols in pagan temples can be eaten by Christians, to the ordering of the Church's worship. The reason that such detailed, and often very mundane, matters are given the kind of attention they are in I Corinthians as well as elsewhere in Paul's letters is because of what is implicit in I Corinthians 1—4 and what is explicit in I Corinthians 12—13. What Christianity is all about is not some set of teachings, some doctrinal system handed down from some place external to the Church itself. What Christianity is all about is the significance imparted to the Church's own life and history by God's presence in it beginning with Jesus of Nazareth. The ordering of the Church's life in all its very practical aspects, both corporately and in the lives of its individual members, is crucial because the Church is, as it is put by Paul in I Corinthians 12, the very body of Christ just as much as Jesus' body was that. That is why the Church's life is to be characterized above all by that concerned-for-the-other love, the Greek word being *agape*, by which Jesus' life was characterized. And that is precisely why the great encomium on love follows right upon chapter 12 in chapter 13.

That kind of alternation between the lofty and the very practical continues through the final chapters of I Corinthians. Chapter 14 applies loving concern to the variety of spiritual gifts present in the Church. Chapter 15 then constitutes a great statement on how the whole human race is destined not for death but for participation in the victory over death which has put in its first appearance in Jesus' resurrection. Then chapter 16 turns again to very practical matters, to collections of money and other such things, as the letter comes to its conclusion. The whole epistle is another case in which "the medium is the message." The statement of what Christianity is which is made in the opening chapters is borne out in what is treated in the epistle as a whole. Paul's argument about the nature of Christianity is reflected in actual practice as he seeks to deal pastorally with the Church that has come into being in connection with his witness to the Christian gospel.

The same point is made in another significant way in terms of the use of that word "gospel" to name just what it is that Paul delivers to those among whom he labors. He uses the word again and again as the designation of the Christian message.[11] "Gospel" is the traditional English rendering of the Greek word *euangelion* which means "tidings," "announcement," etc. The origin of its use in the early Church—Paul's use of it seeming to indicate that it did not originate with him and was already a part of the taken-for-granted vocabulary of the Church—seems to lie in its use in the Greek translation of the prophecies in Isaiah to render the Hebrew word *mebasereth*, which has the same basic meaning. Here is one of the well known places where it is used:

Upon a high mountain climb and take your stand,
O bringer of good tidings, O Zion.
Lift that voice of yours to its highest volume,
O bringer of good tidings, O Jerusalem,
Lift it up and be not afraid.
Say to the cities of Judah,
"Behold! Your God!"
For behold, the Lord Yahweh is coming in might,
The divine power is assuming sovereignty.
Behold God's reward (to Israel) is part of that,
God's payment part of the divine entourage.
Like a shepherd is God feeding God's own flock,
The divine power is gathering them in.
Lambs are nestling in God's bosom,
As God also gently leads the pregnant ewes.
(Is. 41:9–11)

The historical setting of that prophecy is the time in which Cyrus' conquest of Babylon is opening the way to Israel's returning to Jerusalem to reinstitute the cult of

Yahweh. The setting in the prophecies in Second Isaiah is one in which the prophet argues that Yahweh, Israel's God, and not the gods of any of the other captive peoples in Babylon, must be the one who has sent Cyrus because Yahweh is the only God who has consistently chosen to be related to Israel through the course of historical events. So, through Cyrus and the events accompanying his rise to power on the international scene Yahweh is acting to comfort defeated and exiled Israel as well as to make it clear that Yahweh is sovereign over historical events. The comfort that is being extended to Israel is pictured in the lovely shepherd imagery. Both the comforting of Israel and the manifestation of Yahweh's sovereignty will take place as the worship of Yahweh once again begins in Jerusalem. That is why Zion—Jerusalem—will be, in its existence as a part of history, a "statement," a "herald of good tidings." Yahweh's sovereignty is being announced in the course of events in which Persia replaces Babylon as the holder of hegemony over the fertile crescent and in which exiled Israel goes home to reinstate the temple cult. Jerusalem—Zion—as the focus of all that historical reality through which, in the faith of the prophet, Yahweh is related to the world, is the proclaimer of an *euangelion*, a reciter of *todah*.

All that is indicative of the content of the word "gospel" which is taken up by the Church as the word which designates the Church's message. It is also indicative of what the earliest Church took to be the nature of its message. The word itself, given its background in Israel's scriptures, signals that the Christian message is not "teaching" of the kind that had divided the Corinthian Church and led it into what Paul takes to be a fundamentally wrong understanding of the nature of Christianity. It is, of course, in the epistle to the Galatians that what "gospel" implies about the nature of Christianity is particularly contrasted with an understanding of Christianity which makes *torah*, "teaching," basic.[12] It is, however, essentially the same issue that is also present in I Corinthians. There Paul draws the contrast in terms of Wisdom versus the dynamic released into history by God in and through Jesus' resurrection. The issue is one with which what we have been tracing thus far in this book has surely guaranteed some familiarity. It has to do with the contrast between *todah* and *torah*. It has to do with whether *eucharistia* (thanksgiving) or *sophia* (Wisdom) is normative for Christian self-understanding.

What Paul is Arguing Against

The research which resulted in some appreciation of the variety of views actually present in the earliest Christian Church has also made it possible for us to have some understanding of just what it was that Paul was arguing against in I Corinthians, of the forms which led to the Corinthians' understanding Christianity to be basically teaching. One of the very earliest interpretations of Jesus is preserved in a form—and here that word is used in the sense in which it is part of the term "form criticism"—characterized by James Robinson as *logoi sophon*.[13] *Logoi sophon* is the Greek for "words of the wise" or "pronouncements of the wise" or "sayings of the wise." The form is one with which we are already familiar in terms of the discussion in the previous chapter of this book. It is what we have seen and discussed as *meshalim*, collections of wise sayings. So it is that the form Robinson discerned in early Christian literature has a long history. It is that form which was obviously used very early on in the Christian community to preserve and hand on the teachings of Jesus, and two examples of it are available to us. One of these is the Gospel of Thomas, a "gnostic" document which was discovered earlier this century at Nag Hammadi, a site near the Aswan Dam in Egypt.[14] The Gospel of Thomas is a collection of sayings of Jesus, of Jesus' teachings. Many of the sayings found in it are also found, even if in different form, in the New Testament gospels. There is no narrative in the Gospel of Thomas. It consists entirely of sayings. The ethos out of which it gives a picture of Jesus is quite clearly the tradition traced in the preceding chapter, a tradition which was very much a part of the cultural and theological world of Jesus and the early Church.

The other example of that genre termed *logoi sophon* by Robinson is found in the New Testament itself. It is the body of material common to Matthew and Luke denoted by New Testament scholars as Q. Matthew and Luke seem both to have used the gospel according to Mark as the basis of what they wrote.[15] It is interesting to note in passing that they thus shared the ancient Israelite custom of building later restatements of the *todah* recital on those that had gone before. Matthew and Luke also, in addition, each has a body of material that is uniquely its own. When, however, the Marcan core and their own unique materials have been identified in Matthew and Luke, it is apparent that those two gospels also have in common another body of material. That is the material denoted as Q. Q nowhere has, to date, been discovered as a document existing on its own, and exists only as a part of Matthew and Luke.[16] Its name, since its existence was originally postulated by German scholars, is simply short for *Quelle*, the German word for "source." It contains teachings of Jesus. Indeed, a good argument could be made for asserting that the Gospel of Thomas is simply an expanded form of Q in which many of Jesus' sayings, identifiable as they are as basically the same as those found in Q, have been embellished along "gnostic" lines.

Q, however, consists of more than the *logoi sophon*, the sayings of the wise, the teachings of Jesus, which constitute the whole of the Gospel of Thomas. In Q, Jesus' sayings are preceded by the account of his temptation in the wilderness (Mt. 4:1–11; Lk. 4:1–13). When that account is read by anyone familiar with the wisdom literature of the ancient

Near East and the Old Testament, its genre, its form, is immediately apparent. It is a wisdom tale. It recounts how a wise person's deportment was both instructive in the art of living and evidence of the claim that person's teachings should have on men and women. Furthermore, it is a wisdom tale clearly affected by the interpretation of Israel's scriptures which came into existence in the exilic and post-exilic period and saw those scriptures to be the embodiment of Wisdom. Not only does Jesus turn aside the temptations of the devil, just as Joseph turned aside the temptations of Potiphar's wife or as Proverbs exhorted humans to turn aside the temptations of the "other woman," but he does so by quoting scripture. Each successive temptation is countered by the recitation of a verse from those sacred writings in which Wisdom had come to be believed to dwell, twice from Deuteronomy and once from Psalm 91. Q's form, therefore, is one that originated in the wisdom heritage which went very far back into ancient Near Eastern culture and became important theologically in Israel in the centuries immediately preceding Jesus and the rise of Christianity. Q is, in form, a collection of *meshalim*, a recording of the teachings of a *hakam*, a wise person, which begins with a tale in which the credentials of the teacher are established. It also, in line with what had come to be believed in later Israel, holds that true wisdom is to be found in Israel's scriptures.

Thus it is that, by its very form, Q presents its own interpretation of the nature and significance of Jesus and of Christianity. The account with which it begins may indeed go back to an experience of Jesus before the beginning of his public career, and Jesus' sayings in Q may indeed report with complete accuracy what he taught. That is not the issue. The issue is that, by putting the account of Jesus' temptation into the form that it does and then following that account with the sayings of Jesus without any further narrative recital of the acts and events of Jesus' life and ministry,

Q is making a very particular and clear interpretation of who Jesus is and what the nature of Christianity is. For Q, Jesus is a wise man, probably the wise teacher *par excellence*, and Christianity consists in learning and following the teaching of that wise teacher. For Q, *torah* is the principle of interpretation and the norm. Once again, as was the case in our treatment of postexilic Judaism in the preceding chapter, that is a descriptive statement and not a value judgment, for it is undoubtedly the case that Q is of extreme value as a collection of the sayings of Jesus.

That Jesus is for Q even more than the wise teacher par excellence seems to be indicated by an examination of the differences between Matthew's and Luke's versions of one particular passage in Q. Luke 11:49–51 follows a series of "woes" pronounced by Jesus on the Pharisees and the lawyers, and charges that the ancestors of the lawyers martyred the prophets while the lawyers themselves now hypocritically erect monuments to the prophets. Jesus then goes on to say, "Therefore also the Wisdom of God said, 'I will send them prophets and apostles, some of whom they will slay and persecute, that every drop of blood shed by a prophet from the beginning of time may be required of this generation, from the blood of Abel to the blood of Zechariah who perished between the altar and the sanctuary.' " Students of that passage have, down through the years, searched in vain for what it is that Jesus is referring to as the source of his quotation when he says, "Therefore also the Wisdom of God said . . ." There are instances, even in the Old Testament itself, of scriptural books being referred to as "the Wisdom of God,"[17] so it has seemed likely that Jesus is here quoting from something in the Hebrew Bible. The search, however, has never turned up a thing like that in any of the literature of Judaism.

That the reason for the unsuccessful search may lie in Q's view of Jesus and Christianity and not in some sacred book having been lost is indicated by an examination of the same

Q passage in Matthew. There the passage goes as follows: "Therefore I send you prophets and wise persons and scribes, some of whom you will kill and crucify, some of whom you will persecute in your synagogues and hound from town to town, so that all the righteous blood shed on earth shall be on your heads, from the blood of innocent Abel to the blood of Zechariah the son of Barachiah whom you murdered between the altar and the sanctuary." (Mt. 23:34–36) In Matthew's version of the Q passage it is clearly *Jesus* who is speaking. Thus, the most likely solution to the search for the source of the quotation in the Lucan version of the same Q passage is that there is, in fact, no quotation. It is simply the case that Jesus himself was speaking in Q, and it is highly likely that Luke has preserved the original form of Q which said, "Therefore the Wisdom of God (i.e. Jesus) said, 'I will send them . . .' " In the original, which Matthew has apparently edited for reasons which will become clear later on in our discussion, Q would have been asserting explicitly that Jesus is the incarnation of the Wisdom of God, the embodiment of that being through which God had come to be believed to be in touch with human beings. Thus, the founder of the Church is indeed the wise teacher *par excellence*, and the Church is the possessor of the final and truest *torah*. And what is there in Q is there also in the Gospel of Thomas with even more explicit embellishment and interpretation along the same lines.

This view of the nature of Jesus and the nature of Christianity is one in which there is neither room nor need for any narrative save that found in the wisdom tale. This view of the nature of Jesus is not interested in the *events* of Jesus' life, of the "mighty acts" of healing and deliverance which constituted Jesus' career and in which his power was manifest, of Jesus' passion and death and resurrection. On the contrary, here there is nothing really significant in what would be presented in a recital of the course of events which were the story of Jesus. In it *torah*—teaching and knowledge and understanding—is what is important rather than *todah*, thankful recital of a course of events into which the reciters have been incorporated by an act of deliverance. This seems to be the view of Jesus and Christianity against which Paul is arguing in I Corinthians when he insists that teachers and their teaching are not the essential point, that the essential point lies in that dynamic set loose in human history by God in and through Jesus' life and death and resurrection.

Furthermore, this may also be the view against which Paul is arguing in those mysterious verses preceding his depiction of the Church as the body of Christ, the historical phenomenon in and through which God's saving history continues to take place in the world. Before that passage on the Church as Christ's body in I Corinthians 12:4–28 come these words: "Now concerning spiritual gifts (or, spiritual persons), I do not want you to have the wrong information . . . I want you to understand that no one speaking by the Spirit of God ever says, 'Jesus be cursed!' just as 'Jesus is Lord' is what is said by one speaking by the Holy Spirit" (12:1,3). Those words have perplexed readers down through the centuries. How could anyone ever possibly have thought that God's Spirit would move someone to pronounce a curse on Jesus? One possible explanation is that the words allude to a belief and practice present in some circles holding Q's view of the nature of Jesus and the nature of Christianity. In such circles it could have been believed that real Christian maturity, real grasping of the point of it all, consisted in coming to the place where one could indeed say, "Jesus—everything that is implied in that human, earthly, historical name—be cursed! Wisdom, the Wisdom that chose to approach us clothed in Jesus' humanity but which itself is the point, Wisdom be blessed!" If there is anything to that explanation,[18] then Paul is asserting something which is central and crucial to his understanding of the nature of Jesus and the nature of Christianity when he insists right at the beginning of his letter to the Corinthian Church, "Christ did not send me to baptize, but to preach the gospel, and not to do that with eloquent wisdom, lest the cross be robbed of its power." (I Cor. 1:17).

The Results of the Controversy in the New Testament

Thus, an issue was joined which can be understood only against the background of the Judaism and the Jewish heritage within which Christianity appeared. Was Jesus, as Q and the Gospel of Thomas maintained, God's perfect bringer of *torah*? Or, was Jesus, as Paul maintained, the means of God's involvement once again in human history which made *todah* once more, rather than *torah*, the appropriate theological response? It would seem that the Egyptian/eastern Syrian areas opted for a *torah* answer to that issue, since the Gospel of Thomas seems to have come from them.[19] It is probable also that the Syro-Palestinian area tended toward a *torah* theology and christology. Q might have originated either there or in the Church in Egypt or eastern Syria. The gospel of Matthew, which as we shall see presently was finally shaped under the influence of a *todah* theology, clearly pictures Jesus as the giver of the true *torah* and the Church as the company that is to *teach* all nations (Mt. 28:16–20).[20] Matthew may very well preserve the flavor of the Christianity found in Syro-Palestine before the Roman destruction which, first in 70 and then in 135 A.D., emptied the area of Jewish population, and so of Christian population as well.

It is also clear that the Aegean area of the Mediterranean, the area whose brand of Christianity was to survive in a way that the Christianity of the other areas did not, opted for Paul's definition of the significance of Jesus and the Church, opted for a *todah* answer to the questions.[21] It was the adoption of that kind of interpretation of Jesus and of

Christianity that led to the development of a literary form, a genre, in which witness to Jesus was made in Paul's rather than in Q's way. That form seems first to have been used in Mark. It is a form denoted by the word already taken for granted by Paul as a fitting designation for the Christian message, the word *euangelion*, "gospel." We have already, in our discussion of Paul, seen how that word carries connotations of "tidings" or "news" or "announcement" rather than "teaching" or "instruction" or "wisdom." In its inherent meaning alone it conveys what is congenital to *todah* rather than *torah*. However, the meaning of *euangelion*, for the early Church and for Paul, included the special content given by its use in Second Isaiah, namely that of the good tidings present in the events and participants of history due to the initiative of God. Thus, the designation of what Mark is to be about with the words, "The beginning of the gospel of Jesus Christ . . ." (Mk. 1:1) conveys something quite different from what is conveyed by Q's "Then was Jesus led by the Spirit to be tempted. . . ." (Mt. 4:1, Lk. 4:1). The one statement has about it the atmosphere of that kind of thankful recital that is *todah*. The other has about it the atmosphere of the wisdom tale.

If the opening words of Mark already indicate the view of the significance of Jesus held in that gospel, the form of the gospel underlines that view. Mark is a gospel characterized by action, by the narration of tremendous events, by recital. It is almost as if, and this indeed could be the case, Mark was written consciously to be contrasted with Q. When the baptism at the hands of John has been described, Mark states that the Spirit did indeed lead Jesus into the wilderness to be tempted by Satan for forty days, but then omits entirely the tale of how Jesus thwarted the tempter in the fashion of a wise teacher.[22] Instead, Mark goes on with events, almost never pausing to report sayings of Jesus at any length at all. What words of Jesus are reported have to do for the most part with actions or events. The word *euthus*—"immediately" or, as in older translations, "straightway"—occurs again and again, leading right from one event to another so that, once again, "the medium is the message," the message being conveyed by more than the content. What the recital leads to is the account of the passion and death of Jesus. The prominence this account has in Mark has elicited the observation that Mark is really a passion narrative to which a comparatively brief account of what led to Jesus' passion has been added by way of introduction. There is certainly no question but that for Mark, as for Paul, Jesus' death by crucifixion, the cross of Christ, is central to what Christianity is all about.

Whether as a conscious reply to Q or not, Mark is certainly the kind of account of Jesus' life and death that would have been produced in those Christian circles whose view of Christianity had been shaped by or squared with Paul's. It is a gospel, and its content is gospel. Its content is, indeed, *todah*, *eucharistia*, a presentation of Jesus and the significance of Jesus and of the theology implicit in all that through recital of the course of events that was the life and death of Jesus. Theology is, in Mark, once again being done in Israel in the way in which it had been in ancient times when the Yahwist and the Elohist and the Deuteronomist and the Priestly Code and then the entire complex of Genesis through II Kings came into being. Furthermore, theology is being done that way not as a result of some teacher's having decided that that was a better way, theoretically. Theology is being done that way because faith is once again discerning a course of events in history as the medium through which God is being revealed to and involved with a human community.

The gospel form which first appears in Mark is then utilized in Matthew and Luke and John. Matthew and Luke obviously bear a particular relationship to Mark. Mark seems to constitute the core on which each of them built in its own distinctive way. What happened was analogous to the way in which, in the Old Testament, the Yahwist was the core on which the other strata of the narrative built, and around which the final, completed narrative came into being. It is the kind of relationship they have with one another that has resulted in Matthew, Mark, and Luke being together known as the synoptic gospels.[23] Matthew and Luke not only have in common, however, their Marcan core. Each of them also embodies Q, in opposition to which Mark may very well originally have been written. How could that have happened?

That kind of question, to refer once again to the discussion at the very beginning of this chapter, arises out of an "orthodoxy-heresy" mentality, and such a mentality had not yet arisen in the earliest Church in the way that it was to arise later on in the history of the Church. The norm for the earliest Church was not an "orthodoxy-heresy" norm, even though Mark, for quite understandable reasons in a situation of controversy, approached applying such a norm in its total rejection of Q. It was a fact that, in so doing, Mark had omitted what were indeed the teachings of Jesus which meant so much to the Church.[24] It is as if both Matthew and Luke saw that, and set out to remedy the lacuna in Mark's witness to who Jesus was and what Jesus had done. They accomplish what they set out to do by incorporating both Q's wisdom tale and its narration of Jesus' temptation in the wilderness and Q's reporting of the sayings of Jesus in the framework provided by Mark. Thus, the *content* of Q came to be preserved for the Church within a *context* which, by its form, implied a quite different view of the meaning and significance of Jesus than the view implied in the form taken by Q. James Robinson characterized the results of Matthew's and Luke's use of Q in this striking way: "[The] gnosticizing proclivity [of the genre represented by Q] is blocked by Matthew and Luke by imbedding Q in the Marcan gospel form."[25]

The gospel of John is the final exemplar of the gospel form in the New Testament. The content of the gospel of John, as well as the specific theological and christological views of that gospel, is very different from that of the synoptic gospels. Furthermore, John does not, as do Matthew and Luke, follow the Marcan outline in its presentation of Jesus' life and death. Finally, the Jesus presented in John is distinctly a teacher, the deliverer of significant discourses. John is indeed very different from the other gospels, and presents its own peculiar issues and problems. When, however, all that has been said, it is still the case that John's form is "gospel" and not "teaching." The framework in which it presents its interpretation of Jesus is a *todah* or *eucharistia* form. What John has in common with the synoptics, indeed what each of the four gospels of the New Testament has in common with the others, does not lie in content or teaching or ideology. It lies in something else. It lies in a *form*, in the utilization by each of them of the "gospel" form as the framework within which each presents its particular content. The four gospels have that in common with one another. They do not have that in common with Q and the Gospel of Thomas, even though the latter, like other writings from the early Church, uses the word "gospel" in its title.[26] What the four gospels of the New Testament have in common, and by implication the unity of the Church, lies in something more subtle than the content explicitly set forth in each of them. Insistence that the unity of the Church must lie in the *content* of its teaching inevitably produces, just as it did in Corinth in Paul's time, division. The *kanon*,[27] the norm, which resulted in the common acceptance of the four gospels included in the New Testament as authoritative witnesses to Jesus and the significance of Jesus was not a content-defined, "orthodoxy-heresy" norm. It was a norm which had to do with form, with whether or not the medium was indeed compatible with the message, which what was implicitly there in the *life* of the Church rather than what was explicitly there in the *thoughts* of the Church. That was the issue perceived by Paul fairly early on in the Church's history, the issue set forth by Paul in a consistent way in his correspondence with the churches.

Important as they are, however, the gospels do not constitute the whole of the New Testament. The New Testament contains, along with witnesses to Jesus' life and death and resurrection, witnesses to the life and history of the Church as bearers in the world of the presence of God. We have already seen how that view of the life and history of the Church was implicit in Paul's view of Christianity. Paul took the smallest, most mundane aspects of the Church's life very seriously indeed because of his insistence that the Church is the body of Christ. His great passage in praise of other-directed love in I Corinthians 13 is no abstract thing, but something prompted by his belief that the Church, that gathering of different kinds of human beings resulting from God's activity in human history beginning with Jesus, is the locus of God's presence in the world. Like Israel of old, the Church sees itself in the present and its history in the present as the medium through which God has chosen to be revealed to and involved with humanity. That is what Paul is saying. To put it in another way, it is a striking and unique thing in the history of religion that the Church is itself one of the articles of its own belief. The body which recites the creed is not external to that in which it professes its faith in the creed, but part of that in which it professes faith. God the Spirit, which is the subject of the Church's profession of faith in the third section of the classic creeds is not some mystical, sheerly spiritual reality. God the Spirit cannot, in the classic Christian creeds, be spoken of without also speaking of the empirical, historical Church. All that was also true for Paul, indeed was first stated by Paul in epistles such as I Corinthians. It was also true for the New Testament as a whole, and that is why the New Testament consists of more than the gospels.

There is one particular reason why the Church which produced the New Testament considered itself, as a result of the activity of God, an article of its own faith. That is that the Church, originating in the Israel of the postexilic period, experienced itself as the place where the prophetic vision of a new, transethnic, transnational, trans-all-natural-human-categories "Israel" had begun to come into existence. For Paul, who had been formed as a Jew in "the strictest sect" of Judaism, the most striking evidence of God's being at work in the Church was the way in which the course of events which had begun with Jesus' life and death and resurrection, and continued through the experience Paul himself had had on the road to Damascus, and included the proclamation of the gospel about Jesus in places like Corinth, had led to those who ought not, by any human standards, to be together being together. Here is Paul's classic exclamation about that:

> Before the faith we now profess arrived, we were imprisoned in our various *torahs*, inevitably separated from one another until faith should come. It was as if our various *torahs* were holding each of us back under guard until Christ should come and we should have our identity by faith. But faith has now indeed come and we are no longer separated and under guard, for in Christ Jesus you are all children of God through faith. For every one of you who was baptized into Christ now wears Christ as the garment by which you are identified. There is no such thing as Jew or Greek, slave or free, male or female, for you now have one identity in Christ Jesus.
>
> (GAL. 3:23–28)[28]

It is that view of the meaning of the Church which is to the fore in Ephesians.[29] The existence together in the Church of both Jews and those whom the Jews had come to think of in the postexilic period as "gentiles" is, in Ephesians, *the* miracle wrought by God through Jesus Christ. It represents the accomplishment of the final purpose God had in mind from the very beginning of creation. Ephesians, grounded as any theological statement ever is in its own cultural milieu, uses terms fraught with meaning in the Wisdom tradition to emphasize the eternal and theological significance of that unity of humanity which has become a fact in history in the Church:[30]

> God, lavishing upon us wisdom and understanding to the fullest degree, has made known to us the mystery of the divine purpose—precisely as the divine desire and pleasure found their focus in Christ—which is manifesting itself at the appointed time. What it is is this: that the whole universe should find in Christ, everything in heaven and in earth, the unity that God had in mind.
>
> (EPH. 1:8–10)

That statement, basic to what Ephesians considers has happened through God's work in Jesus Christ, is very much like the wisdom literature in its scope and concern and terminology. But the actual way in which the unity of the cosmos of which it speaks is being realized, the evidence that that unity has been achieved, is found in the empirical, historical phenomenon that is the Church. Non-Jewish Christians are addressed as follows:

> Now in Christ Jesus you who were completely separated from God's Israel have been brought near to Israelites through the shedding of Christ's blood. Christ is indeed the peace that unites us. Jews and Gentiles has Christ now made into one. In his own human body Christ destroyed the enmity between them which stood there like that wall in Jerusalem's temple which kept Gentiles out of the most sacred precincts. He set aside *torah* with all its potentially divisive specifications, thereby himself becoming the basis on which one new humanity came out of those separated two. That was the peace Christ brought about. Christ reconciled

> the two of us to God as one, single body through the cross. Yes, the cross was the place where he destroyed that enmity that divided us.
>
> (EPH. 2:13–16)[31]

What Paul sees as happening in the Church is the realization of what God had in mind in forming Israel in the first place. For Paul, the Church, as it comes into being in cities around the Mediterranean and then begins to live its life of *todah*, *eucharistia*, represents that universalization of Israel which the prophets had foreseen as the outcome of those events in which Israel's national existence, its existence as a *goy,* was brought to an end. It is the epistle to the Ephesians in particular which sees the existence together in the Church of Jews and Gentiles, a miraculous happening in light of the separation which actually existed between them and which found expression in ghettos and in that sign on the temple wall forbidding entrance to Gentiles under threat of death, as evidence that the whole cosmos was being reconciled in unity to God through Christ. The New Testament equivalent of *'am* or *kahal* or *'adath ha'elohim*, "people" or "congregation" or "assembly of God," is the Greek word *ekklesia*. That word is derived from the preposition *ek*, "out of," and the word *klesis*, "call" or "calling" or "invitation" or "vocation." The counterpart of *ekklesia* in the Greek of the New Testament is *ethne*, the equivalent of *goy* in Hebrew. The basic meaning of *ethne* is indicated by the fact that it is the word from which the English adjective "ethnic" is derived. Like *goy,* it denotes what a person is by nature, by birth. Thus, the Church, for the New Testament and particularly for Paul and Ephesians, is that real, historical *people* called by God out of its varied ethnic backgrounds and made the locus of a new humanity. It is the manifestation on the human scene of the redemptive reconciliation of the whole fallen and divided cosmos that God is about in and through Jesus Christ.

For Paul and Ephesians and the New Testament as a whole, all that is not an idea, a doctrine, a concept. It is something which is happening in a traceable, describable course of events which runs from Jesus' life and death and resurrection through the coming of the Christian message to those places where the Church actually exists and to the present, real existence of the Church in those places. It is happening as people of various ethnic identities hear the call to find their existence in God's *ekklesia*. It is found as the *ekklesia* exists in and through its recounting of that course of events, as the *ekklesia* gives thanks for that course of events, as the Church identifies itself in *todah*, in *eucharistia*. That is why the gospels do not constitute the whole of the New Testament. That is why the story of Jesus' life and career and death and resurrection is not the *whole* story. Indeed, that is why the resurrection has to do with a life that goes on in that body, the Church, which exists in Corinth and Galatia and Ephesus and all those other places. That is why the New Testament, even though it comes from a very short period of the Church's history, nevertheless includes witness to what is happening in the life of the Church right up to the time at which its constituent parts came to be written.

We have already seen how central all that is to what Paul says. Paul deals with it most explicitly and in the most organized way in Romans, the most systematic of his epistles most of which are *ad hoc* responses to specific situations and issues in the life of the Church. Paul appears to have wanted to make a careful exposition of his views on the nature of Christianity so that they could be considered by the Roman Christians before his arrival in that city. The best known section of Romans is chapters 1–8, chapters 5–8 in particular having become famous as the biblical basis for the Reformation doctrine of justification by faith. However, those opening chapters of Romans about God's work of salvation in Christ and faith as the means by which human beings appropriate salvation do not stand on their own. They are misunderstood when they are taken to be a treatise on salvation in Christ unconnected with the history continuing to flow from Christ and with the historical present in which they are written. Romans 1—8 leads directly to, is indeed the introduction to, what Paul has to say in that hard-to-understand section, Romans 9—11. The New English Bible is quite correct in entitling that section "The Purpose of God in History." Difficult to follow as Paul's reasoning about why Gentiles are coming into the Church before and in greater numbers than Jews may be, and strange as Paul's answer to the dilemma with which he struggles may sound today, it is an inescapable fact that his understanding of the nature of the gospel leads directly to his having to deal with the consequences of the introduction of the gospel into the history of the human race. Furthermore, the consequences of the gospel do not require simply theoretical consideration of the meaning of the history it sets in motion. They require that the life of the Church in the world, both corporately and in the lives of its individual members, be taken seriously. That is why the New English Bible also rightly entitles the final section of Romans, chapters 12–16, "Christian Behaviour." Reformation emphasis on the opening chapters of Romans to the contrary notwithstanding, the two concluding sections of that epistle are as integral to Paul's understanding of the gospel as are chapters 1–8.[32]

Just as the consequences of Paul's view of the significance of Jesus seem to be worked out, in very different ways, in the gospels which came to be included in the New Testament, so the results of Paul's views on the significance of the history which continues from Jesus into the life of the Church were also influential. Looked at against the background of our present discussion, the gospel of Mark, even though its narrative covers only Jesus' life and death and resurrection, does not confine the meaning and significance of Christianity to what is presented in that gospel. It is probably significant that Mark begins, "The *beginning* of the gospel of Jesus Christ the son of God." That heading may very well have been meant by the writer to be more than merely the introduction to the preaching of John the Baptist and Jesus' baptism. It may very well have been meant by the writer to be the heading of the whole gospel.[33] In that case, the heading is saying something very significant, something which radically separates Mark from that modern, romantic kind of Christianity which assumes it would be preferable from a Christian point of view to have "lived in the time of Jesus." The heading of Mark may be implying something like this: "What is written here is only the beginning of the gospel, that *todah*, that *eucharistia*, that thankful recital made possible by God's initiative in Jesus Christ, only the beginning of that gospel which goes on as the dynamic introduced into history in Christ continues to live in the Church and its history." To modern, romantic Christians Mark would have insisted that "the time of Jesus" was not only a then but is also a now.

Understanding of the beginning of the gospel of Mark can be balanced by a possible understanding of the ending of Mark, an understanding which is admittedly much more symbolic than scientific. Many of the earliest manuscripts of Mark end quite abruptly. The conclusion of Mark found in older translations such as the Authorized (King James) Version in verses 9–20 of chapter 16, as more modern translations such as the Revised Standard Version and the New English Bible indicate, is not there in a lot of the ancient copies of the Greek text of Mark. Even though it is there in other ancient manuscripts, it seems more likely that the material in Mark 16:9–20 was a later addition to the original than that it was dropped out of some manuscripts. That judgment is supported by the fact that the manuscripts of Mark which do continue after Mark 16:8 have significant differences in what they include in the conclusion to the gospel.[34] Not only is it the case that Mark seems originally to have ended with Mark 16:8, it is also the case that the usual structure of the Greek language would seem to indicate that Mark 16:8 ends in the middle of a sentence. The particle *gar,* with which 16:8 ends, does not normally end a sentence. The effect of its being there—structurally, not in terms of its meaning—is to make the sentence break off without a proper conclusion, in spite of the way in which the various English translations make it seem otherwise. The effect is something like this: "And they (Mary Magdalene and Mary the mother of James and Salome) left the tomb and fled because of the terror that gripped them, and they said nothing about it all to anyone because of their fear of . . ." Could it possibly be that Mark actually ended that way originally, that the lack of an ending which characterizes many early manuscripts is calculated and not an accident? Could it be that this gospel which begins its narrative of the life and death and resurrection of Jesus with the assertion that "What is recounted here is only the beginning of the gospel of Jesus Christ" also emphasizes that at its conclusion by, in fact, not having a conclusion? Such a thing would certainly fit with the views Paul held of the nature of Christianity. Furthermore, it would be in line with what we have seen again and again to be true in the biblical material, namely that "the medium is the message."

The point which seems intentionally to be made in Mark in line with the views which find expression in Paul and Ephesians is also taken seriously in the other gospels. The atmosphere of Matthew is, of the gospels of the New Testament, most like that of Q and the Gospel of Thomas. Nevertheless, it is not only true that Matthew makes the Marcan genre "gospel" the context within which Jesus is presented as the great, neo-Mosaic teacher, it is also true that Matthew specifically connects the narrative of Jesus' life and teaching and death and resurrection with what continues from them in the life and mission and history of the

Church. The last words of Matthew's gospel are words spoken by the risen Jesus: "Authority over everything in heaven and on earth has been committed to me. So go forth and call disciples out of every brand of humanity (*ethne* is the word), baptizing them into the story of the Father and the Son and the Holy Spirit,[35] and teaching them to observe all the commandments I have given you. You can be sure that I am with you through every one of the days leading toward history's end" (Mt. 28:18–20). It is remarkable to note the extent to which Matthew, whose views are not at all like those of Paul, not only concludes with an insistence on the significance of the life and history of the Church which continue on from the life and history of Jesus, but implies in that conclusion themes with which we have become familiar in our examination of the Pauline literature. While the content of the Church's mission is conceived much more as *teaching* than Paul would have liked, that mission does involve gathering a people out of every *ethne*, and its own life and history are the place where Jesus continues to be present as history goes on.

The same kind of thing is true also in Luke, in an even more concrete and significant way. Not only does the gospel of Luke conclude with its own version of a promise by Jesus that he will continue to be with the Church in the time following what has been narrated (Lk. 24:44–49), but the gospel of Luke is only the first volume of a work which continues in the Acts of the Apostles. Acts carries on the story of God's involvement in the course of events which is the Church's life in history down to Paul's arrival in Rome. The view of the nature of Christianity and the meaning of the life and history of the Church held in Acts is quite different from the view held by Paul. Once again, however, the very fact of what is done says something much more significant than does the specific content. The existence of Acts is a testimony to that faith, which we first saw enunciated in Paul, that, beginning with Jesus of Nazareth, the God who was involved of old in the history of Israel has once again chosen to be related to the human race through a traceable course of events.[36]

The same is true of the gospel of John. There is a sense in which a Wisdom-like mysticism is very much to the fore. There is an unworldly quality about the Jesus it pictures, a quality verging on what is found in early Christian writings which seem not to have satisfied the *todah*, *eucharistia* norm and so not to have been finally included in the New Testament.[37] Once again, however, *content* is not the primary basis on which the adequacy of witnesses to what Christianity was all about seems to have been assessed in the period before "orthodoxy-heresy" came to be a standard. John is there in the collection which came to be recognized as authoritative because its *form* is clearly "gospel." Moreover, it is there also because of the way in which, even if in its own fashion, it identifies the Church which emerges from Jesus' life and death and resurrection as the locus of God's involvement with human beings. John 20:21, presented as words of Jesus to the Church after the resurrection, voices what is said or implied many times in John: "Even as the Father has sent me, I send you. . . ." The Church and its life and mission are, in the gospel of John as elsewhere in the New Testament, the medium of God's presence in the world in a history which has to be recited beginning with Jesus.

Even the final sequence of the books included in the New Testament seems to witness to that belief in the Church and history as the medium of God's involvement with human beings which is there in all the gospels. It could very well be that the reason that Luke and Acts are now separated by the gospel of John is that, having decided to put the four gospels in what they took to be the order of their composition the collectors of the New Testament then separated Acts from Luke and put it after the gospels in order to have the

New Testament's form say what its individual books said: that the life and death and resurrection of Jesus are not a finished reality, but that the reality introduced through them by God into human history continues on in the life of the Church. The inclusion of the epistles in the New Testament after Acts witnesses to the same thing, that the real life of the Church is of such significance that its correspondence files can be considered scripture. Finally, following out the logic, the Revelation to John is a fitting conclusion with its apocalyptic vision of the end to which it is all moving as the Church lives in that history which God began in Jesus.

THE CHURCH AS GOD'S ISRAEL

We must remember that it was considerably later than the time in which they were written that the books which make up the New Testament came to be thought of by the Church as "Holy Scripture." To the earliest Church "Bible," "Scriptures" meant what we know as the Old Testament. The Church considered the Old Testament to be its sacred writings. The extent to which the Old Testament is quoted in the New is great indeed, and considerable study and writing has been devoted to that phenomenon.[38] Given the modern assumption that Christianity was a new and distinct religion, that people like Paul became converts to a new faith, it is surprising that the Church should have made the use it did of the scriptures of Israel. The fact is, however, that that assumption itself is the problem. It was not a case of one religion's borrowing the writings of another religion. The earliest Church considered itself to be a part of Israel, understood itself to be the result of the latest series of acts by Israel's God. Paul would have been astonished at being thought of as a "convert" from one religion to another. He, in fact, became part of a group within Israel of which it is written, "Participating in worship in the temple on the same daily basis on which they took their meals at home, they received their food with glad and generous hearts, giving praise to God and being respected by all the people (i.e. the Jewish community)" (Acts 2:46–47).[39] The issue for Paul, as well as for the earliest generation of the Church as a whole, was not that of one religion over against another. It concerned the validity of the significance Paul and others were giving to the course of events in history which had begun with Jesus of Nazareth on the basis of the scriptures which were the common property and heritage of all involved in the discussion.

In two respects in particular did the Old Testament shed light, for the earliest Christians, on what had transpired and was continuing to transpire beginning with Jesus. First, they discovered as they read the Hebrew Bible in light of what they themselves had experienced that another "people" had had a similar experience. What the earliest Christians were experiencing was God's presence in an historical course of events in such a way that that course of events had to be recited in order to make theological statements or to render praise to God. When they read the Hebrew Bible they found that that was precisely what had happened to the children of Israel from their remote beginnings down to the fall of Jerusalem to Babylon. The experience of the earliest Church made sense on the basis of what had happened to ancient Israel. The same God seemed once again to be at work in the same kind of way. Thus the early Church could readily identify with Old Testament events, and could, for example, easily speak of Jesus' resurrection in terms of Israel's exodus from Egypt.[40] Here is the basis for Paul's arguments with the kind of interpretation of the Old Testament which developed out of an understanding of Wisdom as the medium of God's presence. In terms which often indicate how much he himself had been formed by and was part of that tradition of interpretation, Paul keeps insisting that modes of finding a relevance for the scriptures appropriate to a situation of exile are irrelevant to a situation in which God is once again involved with a human community through an historical course of events. That is why, in Galatians in particular, Paul argues so forcefully for an abandonment of the kind of understanding of the relationship between God and human beings that grew out of the appropriation of Wisdom as a theological idiom in the exilic and postexilic era.[41] It should be noted, however, that he is arguing with those of his own community of faith about how they should understand the scriptures they all assume to be their own. There is no indication whatsoever that anyone thinks in terms of the Hebrew Bible being the scriptures of another, separate religion.

The second respect in which the Old Testament shed light for the earliest Christians on what was happening among them had to do with the nature of the Church as *ekklesia*, a people called out of various human, ethnic identities by God. Particularly in the promises of the prophets, which themselves were based on what ancient Israel had taken to be its essential nature from premonarchical times, the early Christians discovered descriptions of a human, historical community which squared with what they found themselves to be as a result of the coming of Jesus and the history that flowed from Jesus. They, therefore, saw the relationship between themselves and God as a *covenant* relationship, and because of that they found themselves in the same kind of tension with the Roman emperors as Israel's prophets had experienced in relation to Israel's kings. Consequently, it was a quite natural thing for the earliest Church to designate itself as "Israel," for it believed itself to exist as a result of the call of that same God who had begun the process of salvation by calling Abraham and Sarah away from what they were as *goy* and into the future God had in mind for the people of God. Again, the Church did not understand itself as the possessor of a new religion in contrast to an old. It understood itself as the latest generation of that people, that Israel, which continued to exist because of the initiative of Israel's God.

In both these respects the Old Testament was the book which shed light on the experience of the early Church. Other books available in the culture of which the earliest Christians were a part did not. Whether Jewish or Gentile in origin, most of the books in that culture understood reality in ways analogous to Wisdom. They did not, therefore, shed much light in a situation where a course of events was being experienced as the medium of God's revelation to and involvement with the human community. Furthermore, the books available in that culture which dealt with the meaning of the human community, whether the epics of Homer or Virgil or the treatises of Plato, were really celebrations of the ascendency of one or another *goy* ness, one or another ethnicity. They assumed the enslavement or restraint or destruction of less qualified ethnicities as normative. They did not, those other writings available in the culture, shed light on history's gathering of a people in which there was neither Jew nor Greek, slave nor free, male nor female. For those two reasons in particular, the Church, from the time of the New Testament onward, insisted that the Old Testament was the normative basis for the Church's self-understanding. That insistence was not the result of some arbitrary, intellectual, doctrinal decision. It was not the result of a theoretical or ideological stance. It grew out of the empirical, historical experience of the Church. Attempts to understand that experience on the basis of other norms resulted in the distortion of the experience in the interest of preserving the norm, as, for example, when Marcion had to excise large sections of the New Testament in order to maintain his stand that the God who acted in Jesus was different from and superior to the God who had acted in ancient Israel.[42]

Once again, we are perceiving a norm which antedates

the later "orthodoxy-heresy" concept. A conceptual "orthodoxy-heresy" norm, based on an understanding of Christianity as essentially teaching, is not what explains the role the Old Testament played in the early Church's life and thought. What is involved is a common, or an analogous, experience. It is the experience which makes *todah*, *eucharistia*, fitting praise of and witness to God. Indeed, it is the experience that *is todah*, that *is eucharistia*.

6

Eucharistia: The Canon Underlying the Canon

THE preceding chapter constitutes only a sketch. It presumes to cover material and issues which have occupied the attention of countless scholars and resulted in prolific publication. It is, however, a sketch which sets forth the basis of the thesis of this book as stated at the outset. That thesis is that, variegated and complex as were the early Church and early Christianity, there was a norm, a *kanon*, by which the earliest Church, like ancient Israel, measured the adequacy of witnesses to its faith. That norm was not one having primarily to do with conceptual content as such. That norm was, rather, one based on liturgical form, on cultic action, on what the Church knew and experienced and was involved in as it identified itself in worship. It was a norm rooted in the liturgy elicited by and appropriate as praise for God's revealing and saving involvement with a people in history. That form, that action, that norm was *eucharistia* which, like *todah* in ancient Israel, was thankful recital in the context of liturgical action in which the human community involved participated with God in the enjoyment of a sacrifice.

It is on that basis that it is possible to grant that early Christianity was indeed a complex phenomenon, yet at the same time to account for the early widespread recognition of certain witnesses to the faith as having normative authority. It is on that basis that it is possible not only to grant but to affirm that orthodoxy and heresy are indeed categories of a later era, yet at the same time to see how there is something which very different witnesses to the faith of the earliest Church have in common. The final question did not have to do with the content of *teaching*. It had to do with a *form* which was discernibly related to the Church's eucharistic act of self-identification, to the Church's eucharistic self-understanding. Furthermore, the final question has to do with that in no content-oriented, teaching-centered, "orthodoxy-heresy" way, based on *eucharistia* but itself still abstract and conceptual. It has to do with that, for the most part quite unconsciously, precisely in terms of the Church's liturgical life. It was not until the time of the Reformation, until a millenium and a half after the Church began, that the Church got around to deciding *in theory* which witnesses belonged in its canon of scripture.[1] What resulted in various witnesses just being used widely and often to such an extent that they were "naturals" for inclusion in a canon when a self-conscious decision had to be made was their compatibility, in form and assumptions and ethos, with the Church's liturgical *eucharistia*. That is why, in terms of the geographical centers and the content of the writings emanating from those centers as identified by Bauer and those who have followed Bauer, it is quite possible for representatives of various emphases in early Christianity to be found side by side in the New Testament. Paul and Mark are representative of Aegean Christianity. Matthew and Luke and John, in various ways, are representative of Syro-Palestinian Christianity. Q, embedded in Matthew and Luke, is representative of eastern Syrian-Egyptian Christianity. At the same time, Q in its original form and the Gospel of Thomas, as well as a number of other works, are in fact not to be found in the New Testament.

It is the thesis of this book that what led to that is discernible only if other factors than "teaching" are taken into account. The criterion that brought the New Testament into being, long before the era of the Reformation, was the ability in the last analysis of any given witness to Christianity to be recognizable as compatible with the eucharistic context within which the Church lived. It was that criterion which resulted in widespread acceptance of certain writings and in the comparatively restricted use of others. The *kanon*—the rule, the standard, the test, the norm—lay in the Church's concrete experience. It lay in the Church's actual liturgical appropriation of what its faith believed, in the Church's actual cultic reliving of that course of events in which it had originated and continued to exist.

The Eucharistic Character of Baptism

Baptism was, in ancient times as it is now, the liturgical act in which a human being was incorporated into the Church. It was the liturgical act in which a person became part of all that which had brought the Church into being and in which the Church continued to exist. Baptism was analogous to what happened in ancient Israel on occasions such as the one described in Joshua 24. There, as a new era of Israel's life and history began in a new land, we see Israel reaffirming its covenant commitment to God. Israel does so by hearing the recital of the course of events which has placed it in the covenant relationship with God, and by restating its assent to the relationship. Israel gives consent to its being incorporated into the story in which God has been and is involved, through which God is in contact with this world and the history in which human beings live. Moreover, there is every reason to believe that an occasion such as this was not only a reaffirmation of loyalty to the covenant by those who were already Israelites. The contemporary studies of the background of the covenant which have shed so much light on what covenant is really all about indicate that, on occasions such as the one described in Joshua 24, *new* families or clans or tribes would come into the Israelite tribal confederation by giving their assent to the covenant and becoming incorporated into the history in which the covenant relationship had originated and in which it continued to exist.[2]

Baptism was the same kind of thing in the early Church.[3] It was not a sacramental act separated from the corporate life of the Church and applied to individuals. It was apparently the custom that baptism took place in connection with the cycle of the Church's year in which the story of Jesus and the beginning of the Church were relived liturgically. Baptism took place as the Easter celebration proclaimed God's validation of Jesus as the formative event in the introduction of a new life and history into the human community. Baptism took place in the context of the celebration of that new life present in the Church as a result of God's gift of the Spirit. Those who were to be baptized were instructed for a considerable period of time in what Christian faith was and meant. What that instruction culminated in, however, was not certification that the candidate had finally mastered *teaching* in such a way as to be qualified to enter the company of the wise, the company of those "in the know."[4] It culminated in an action in which the candidate gave up his or her ethnic identity as the primary truth about who he or she was. In this action the candidate received a new identity as a participant in that course of events in which God through Jesus was present in a human fellowship (*ekklesia*) whose story was gospel.[5]

The type of statement of faith denoted as "creed" apparently originated in connection with baptism as the equivalent in the Church of Joshua's recital in the covenant renewal ceremony to which Israel gave its assent and was thereby incorporated into the life of the people of God.[6] The Christian recital consisted of three major parts: the story of God as creator and sustainer of all things; the story of God as the One whose call had constituted Israel and whose call was universalized so as to include all peoples in the life and death and resurrection of Jesus of Nazareth; and the story of how God continued to be present in the Spirit in this world in the life and history of the Church. It seems to have been the case that, when a candidate came actually to be incorporated into the Church by the baptismal act, that that recital was central. The candidate would be questioned as to his or her readiness to put faith and trust in the God who is creator. The answer would be the recital of the first part of the story by the candidate, or assent to that recital, followed by immersion in the baptismal water. The same thing would happen with regard to faith and trust in God in Christ, and finally the same thing would happen with regard to God in the Spirit in the Church. What was happening, as the candidate successively went down into the water (water being from ancient times a symbol of destructive chaos) was death to the candidate's ethnic identity. That dying was accompanied by a recital of or assent to the recital of God's involvement with the world as the candidate was incorporated into that story, incorporated into the course of events in which God's purpose of reconciliation and salvation was being worked out. The candidate's identity in this or that *ethne* was being erased, and the candidate's real identity was becoming part of that story which was the story of the Church. Furthermore, it was a corporate thing that was taking place as the Church as a whole celebrated Christ's resurrection and the coming of the Spirit on Easter and Pentecost. The Church too was giving its assent to the recital, joining in the recital, after the fashion of Israel under Joshua on the banks of the Jordan. The Church too was dying to the ethnic identities which had produced its various members, was being reincorporated into the gospel story. The genre "creed" seems to have originated as the form of words in which the recital took place in the total liturgical celebration which was baptism.

It should be noted that what we have just been describing probably explains concretely what Paul means when he talks about dying to self and living to Christ, about dying with Christ in his death and rising with Christ in his resurrection. For the Paul who thought of the Church as the body of Christ and of the seemingly most insignificant aspects of its life and of the lives of its members as, therefore, of great consequence, those phrases surely could not have had some sheerly mystical connotation divorced from life and history in this world. That kind of meaning comes to be seen only when they are read as abstract sets of words with no concrete, physical, liturgical setting. What Paul was talking about when he used those phrases would have been recognized automatically by his original hearers and readers because of their participation in the liturgical life of the Church. He was talking about the reality of what the Church was when it acted out that reality in baptism. The real source of Paul's imagery about Christian existence as dying and rising with Christ was not some otherwordly, sheerly spiritual experience. It was the life and liturgy of the Church, the people of God, to whom Paul was speaking.

It should also be noted that "creed," understood in terms of its origin as a form, as a genre, is not primarily a statement of doctrinal tenets. That the word "creed" came to be understood in that way, and is so understood by both proponents and opponents of creeds, is due to the rise of an "orthodoxy-versus-heresy" understanding of the nature of Christianity. It is due to concern for correct interpretation leading to a situation in which interpretation really becomes more important than what is being interpreted. It results in lots of honest people having difficulties about Christianity which really have nothing to do with Christianity's essential nature. "Creed" in its origin and in terms of the function it originated to serve was not a definitive, conceptual, doctrinal, dogmatic statement at all. It was a witness to, a sign which pointed toward, a "symbol" in the classic sense of that word of the life, the history, the course of events in which God had chosen to be involved with human beings. "Creed" was the recital accompanying the liturgical action in which the present was caught up into that life, that history, that course of events. To examine every single statement of a creed with a philosophical magnifying glass, whether the examiner be procreed or anticreed, is to misunderstand what a creed really is in origin and function. It is, therefore, to misunderstand Christianity as it was understood by those amongst whom the creeds originated. Creeds are living, liturgical, recitative statements. They are not abstract, doctrinal, dogmatic statements. They are meant to be recited in the context of a liturgical drama. They are not meant to be the subjects of abstract arguments.

It should be noted finally, therefore, that creedal unity in the early Church was not fundamentally a doctrinal thing. It was a unity with one another existing among those who participated in the Church's liturgy and life and history. It originated in the action which constituted the Church as Church and which brought the members of the Church out of separated ethnic identities into identification with the course of events in which God was working to bring fragmented humanity together with itself and with God. It was that unity as concretely experienced which was the basis on which the adequacy of various witnesses to Christianity and its significance came to be adjudged in practice. It arose out of an ethos common to both ancient Israel and the early Church, an ethos which resulted in *todah* rather than *torah* being normative, in *euangelion* and *eucharistia* rather than teaching or orthodoxy in a later sense being normative. "Creed" stands alongside "gospel" and "eucharist" as a form appropriate to that kind of witness to God which first made *todah* normative back in ancient Israel. That is because the origin of "creed" lies in baptism, central to which is *eucharistia*, thankful, witnessing recital.

The Eucharist Itself as Normative Eucharistia

Baptism was the liturgical act in which human beings were born into a new identity in the Church. It was also the liturgical act in which the Church itself was born anew as the nonethnic people of God. Baptism was a once-in-a-lifetime liturgical action for individual Christians, an annual act of renewal for the Church as a whole. Baptism was not, however, the regular, ongoing liturgical act in which the Church identified itself as Church. The liturgical act in which, from the very earliest stage of its existence, the Church identified itself regularly week by week as God's *ekklesia* was the Eucharist. That act took place, originally and normally, on the first day of the week, which Christian tradition held to be the day on which Jesus' resurrection had taken place.[7] For the earliest Church the primary significance of the resurrection lay in its being the event in which God affirmed the crucified Jesus as the beginning of that course of events in and through which God was reconciling fragmented humanity to itself as well as to God. Observing that first day liturgically as "the Lord's Day" was, therefore, in and of itself saying something significant, making a witness. It was proclaiming when and where and in whom the history which really mattered had got underway. It is important to understand this in the context of the discussion of the meaning of covenant given earlier in this book. The earliest Christians, in the days before the emperor Constantine removed the legal strictures against membership in the Church, did not make their way furtively through cities in the Roman empire to the house where the Church was gathering on the Lord's Day at the threat of imprisonment and torture and death in order to "get a lift" or to be impressed by a fine sermon or to hear good music. They were not "going to Church" in the modern sense. They were bearing their witness to the One who was the true emperor by observing the day on which the reign of the true emperor had begun. They were gathering to witness to that to themselves, individually and corporately, as well as to the world in general. If that witness turned out to mean death, then death became testimony to just who it was who was the true emperor of the universe. Indeed, the Greek word the English form of which is "martyr" means simply "witness," "one who testifies." It was the nature of the witness given by early Christians which gave the word "martyr" the connotations it now has. And that witness was *liturgical* witness, just as recantation of loyalty to Christ as emperor took the *liturgical* form of offering incense to the Roman emperor.

The liturgical act in which the Church engaged when it gathered on the Lord's Day to identify itself as the people called together by the true emperor followed a certain form. After the gathering had been convened by one authorized to do so, and words about God's presence in Christ had been spoken, and prayers for the Church and the world offered, a liturgical action consisting of certain established elements took place. A table was set, and bread and wine placed on it. The bread and wine were blessed by thanks being offered to God over them. The bread was broken, and it and the wine offered to the gathered Church. Finally, the bread and wine were consumed by the Church with thanks.[8] It is that liturgical action—not the specific words used or the elaborateness or simplicity with which the various parts of the action were done—which constitutes the Eucharist and makes it recognizeable in different languages and different settings and different cultures. In that action the Church was acting out the kind of relationship it had with the God who had brought it into being in that course of events which had begun in Jesus' life and death and resurrection, and which was analogous to the course of events in which the same God had in former times brought Israel into being. In that action the Church identified itself for what it really was. It was the Church's normative act of liturgical self-identification.

Given the Church's deep awareness of the likeness of its experience and nature to the experience and nature of ancient Israel, it is interesting to note the ways in which that liturgical action parallels the *todah* sacrifice in ancient Israel. In the *todah* sacrifice the victim was brought to the priest at the sanctuary, thanks was given over the victim to be offered for the deliverance which had prompted the sacrifice (here is the origin of the psalms of thanksgiving), and then the victim was sacrificed to become both an offering to the divine deliverer and a meal at which family and friends, whose praise Israel's God preferred to that of a heavenly court, celebrated with the one who had been delivered. There is, of course, no way of proving that the earliest Church had knowledge of the procedures followed at ancient *todah* sacrifices, and the question of where the origins of the shape of the Eucharist are to be sought has been the subject of an immense amount of scholarly work.[9] Our contention here, therefore, is not that there was a self-conscious copying of an ancient cultic act. What is contended, however, is that the memory of that *todah* cult, of its ethos and character, was preserved in exilic and post-exilic Judaism. The atmosphere and tone of *todah* were present in the Passover *haggadah*, in the *berakoth* ("blessings") used in the synagogue and at meals, and in the various "freewill" sacrifices offered by individuals at the Jerusalem temple certainly up to 70 A.D., and quite possibly until 135 A.D.[10] It was so much a part of the heritage which had come down to Judaism from ancient Israel that, and this is the thesis of this book, it was inevitably appropriated by the Church when an experience analagous to the one which had made *todah* normative in ancient Israel in the first place demanded celebration.

At the heart of the liturgical action lies the prayer by which the bread and wine were blessed as they were offered to God and sanctified for the communion meal of the Church. In the prayer God was praised and thanked for what God had wrought in and through Jesus, for that course of events which had brought the Church to the eucharistic gathering in which it was presently engaged. It was a recountal of the Christian story into which the members of the Church had been incorporated in baptism and in which the Church continued to live, a recitative prayer like both the *todah* psalms of the Old Testament and the *berakoth* of post-exilic Judaism. The prayer connected the *mirabilia Dei*, the mighty acts of God, with their *re*-presentation in a sacred, liturgical action which was the central means by which the Church proclaimed what it was.[11] It recited the same story underlying the baptismal creed, the story of the course of events which had begun with Jesus' life and death and resurrection and was continuing even now as the Church was gathered around the table. The recital brought Jesus' story into the present and included the Church in that story, which made the meal the Church was participating in the heavenly banquet, which made the bread and wine on the table the body and blood of Christ.

A classic example of such a prayer is found in the *Apostolic Tradition* of Hippolytus from the middle of the third century. This prayer is offered as a model for the use of a newly ordained bishop. It seems to be more reminiscent of forms which prevailed much earlier in eastern Syria than what was typical in the Rome in which it was written at the time it was written. That its author seems to have been antiquarian in taste is to our advantage, for he provides us with a look back into tradition.[12] After directions that the deacons should present the offering of bread and wine to the bishop and after the opening dialogue of the *sursum corda* ("lift up your hearts"), the prayer itself goes as follows:

> We give you thanks, O God, through your beloved Child Jesus Christ, whom you have sent us in the last times as savior, redeemer, and the messenger of your plan; who is your inseparable Word, through whom you have created all things, and whom, in your good pleasure, you have sent down from heaven into the womb of a Virgin, and who, having been conceived, became flesh and was shown to be your Son, born of the Holy Spirit and the Virgin. It is he who, fulfilling your will and acquiring for you a holy people, stretched out his hands while he was suffering that he might free from suffering those who have trust in you. While he was being betrayed to his voluntary suffering, in order to destroy death and break the chains of the devil, tread hell underfoot, bring forth the righteous into light, set the guiding principle, and manifest the resurrection, taking bread he gave thanks to you and said: Take, eat; this is my body which is broken for you. Likewise the cup, saying: This is my blood which is shed for you. When you do this, do it in memory of me.
>
> Wherefore we, being mindful of his death and resurrection, offer you this bread and this cup, giving thanks to you that you have deemed us worthy to stand before you and to serve you as priests.
>
> And we beseech you to send your Holy Spirit upon the oblation of holy Church. And in bringing them together, grant to all those who partake of your holy mysteries to partake of them in order that they might be filled with the Holy Spirit, and for the strengthening of their faith in truth; that we may praise you and glorify you through your Child Jesus Christ, through whom be to you glory and honor with the Holy Spirit in the Holy Church now and forever. Amen.[13]

Father Bouyer, in his book *Eucharist*, presents a convincing case for the embodiment in that prayer of a form—his terms are a type, a schema, a living *anima*—which goes back through the beginning of the Church to the Jewish *berakoth* (blessings). It should be emphasized that what is being talked about is a *form*, not a script or a set form of words, which lies behind later variations and corruptions. The *form* in that sense is the basic thing.[14] It is the thesis of this book that the roots of that form ultimately go back even further than the postexilic *berakoth*, that their remote origin lies in the *todah* recital which was integral to the *todah* sacrifice in ancient Israel. *Eucharistia* is the name of that form, and *eucharistia* is the Greek translation of both *todah* and *berakah*, the singular of *berakoth*. Like theirs, its meaning is "blessing" or "thanksgiving," blessing or thanksgiving given through a recital of what is the reason for or the subject of blessing or thanksgiving. It is the recognition in our own time of the extent to which the *eucharistia* form underlies both the entire liturgical action which is the Church's central act of worship and the prayer lying at the heart of that action which has resulted in the increased use of the word "Eucharist" to name it.[15] Down through the centuries it has been variously called the Lord's Supper, the Mass, the Holy Communion, the Liturgy. Those designations emphasized various aspects of that liturgical action, but there is also a sense in which they have resulted from a loss of consciousness of the fundamentally *eucharistic* character of the action and have obscured its character.

It is, though, the case that the earliest Church out of whose life the action originally came characteristically and normatively identified itself by doing *eucharistia*. That was so routine in the Church out of which the earliest writings came that it was simply taken for granted. Paul refers to it in I Corinthians 11. The synoptic gospels connect it with that last meal with the disciples at which Jesus "gave thanks," "blessed" bread and wine. While the gospel of John does not include the founding of the Eucharist in its narrative, it clearly takes it for granted as the very setting of what the gospel is setting forth, and Jesus' discourses in John bespeak the Church's communion with Jesus in the Eucharist (cf. Jn. 6 and Jn. 15). It was just *there*, a centrally fundamental part of the Church's existence.

Hence, inevitably, *eucharistia*, that central liturgical action of its life by which the Church identified itself as God's people and from which it got its identity as God's people was the *kanon*, the standard, the rule, the norm, by which it recognized what was authentically Christian in shape or content. *Eucharistia* was the *kanon* by which Paul deemed that frantic search of the Corinthians for the correct teaching and the authoritative teacher to be based on a fundamental misunderstanding of the nature of Christianity. It was on the basis of that *kanon* that he directed their attention to their *life as Church*, their life as an historical people, as the locus of God's presence. *Eucharistia* was the *kanon* by which Paul found that running of the Galatians after the correct instruction in cultic and moral matters to be a distortion of what God had wrought in and through Jesus. It was on the basis of that *kanon* that he called them to the free, thankful celebration that results from faith in what Christianity is really about. *Eucharistia* was the *kanon* by which the Church—without ever engaging in any conscious, content-centered decision—simply *made use of* the writings that eventually came to be the New Testament but allowed Q in its original form and the Gospel of Thomas and lots of other things to fall into disuse. Later, formal, self-conscious decisions about these matters usually only ratified what had already been decided in the life and use of the Church on the basis of that *eucharistic kanon* which was just inhaled in the liturgical air breathed by the Church.

Furthermore, the nature of the Church's experience was such that it found itself driven to do theology in a eucharistic way. Just as the Yahwist and the Elohist and the Deuteronomists and the Priestly Writers and the Chronicler did theology by creating an interpretative narrative, so did Mark and Matthew and Luke (in both the gospel and Acts) and John. Moreover, that tradition continued in the Church. Just as ancient Israelite writers rethought the meaning of Israel's involvement with God at certain points of transition in Israel's life by an interpretative recounting of Israel's history, so did Eusebius do the same thing for the Church when the Roman Empire recognized Christianity, and so did Augustine when the empire began to collapse before the barbarians.[16] The reason was twofold. First, in the same kind of way as had ancient Israel, the Church experienced the course of events that made up its own history as the medium through which it was related to and involved with God. That history, therefore, was a necessary basis for theology. Second, those who produced the gospels and the Acts of the Apostles, as well as later Christians such as Eusebius and Augustine, were formed spiritually and mentally by their regular participation in the Christian *eucharistia*. That formation led, therefore, to the recitation of God's involvement with the Church being the logical way to do theology. *Eucharistia* was not only the *kanon* by which the adequacy of statements about God and God's relation to the world was adjudged. It was also the ethos out of which such statements arose.

The Loss and Rediscovery of Eucharistia as the Norm

Through the centuries following the writing of the New Testament witnesses to the gospel, particularly from the third century on, consciousness of *eucharistia* as the norm for Christian self-identification and for statements about the nature of God and the nature of God's relation to the world declined.[17] The eucharistic *kanon* which the earliest Church applied unconsciously out of its liturgical experience faded into obscurity in the Church's consciousness. The reason lay in the necessity for the Church to understand itself in terms present in the culture in which it existed. As its existence was made legal by the Roman empire and Christianity came gradually to be the religion of western culture, the Church had to understand itself and explain itself in the idiom of that culture whose view of reality was not, on the whole, historical and eucharistic and eschatological. Rather it was really a demythologized and rationalized form of the view which had prevailed in the ancient Near Eastern culture which was the setting of ancient Israel's life and history. It was an ontological view of reality, a view which posited being (*ontos*) as the fundamental reality underlying all specific manifestations of reality. As a view it led to interest in the nature of being rather than interest in particular manifestations, to priority being put upon speculation about and mystical contact with being rather than on affirmation of the things and events and human beings inhabiting this world and the history which goes on in this world. Just as ancient Israel had had to assert that Yahweh was indeed God in terms which would mean something to ancient Near Eastern culture and then, later, in terms which were understandable in the Wisdom ethos, so the Church had to acclaim the God who was manifest in Jesus and the Church itself in terms which would mean something in the culture in which it was now existing.

That process occupied the Church through the first five centuries of its existence. The period was as fraught with differences and controversies, as characterized by widely varying theological statements, as was the history of Israel in the context of ancient Near Eastern culture. The problem was that the nature of Christian faith was such that it strained the concepts in which the Church had to try to state the faith.[18] As it had been in ancient Israel, so it was in the Church. Neither those who refused to have anything to do with the culture and the ways the culture thought and expressed itself nor those who simply put the Christian God into the categories and concepts of the culture really got the job done. It was those who worked within the tension who accomplished the theological task. When the process had run its course, and the age of the ecumenical councils—at which decisions were made about which statements regarding the nature of Christian faith were generally acceptable—was over, something analogous to what happened to Israel's epics and prophetic books in the exilic and postexilic era had taken place.[19] The form "gospel" had remained normative, and the form "creed" had remained normative. *Eucharistia* remained normative. Nevertheless, just as Israel's scriptures came to be perceived as repositories of Wisdom rather than statements of *todah*, so "gospel" and "creed" and *eucharistia* came to be perceived as repositories of "revelation." "Gospel" and "creed" and *eucharistia* had come to be understood as repositories of the truth about that Being which gave all particular things their meaning, and that Being had come to be identified with God in Christ. The *forms* had been retained, but the content was now understood in quite different terms from those which had given rise to the forms in the first place.

The way in which this change in perception affected the central Christian act of liturgical self-identification almost completely obscured its origins in *eucharistia*.[20] Rather than being understood and participated in as the recital of the great works of God in which the Church celebrated its own historical existence as the medium of God's involvement with the world, the central Christian liturgical act came to be understood as the mystical transaction in which the Church was put into contact with the transcendent Being which alone really meant anything. The great prayer at the heart of the liturgy ceased to be understood as *eucharistia*, and came to be understood as the consecration formula which transformed bread and wine into the body and blood of Christ through which the Being that mattered could enter human lives. The significance of the recital which was *eucharistia* having been forgotten, significance came to be focussed on Jesus' "words of institution" as the *formula* which effected "consecration". The great story which was the context of those words then tended to become more and more truncated. Thus the theology of the era fed the understanding of the liturgy, and the form and understanding of the liturgy had great effect on theology. A liturgy centered on a formula of consecration and a theology consisting of dogmatic formulas went right together.

The consensus coming out of the great councils of the first five centuries, in which Christian faith was stated in terms native to the culture which had become the Church's home, prevailed in a Christendom which existed in Europe for centuries.[21] Church and state and society and culture were intertwined as one, as were philosophy and "science" and the arts and theology. The participants in that culture all over Europe, whatever differences of background there might be, lived together in relation to a common set of realities and spoke a common language, Latin, about those realities. The time came, however, when "Christendom" began to come apart. Indeed, in the long perspective of history, it can be seen that that began to happen almost as soon as "Christendom" came into being. Men and women began to find their identities in terms of different and more local and less universal realities than the ones which had been universally assumed. Different nations began to wield the power which had, theoretically at least, been wielded by the successors of the Roman emperors, and men and women began to be conscious of nationalities which had not existed before in a conscious way. The economy began to change, and new classes came into being. The power which had earlier belonged to the nobility shifted into the control of manufacturers and merchants. New technologies developed, and guilds and other self-conscious alignments of people related to their work arose. In general, a new variety of human consciousness seemed to appear. Certainly by the fifteenth and sixteenth centuries people began to be aware of that, and to be insecure and fearful as people inevitably are at times of historical transition.

That collapse of "Christendom," its transformation into something which had not previously existed, is the background against which the Reformation is probably best understood. It may very well be, as the passage of time results in our having more perspective, that we will come more and more to see that the Reformation marked response to the end of an era rather than initiative in creating a new one. With better perspective it may very well be that the Reformation will recede in importance as a creative and critical era in the Church's history. With better perspective it may very well be that the first five centuries and the eighteenth and following centuries will come to be seen as the two really critical and creative eras in which the Church was called upon to understand itself and preach its gospel in new cultural settings. What the Reformation, on the other hand, really represented, in different self-conscious national and cultural areas where the universal consensus of Christendom was collapsing, was attempts to state what was really central to and authoritative for Christianity. Attempts like that, the search for authority, always spell the collapse of the structures in which authority has previously resided and been taken for granted.

Those areas which, in particularly significant ways, had come to new self-consciousness over against the older consensus understandably looked in new directions for what was central to and authoritative for Christianity. Those Christian institutions and structures which had been associated with the older order which was passing must, in the view of those who found themselves in new and different historical places, not really have been the fundamental things. Thus, in parts of Germany and France and Switzerland and in England, when the political authority of the Holy Roman Empire began to collapse and the theological and spiritual authority of the papacy to come into question, a search for the original and basic source of authority in the Church led to the early Church and the Bible. Thus also, in those areas where the structures inherited from the old order remained comparatively intact or where Christians had problems about accepting newer views and structures—in other parts of Germany and France and Switzerland and in Italy and Spain—newer and more self-conscious reasons for the centrality and authority of the papacy and the tradition which had produced the papacy were found. Both groups, however, Protestants as well as Catholics, had in common the heritage of the era that lay behind them in history. Protestants might rest their appeal on the scriptures and the creeds of the earliest Church uncontaminated by the doctrinal accretions of intervening centuries, but the way in which they interpreted and considered the Bible and the creeds authoritative had in fact been learned from the intervening centuries. Bible and creeds were, for the Protestants as for their predecessors, repositories of revealed truth of an, ultimately, ontological kind. Catholics might appear to take ongoing history seriously as a medium of God's involvement with the Church and the world, but in reality the "tradition" deemed authoritative alongside the Bible by the counter-Reformation Roman Catholic Church was a deposit of revelation, a repository of revealed truth, just as the Bible was for Protestants.

What was taking place, in different geographical and demographic and theological areas splitting away from one another as Christendom collapsed, was a codification of the Christian heritage so that it would not be lost in the strange, new world in which the Church now found itself. It was not unlike what had happened in Israel when the fall of Jerusalem to Babylon and the strange, new world of exile led to the collection and collation and codification of Israel's traditions so that they would not be forgotten.[22] The Hebrew Bible and the collection of writings which came to be known as the New Testament had, for a long time, been commonly recognized as authoritative just because of their use in the Church. It is the thesis of this book that that authority originally arose from their eucharistic character. It was, however, only at the time of the Reformation that the Church found it necessary officially to define the limits of the biblical canon, to make official statements as to just which books actually were the repositories of God's revelation.[23] A view of the nature of God and of God's relation to human beings unlike the one presupposed by ancient Israel and the early Church underlay what was happening. So too did the insecurity which always goes with the end of one era and the beginning of another. That Reformation definition of just which books were authoritative led to the Roman Catholic Church's adoption of the ancient Greek translation of the Hebrew Bible—the Septuagint—as its recognized Old Testament, while the Protestant Churches recognized only those books contained in the Hebrew Bible itself. The Septuagint contains some books and sections of books which are not found in the Hebrew Bible. This overplus, following Jerome, is what is called the Apocrypha. Like the Protestant Churches the Anglican Church separated the Apocrypha from the "canonical" Old Testament books, but like the Catholic Church it uses some of the apocryphal writings, considering them edifying but not doctrinally authoritative.[24] What happened with regard to the Apocrypha is illustrative of how all parties in the Reformation shared, even as they sharply defined their differences, a common set of presuppositions about God and the mode of God's contact with the Church and the world. Those presuppositions involved "revelation" of the truth about Being as crucial, and the derivative necessity to define just which books and/or set of traditions contained that truth.

It is significant that the Reformation occurred just as Gutenberg's invention of moveable type made the mass production of books a factor which was to be extremely important in western culture.[25] Before the Reformation and the invention of moveable type Christians knew the Bible not as a book. They knew its various sections as parts of the Church's heritage as they were read at appropriate times in the Church's year and at appropriate places in the liturgy. Furthermore, the liturgy itself was preserved and its continuity maintained from age to age in the centuries before the Reformation in terms of its *form*—its shape, its structure—rather than as a script of written words. Various rites were used in various areas and places, their basic *form* being the basis of their unity. The Reformation search for the authoritative deposit of the Church's revealed truth combined with the technology of moveable type, however, led to the Church's becoming a people of the book. For classical Protestants that book was the Bible, the parameters of which were now sharply defined. For Roman Catholics that book was the Roman Missal which, with a few exceptions, replaced all the varied, local rites which had existed in the pre-book-oriented era with a written script based on the rite of the Church in Rome. For Anglicans that book was the Book of Common Prayer, which also unified the varied rites existing in England and put them into the vernacular.

The result of all this was, to all practical intents and purposes, the total disappearance of any liturgical life in the Church in the sense that such a life, *eucharistia*, had been the ethos out of which theology and spirituality and service of the world arose. In the Roman Church the priest "said Mass" out of the book, and the people "heard Mass" out of the book, quite possibly also reading some devotions out of a little book of their own while the priest read the script of the liturgy out of the missal. In the Protestant churches the doing of liturgy was almost entirely replaced by reading and hearing the reading of the Bible and then expounding or hearing the expounding of what had been read. When liturgical things like communion or baptism were done in Protestant Churches, they were justified by texts from the

Bible which gave warrant for what was taking place. In the Anglican Church active participation in liturgy was replaced by the officiant's reading of the script of the liturgy from the Book of Common Prayer and the congregation's following of the reading from their copies of the Prayer Book. Indeed, pews in Anglican churches came very often to be built and located so that worshippers could not see what was happening liturgically but participate only by following what was being read from the book.[26] Once again, the mode of doing theology in a given era fed the understanding—indeed, in this case the disappearance—of liturgy. Furthermore the form of the liturgy—or the lack of liturgy—had great effect on theology. The substitution of the reading of a book for the doing of liturgy and the grounding of theology in the interpretation of authoritative books went right together. Neither in liturgy nor in theology was *eucharistia*—thankful recitative, acted out praise of God—any longer the norm. "Canon" had come to mean either a set of authoritative books or the set prayer read from an authoritative book.

It needs to be said at this point, just as it was said at the conclusion of our discussion of how ancient Israel was replaced by exilic and postexilic Judaism, that what has been said above is meant to be simply descriptive of what took place in the era of the Reformation. It is not meant to constitute a set of value judgments. Both that adaptation to a culture and its way of thinking and expressing its thought which coincided with the rise of Christendom and the Reformation codification of the Christian heritage which coincided with the collapse of Christendom represented continuing attempts on the part of the Church to understand and articulate its faith in the context of the historical and cultural situation in which it found itself. Just as the Old Testament simply would not have been available to shed light on and nourish the early Church's eucharistic understanding of God and its existence if rabbinic Judaism had not found a meaning in the old writings which made sense in exile, so the very possibility of setting out what has occupied us in this book would not have been possible if the Christians of the Reformation era had not preserved the biblical heritage in the way they did or if their predecessors had not tried to make sense of that heritage in the culture of Christendom. What we have been saying here does have the ring of negative judgment about it when it is said against the background of our discussion of the early Church, but it too describes stages in that course of events through which—to follow out the logic of *todah* and *eucharistia*—the witness of ancient Israel and the early Church has come to us in the present. The very criterion by which it would all seem to be judged is a criterion which ultimately demands that it all must be celebrated.

The collapse of Christendom, that western culture in which the Church and the gospel had lived for a thousand years or more, led to the rise of a new culture the outlines of which began to be discernible in the seventeenth and eighteenth centuries and which came to be dominant through the nineteenth and into the twentieth centuries.[27] While that culture is fundamentally secular, it was and is very deeply formed and influenced by the dynamic introduced into the history which produced it by Israel and the early Church. Indeed, there are many ways in which, in spite of secularism and surface impressions, that dynamic is much more embodied in the new culture than it was in the defensive codifications produced in the Reformation and the Counter-reformation. For one thing, the new culture came to be characterized by a consciousness of the reality of history—parallel to a similar consciousness present in ancient Israel and the early Church—which had been lost in Christendom and the Church of Christendom. There were those who responded to the new perspectives and consciousnesses which came as Christendom collapsed by seeking to trace just how it had all come about. As a result, history as a discipline came into being and came to be important in the intellectual life and educational structures of western culture in a way in which it had not been important before.[28] History once again became the basis, as it had been for the framers of the Israelite epics and Israel's prophets and Paul and the evangelists and Augustine, on which a Vico meditated on what things were all about.[29] The historical shift in which social and political and economic structures that had been taken for granted gave way to new structures led to conscious interest in such structures and to the rise of the social sciences as important factors in the intellectual and educational life of western culture. They had not existed before. Furthermore, the historical shift in which one culture was replaced by another resulted in a shift of attention from the Being which underlay a stable order to the human beings who were the continuing occupants of a world which changed in other respects. Fascination with human beings and what makes them what they are eventually led to psychology and the disciplines associated with it becoming important parts of the intellectual and educational life of western culture. Thus, the perspectives of history and the social and human sciences, rather than the categories of philosophy and ontology, came to provide the basis on which human beings pondered life and meaning.

If history and the content of history were viewed in very new ways in the culture which succeeded Christendom, that culture also viewed nature in a significantly new way. Nature ceased to be the manifestation of Being and the various supernatural beings, and came to be regarded as something interesting and challenging and useful in its own right, something to be investigated and brought under human control and utilized for human purposes.[30] Thus the various physical and biological sciences developed as part of the intellectual and educational life of the new culture. These sciences had not existed in a culture the attitudes of which toward nature were those of Christendom. Furthermore, the new attitude toward nature resulted not only in modern science. It resulted also in the development of all those technologies through which—in food production and the retrieval of riches within the earth and the atmosphere not dreamed of before and transportation and communication and the healing of illness and birth control—the human community came to dominate the forces of nature and use them for its own purposes and ends.

Those two ways of looking at things—viewing human history as a self-contained reality the movement and structures of which explained the present, and viewing nature as a resource to be controlled and dealt with by human ingenuity—were the primary characteristics of a culture that was *secular*. "Secular" comes from the Latin word *saeculum* which means "world" in the sense of "eon" or "age," and so a secular culture is one which sees the world of time and space within which the human race finds itself as the location of all the reality there is. There is, for a secular culture, no other realm or course of events or set of beings, decisions and activity in and among which explain what the human race experiences in this world. The secularism of the culture which succeeded Christendom was a freeing and exhilarating thing, and it was responsible not only for the vast accomplishments of the social and physical and biological sciences and the conquests of earth and sea and sky and space by modern technology. It also produced significant achievements in literature and the arts and the meeting of human needs. Moreover, secularism has moved from original self-awareness to a heady, self-confident optimism to contemporary disillusionment and despair. For there is no doubt in the latter quarter of the twentieth century that humanity is disillusioned with the historical process and the structures involved in that process. That disillusionment is manifest in the small percentage of citizens who exercise their voting rights, in an increase in terrorism, in a widespread cynicism about the officers and structures of government and private enterprise, in a general ennui. Furthermore, even at a time at which the accomplishments of technology are astounding, there is despair about nature and its resources and what seems to be the demise of nature's promise to secular humanity. Human beings living in the latter quarter of the twentieth century are beginning to grasp that nature is finite, that its resources are limited and running out, that the end of its ability to support human life and history is quite conceivable. The assumptions which made optimistic, confident secularism viable are eroding, and the secular human community which has conquered all kinds of problems and diseases cannot seem to shake off the depression which is its present most besetting infirmity.

Thus it is that those of us who live in the late twentieth century find ourselves the heirs of a doubly negative heritage, particularly those of us denizens of the secular culture who remain within the Church. First, we still live in the aftermath of the collapse of a theological view of life which came with the fall of Christendom, and the defensiveness of the Reformation attempts to deal with that is still very much with us. For the most part, within ourselves individually as well as corporately as the Church, we do not allow our faith to come right up against secularism. That is dangerous, and we fear it. Those of us who are most "orthodox" fear it most of all, and insist on the maintenance of a separation which will leave faith unthreatened by a wholly different set of assumptions and presuppositions than the ones which produced faith.[31] What is more, we live in the era of the collapse of secularism as a positive faith, and are no longer convinced of the viability of the secular assumptions of inevitable progress and limitless opportunity and the triumph of sheerly human values. We are at a place at which optimistic, I-am-the-captain-of-my-fate, ideological humanists appear as out of place and anachronistic and quaint as believers in miracles and angels and divinely revealed truth.

We have trouble admitting it, but the rhetoric produced by the secular culture which has produced us rings hollow. Sometimes those Christians among us who are "liberal" hate to admit that most of all because of the way in which they had seen modern, scientific, secular culture to be the culmination of God's progressive purpose.

Other things, however, can be said. If we will but look at things from a biblical, Christian perspective broader and longer than the one provided by Christendom and the Reformation, we shall see that the culture which succeeded Christendom is in many ways more like that of ancient Israel and the early Church than was Christendom itself.[32] Unlike the mythology of the ancient Near East and the philosophy of the world into which the Christian Church first emerged, modern culture invests the history in which human beings live and make decisions and act a crucial, even an ultimate significance. Unlike the mythology of the ancient Near East and the philosophy of the world into which the Christian Church first emerged, modern culture holds a view of nature which is empirical and pragmatic rather than mystical. In both those respects modern, secular culture has much in common with ancient Israel and the early Church. Indeed, it can be argued that it is much more the result of the influence of the biblical world view than either secularists or many Christians understand. The basic assumptions of modern culture are more in line with the assumptions of Israel's historical epics and the assumptions of the first chapter of Genesis than with the assumptions about history and nature held by the theology of Christendom.

Furthermore, it was precisely when the critical historical method which developed out of the assumptions of secular culture was applied to the Bible and its background, as well as to the Church's heritage and history, that it was possible to gain some understanding of them in terms of their own assumptions, to look at them without reading into them the assumptions of Christendom or the Reformation. The story of the application of critical historical method to the Bible and to the life of the early Church is long and complicated,[33] a story in which the extent to which we have substituted our own, modern, secular assumptions for those of Christendom and the Reformation can be discerned again and again at different levels. It is a story leading from the discovery of different literary sources in the individual books of the Bible to the mistake of assuming that the discovery had solved all the problems and that the biblical literature was the product of authors in the same sense that modern literary writings are the products of individual authors. It is a story leading from an appreciation of the distinctiveness of the theology of the Bible as compared with later theologies to the mistake of assuming that the communities which produced the Bible thought in the same, idea-centered, abstractly conceptual ways in which modern people think. Nevertheless, continual critical examination seeks to correct mistaken assumptions, form criticism has come into being to correct the mistakes of source analysis, and tradition criticism and redaction criticism have built on and corrected form criticism. Happily, results are continually being questioned and modified as continual examination of all the evidences of the atmosphere and assumptions of the culture out of which the Bible and Christianity originated takes place. More and more understanding of the Bible and the earliest Christian Church *in terms of their own assumptions* is being gained.[34] It is precisely when those biblical and early Christian assumptions about the significance of history and of the human community and the nonsacral character of nature are uncovered that we begin to appreciate how much the culture which gave us the method to uncover them is the product of those biblical and early Christian assumptions.

Yet it is clearly the case that the biblical and early Christian assumptions differ from modern assumptions in one most important respect. Ancient Israel and the earliest Christian Church held human history and the human community to be significant not just of themselves, but because the One who is finally sovereign had invested them with significance. They held, likewise, that nature is not sacral, not the manifestation of beings standing behind it, because the One, experience convinced them, who is in charge had removed that significance from nature. Furthermore, ancient Israel and the earliest Church differ from modern culture in those ways not because they hold different *ideas*. They differ on the basis of their involvement in the course of events which is their history with One who has to be defined and witnessed to be reciting that One's story, by engaging in *todah*, *eucharistia*, rather than by classifying that One in some theoretical way. Ancient Israel and the earliest Church differ from modern culture in the ways they do not because they are *theists*, not because they "believe in God" in some theoretical way while modern folk do not "believe in God" in some theoretical way. They differ from modern culture, in fact, at exactly that point at which modern, secular culture still participates in the assumptions of the culture of Christendom.

The culture of Christendom, like the culture of the ancient Near East which preceded it and so deeply affected it, assumed that reality was finally located in Being or divine beings, in *something* underlying the events of history and the phenomena of nature. The search, therefore, of the framers of myths and the philosophers and the theologians of Christendom was for that *something*. For the framers of myths that something was symbolized in the gods and their relationships and struggles. For the philosophers it was captured in theories and concepts. For the theologians of Christendom it was stated in dogmas and doctrines, and rested on the theory that that something fitted into the category "god" and expressed itself most clearly in the truths stated in the Bible and Christian tradition. The basis of the *dis-*

agreement between modern, secular culture and Christendom lies basically in modern culture's rejection of the *theory*, the *concept*, the *category*, the *idea* "god." The basis of the disagreement is the rejection by modern culture of the abstraction "theism" *and* the espousal of the abstraction "atheism," or the abstraction "agnosticism," or the abstraction "secularism." There is, however, *agreement* between modern culture and Christendom at a fundamental level. Modern, secular culture has continued, in spite of the empirical, pragmatic methods it has developed in so many areas, Christendom's assumption that what is most real is the idea, the abstraction, the concept which embraces the realities of history and nature. There is agreement between modern, secular culture and Christendom in the priority both of them assign to thoughts and theories *about* things. Modern culture may use terms such as "theory" and "meaning" instead of "doctrine" and "dogma," but it is finally, at bottom, more like the Christendom it replaced than it is willing to admit. We see that clearly when we look at both of them in contrast to ancient Israel and the earliest Church.

Furthermore, the contemporary Christian Church is indisputably a part of the modern culture in which it lives. The contemporary Church is involved in the assumptions and the methods of the culture in which it exists, whether by reacting against those assumptions or affirming them in the carrying on of the theological enterprise. Those assumptions are deeply present in both "conservatives" and "liberals," in both "orthodox" and "radicals," in both "traditionalists" and "modernists." The conservative may insist on holding onto the doctrines and dogmas of Christendom and the Reformation era, while the liberal may seek other ways of theologizing which seem to connect more directly with the experience and vocabulary of contemporary men and women. Both, however, are for the most part still dealing in concepts and ideas and abstractions. Both take theology, the discipline of trying to say something about God, really to lie in our *thoughts about* the world and history and the Bible and the Church's tradition and liturgy. Both take the truth to lie finally in statements like "God can indeed work miracles" or, conversely, "the biblical miracles can be explained naturally and rationally." Both take the truth finally to lie in abstractions rather than in the events, the data, on which the abstractions are based. They both tend to make interpretations more important than what is being interpreted and then to be divided on the basis of the differing interpretations rather than united in their common relation to what is being interpreted.

It is the thesis of this book that, as a result of the critical, historical study of the Christian heritage which has taken place for the past two centuries or so, another fundamentally different alternative can be discerned. That study's recovery of the ethos and assumptions of ancient Israel and the earliest Church results in our catching a glimpse of the way in which *todah*, *eucharistia*—thankful, liturgical recital of the works of God in history in relation to the people of God—was the basis of theology in ancient Israel and the earliest Church. But we are, it should be emphasized, dealing with a fundamentally different alternative. We are not dealing with another alternative among all those which share the assumptions of Christendom and modern, secular culture. *Todah*, *eucharistia*, is a basis for theology the concentration of which is not concentration on *theos*, the concept or category or *idea* "god." Its concentration is on the One who alone deserves finally to be assigned to that category because of who that One is as manifested in the events remembered in the *todah*, *eucharistia* cult and as manifested in the *re*-presentation of those events in that cult. The method of *todah*, *eucharistia* theology is not abstract reasoning. Its method is participation in and observation of the course of events which is the history in which the Church, the eucharistic community, lives and moves and has its being along with all humanity. Its method is not primarily thinking about and lecturing on tradition and liturgy and cult. Its method is participation in liturgy and cult which puts a person and a congregation right into the tradition. We are not, if we grasp what emerges from the kind of examination we have made of Israel and the Church, thinking about a theology *of* the Eucharist. We are talking precisely about *eucharistic theology*.

Louis Bouyer, near the beginning of the book which was one of the principal starting places of the thinking which led to this book, puts it beautifully:

> Obviously what we have here is a theology with which our modern manuals have not familiarized us—and this is surely why its discovery can be so delightful! This theology, as exacting as it may be (and it is in its own way), remains very close to the first meaning of the Greek *theologia*, which designates a hymn, a glorification of God by the *logos*, by [expressed human] thought. This thought is obviously rational in the highest degree, but rational in the way harmony is; it is an intellectual music whose spontaneous expression is therefore a liturgical chant and not some sort of hair-splitting or tedious labeling.[35]

This book has really been written to lead up to the presentation of that alternative. What critical, historical research has uncovered and the way the results of that research have been used in liturgical revision in the Church have opened up wonderful possibilities. Not only have those discoveries and their application in liturgical revision made it possible for contemporary Christians once again to worship in the atmosphere and structures of the *eucharistia* cult of early Christianity. Not only have those discoveries and their application in liturgical revision made it possible for contemporary Christians to reappropriate the truly traditional ethos of their liturgy which was obscured by "modernizing" accretions in medieval and Reformation times. Those discoveries and their application in liturgical revision have also reintroduced *todah, eucharistia,* as a possible basis for faith and theology which cuts right across medieval and Reformation alternatives.[36] *Theology as thanksgiving*, growing out of and expressed in a gathered human community's participation in the Eucharist, can once again be seen as a possibility on the basis of what we know of the life of ancient Israel and the life of the earliest Church.

Through the participation of a human community—an *ekklesia*, a Church—in that kind of eucharistic theology, God may very well continue to accomplish what ancient Israel and the earliest Church believed God had accomplished in and for them. Contemporary human beings disillusioned with the history which has brought them to where they are and in which they participate might find that history redeemed from the meaninglessness which overwhelmed it when human beings looked for meaning where God had not in fact located it. *Eucharistia* might begin to include a recital of that course of events, running from the collapse of Christendom into the twentieth century and resulting in human historical consciousness, which has recovered *eucharistia* itself as a theological alternative for us. By celebrating the way we ourselves have come to be included in what *eucharistia* celebrates, we might begin to bring to the world of which the Church is a part precisely a belief in the viability and worth of the enterprise which goes on in that world. Such a belief cannot be generated by abstractions which finally locate worth elsewhere than in that enterprise.

Through the participation of a human community—an *ekklesia*, a Church—in that kind of eucharistic theology, God may very well be able to reconvince human beings of the worth of their humanity. In subtler and possibly even more destructive ways than in the ancient past, human beings still fear and resent the limitations inherent in their various *goy*, *ethne* identities. They still, in their defensiveness in the face of those limitations, "put down" *goys* and *ethnes* who differ from themselves. In exalting and defending their nation, their class, their race, their sex, their ethnicity, human beings devalue the humanity which binds them together with every *goy* and *ethne*. The *eucharistia* of a human community gathered out of various ethnic identities in those actions of God celebrated in *eucharistia* could once again, as it did in ancient Israel and the earliest Church, restore both confidence in themselves and respect for others in and among human beings.

Through the participation of a human community—an *ekklesia*, a Church—in that kind of theology, God may very well be able to free humanity from the despair in which it increasingly finds itself over the foreseeable expiration of the resources for life in the universe. The *todah* of Israel and the *eucharistia* of the Church celebrate God as creator of nature, not nature as the embodiment of the gods. They do not, like modern culture, see nature as self-explanatory and self-contained. *Eucharistia* to the creator God, therefore, produces a set of assumptions which do not see the demise of nature as the end of every possibility. What is celebrated in *eucharistia*—the rescue of Israel from hopeless oppression and the course of events which showed that death could not stop what God was about in Jesus of Nazareth—leads to a faith that God and God's purpose still have a future when every possibility calculable by natural means has run out. What is celebrated in *eucharistia*, God's record so far, indicates that it is God's purpose to include humanity in that future. Such a faith has the possibility about it of setting human beings free to work responsibly as stewards of the resources of nature without being paralyzed by the presumptuous despair produced by confining future possibilities to what can be measured by human definitions.

The mission of the Church to the world consists of things such as those outlined in the preceding paragraphs. Those things do not, however, arise out of proper thoughts, out of right attitudes, out of private, inner piety. They are not self-generated. They arise out of participation by the

Church in that recitative, liturgical, thankful life with God which is Eucharist. That life, by the nature and logic of what it is, also directs its participants toward thankful participation in the history and humanity and world in which God has placed them. The first vocation of the Church is to be open to such a mission, to participate in that eucharistic action in which it identifies itself as Church. Its mission is simply and exclusively there in that action and what is implied in that action. If the Church will live within the Eucharist, will do so faithfully, will look at all that is implied in what it is doing and listen to the One to whom *eucharistia* is appropriate praise, then all the families of the earth may indeed come to have a vision of the worth of their humanity and their history which is the blessing God has in mind for them.[37]

Author's Notes

Chapter 1 Hymn and Thanksgiving: The Transformation of a Myth

1. Cf. Gunkel and Begrich, *Einleitung in die Psalmen,* and Gunkel, *The Psalms.*

2. Among others, cf. Mowinckel, *The Psalms in Israel's Worship;* Leslie, *The Psalms;* Johnson, *Sacral Kingship;* Weiser, *The Psalms;* Kraus, *Psalmen* and *Worship in Israel;* Guthrie, *Israel's Sacred Songs.*

3. Where most English translations of the Old Testament use "LORD" (in capital letters), the Hebrew text sets down the actual proper name of Israel's God. The consonants of that name are YHWH or JHVH. Since the Hebrew text consisted for centuries of the consonants alone and since reverence resulted in the pronunciation of the name being replaced by the Hebrew word for "Lord," the actual, original form of the name is a subject of speculation. There is general agreement that "Yahweh" is probably more accurate than "Jehovah." Here as elsewhere in this book the translations of biblical material are my own. In the case of the psalms, reasons for my translations can be found, in most cases, in *Israel's Sacred Songs.*

4. For anthologies of ancient Near Eastern literature, cf. Pritchard, *Ancient Near Eastern Texts,* and Thomas, *Documents from Old Testament Times.*

5. Cf. Frankfort *et al., The Intellectual Adventure of Ancient Man,* chapter 1.

6. It is the difference between Mesopotamian and Palestinian climate and mythology which accounts for the ambiguity of the Jewish calendar in which New Year is celebrated on the first day of the seventh, rather than the first, month. The ancient Palestinian calendar undoubtedly began the year at the fall equinox when the summer drought gave way to the fall rains. The Babylonian calendar began at the spring equinox when the late winter floods receded. In the exile Israel took over the Babylonian calendar in which the first month came in the spring, but continued the ancient custom of observing New Year in the fall, thus celebrating the beginning of a new year in the middle of the calendar year.

7. On laments as the cultic background against which thanksgivings must be understood, cf. my *Israel's Sacred Songs,* 118–147. References to other treatments of the cultic setting are given there.

8. Treatments of "righteousness" in such standard reference works as Richardson's *Theological Word Book of the Bible* stress the way in which "righteousness" (*zedek*) involves God's rescue of the needy and can mean "pity." Realization of the cultic location of the word and concept underlines its significance along those lines.

9. Cf. Jacobsen in Frankfort *et al., The Intellectual Adventure of Ancient Man,* especially pp. 203–207.

10. Cf. the bibliography.

11. *The Praise of God in the Psalms,* p. 18.

12. Cf. the table of contents of *The Praise of God in the Psalms* for a glimpse into the way in which Westermann substitutes "declarative psalms of praise" for thanksgivings and "descriptive psalms of praise" for hymns. His terminology reflects the verb forms characteristic of the two types as described above.

13. That is why form-criticism and tradition-criticism seem to me still to be the most promising means of getting at the background and meaning of poetry such as that found in the Psalter. Recent work in what is called structural criticism seems to me to treat biblical material in such a way as to overlook its cultic background.

14. The Gilgamesh Epic from ancient Mesopotamia is the classic example of tragic literature originating in the ancient Near East. Cf. Pritchard, *Ancient Near Eastern Texts*, pp. 72–99. For king lists, cf. pp. 265 and 271ff. of the same work.

15. For a more detailed description of the social order which gave rise to the hymn and the mythology which was the setting of the hymn, cf. my *Israel's Sacred Songs,* pp. 59–71, and the references given there.

16. Re the Amorites, cf. Bright, *History of Israel,* p. 42ff. The term is used, of course, in the Old Testament in various ways. Ezekiel 16:3 preserves a memory of how Israel's ultimate origins lay in peoples such as the Amorites.

17. The letters in question are the Amarna Letters, selections from which are to be found in Pritchard, p. 483ff. Because of the similarity between "Hebrew" and "Habiru," the Amarna Letters have been extensively studied by those interested in Israel and its history. For a stimulating discussion of all the issues involved, cf. Mendenhall, "The Hebrew Conquest of Palestine."

18. Cf. Pope, *El in the Ugaritic Texts,* p. 94.

19. Israel in the days before the monarchy was clearly a league, a confederation of *different* tribes. It was an "amphictyony," into which different tribal groups came out of loyalty to and service of a common God. The work which first set forth this now commonly accepted view of the nature of the earliest Israel was Noth's *Das System der zwölf Stämme Israels.* Cf. Noth, *History of Israel* (2nd edition), pp. 53–138. Mendenhall's "The Hebrew Conquest of Palestine" may be cited again as a most enlightening treatment of the character of pre-monarchical Israel.

20. It is a fact that Israelites only call themselves Hebrews in the Bible when that is necessary in order to make other peoples understand who they are. Cf. Genesis 40:15, Jonah 1:9. On the other hand there are several places where *other peoples* call Israelites Hebrews. Cf. Genesis 39:14,17; 41:12, and many places in the early chapters of Exodus as well as elsewhere. It seems to have been the case that the Israelite tribal league was made up of a number of Habiru groups. On the other hand, there must have been many Habiru who were not Israelites. Greenberg's *The Hab/piru* provides a good summary of scholarly work on the Habiru.

21. Again, cf. Mendenhall, "The Hebrew Conquest of Palestine" for the best historical reconstruction of the experience about which this paragraph is speaking.

22. For a discussion of the way in which creativity and forms provided by a culture are always related to one another, cf. von Rad, *Old Testament Theology*, vol. II, pp. 70–79.

23. Cf. Guthrie, *God and History in the Old Testament*, pp. 20–29 and *Israel's Sacred Songs*, pp. 53–58.

24. Cf. Cross, "Notes on a Canaanite Psalm in the Old Testament."

25. For an argument that Psalm 29:9 is explicitly about fertility, cf. Guthrie, *Israel's Sacred Songs*, pp. 77–78 and especially footnotes 28 and 30 on pp. 213–214.

26. For a passage in the Ugaritic literature in which Baal is pictured as manifesting his power in thunder, lightning, and rain, cf. Pritchard, *Ancient Near Eastern Texts*, p. 135, column 1.

27. It is interesting to note that the word for "death" in biblical Hebrew, *maweth*, is obviously etymologically the equivalent of the name Mot. For a commentary on the Psalter which emphasizes all possible connections between Israel's psalms and the Ugaritic literature, cf. Dahood, *Psalms*.

28. While Psalm 29 is the most obvious example of a place where this has been done, the same kind of thing is present again and again in Psalter. Cf. Guthrie, *Israel's Sacred Songs* and Dahood's *Psalms, passim*.

29. It is interesting to note that the genre represented by Deuteronomy 32, in which Israel is called to accountability under the covenant, is represented in the Psalter by only Psalms 50 and 81. That is undoubtedly because the Psalter preserves the songs used in the Jerusalem temple, the cult of which undoubtedly was more closely related to the Canaanite city taken over by David than to Israel's pre-monarchical traditions. That may be why the song in Deuteronomy 32 is preserved in a book which self-consciously sets forth the ancient covenant traditions rather than in the Psalter.

30. The traditional Hebrew text, the massoretic text, says in verse 8b, "That Ruler fixed the number of different peoples so that it conformed to the number of the children of Israel." Our translation, like the RSV and most modern English translations, has followed the Septuagint, the ancient Greek translation of the Hebrew Bible. While it is impossible to explain how the reading in the massoretic text might have been changed to that in the Septuagint, it is quite understandable how, once monotheism had come to be commonly accepted, the text was changed to remove a statement that was clearly originally polytheistic. Thus, that reluctance of modern commentators (cf. Wright in *The Interpreter's Bible*) to accept what the text obviously said began at some point after the Septuagint was translated from the Hebrew and before the massoretic text reached its accepted form in the early centuries of the Christian era.

31. Scholarly opinions as to the date of the Song of Moses have varied greatly. It is difficult to assign dates to such songs just in the nature of the case, their *form* and its use being more important issues than specific dates of authorship. It could, in the form we have it, be early or late, for it was probably only sometime after II Isaiah in the latter half of the sixth century that anything like what we would call monotheism existed in any explicit way.

Chapter 2 Theology as Thanksgiving: The Israelite Epics

1. Cf. Tablet VI of *Enuma elish*, Pritchard, *Ancient Near Eastern Texts*, p. 68.

2. The issue of polytheism *versus* monotheism in the Old Testament is a complicated one, chiefly because the issue is, as a theoretical issue, of concern to modern students in a way that it was not of concern to the Israel which gave

us the Old Testament. The vitality of earliest Israel's faith that "Yahweh is your God, Yahweh alone" arose precisely because of the options over against which that affirmation was made. It is the present writer's opinion that Israel's *de facto* faith that only one God mattered goes clear back into the era of the pre-monarchical tribal league, but that *theoretical* monotheism is given explicit statement only by II Isaiah—and then in imagery derived from the polytheistic mythology of the ancient Near East. Cf. Isaiah 41, 46, etc.

3. In the judgment of the present writer this type of oracle is one common to "prophetic" figures whose function it was in royal courts in the ancient Near East to announce to kings what was transpiring in the heavenly assembly of divine beings. It probably became part of the heritage of Israel through institutions and offices inherited when David took over the Canaanite city-state of Jerusalem as his headquarters. A prophet like Isaiah has to be understood against this background, while a prophet like Jeremiah is rooted in the tradition of the covenant mediator of pre-monarchical days whose prototype is Moses. The rendering of Psalm 82 which follows is really a paraphrase calculated to dramatize the sense of the poem.

4. The sense of the Hebrew is to emphasize Israel's God's statement, "*I* am the one;" and then, by use of the perfect form of the verb to continue, "who *made* the pronouncement that you should be gods." That, then, is the background against which God *now* says that the gods are sentenced to the death which is the lot of mortals.

5. *'Adam* has here been translated "human being(s)" or "humanity," because that is its real sense in Hebrew, and it is made clearer that way than by leaving the reader to understand that it means "man" generically. Also, in Genesis 1:27, *zelem 'elohim* has been translated "in the image of the divine beings" because, given ancient Near Eastern mythology, that seems more likely to be what is meant than "in the image of God."

6. Because the Greek of the New Testament is significantly different from the classical Greek of the poets and philosophers, Christians long held that it was the Holy Spirit's special, divine dialect. Modern discovery, however, of business documents in Greek demonstrated that the New Testament is largely written in *koine* or "common" Greek, the language of the street and the marketplace. The Good News had to be conveyed in an idiom understandable to the people who were delivering and receiving it.

7. For what follows, cf. Baltzar, *The Covenant Formulary,* and a large body of literature, the most striking of which is still Mendenhall's "Law and Covenant in Israel and the Ancient Near East" and "The Hebrew Conquest of Palestine." Cf. also chapter 1 of my *Israel's Sacred Songs*. Covenant formularies are much more pervasive in the Old Testament than the examples cited here, including Psalms 50 and 81 and numerous passages in the books of the prophets.

8. Indeed, the deuteronomic history of Israel's life in the land of Canaan which runs from the Pentateuch through II Kings is organized around a succession of prophetic figures—officers of the covenant in the tradition of Moses—and a rhythm of prophetic predictions and their fulfillments more than around the succession of kings. Cf. von Rad, *Studies in Deuteronomy,* chapter 7.

9. Cf. Isaiah 41:2–4 and Isaiah 45:1–7. Cf. also the Chronicler's history of Israel (I and II Chronicles, Ezra, and Nehemiah) in which, once the Davidic dynasty has established the temple its role as "civil" protector of Yahweh's cult is taken over by "foreign" powers who are in every respect Yahweh's agents. In this respect it is interesting to compare the account of the death of Josiah at

the hands of Pharoah Necho in II Kings 23:29 with the account in II Chronicles 35:20–27. Influenced by II Isaiah, the latter understands the Egyptian ruler as one who not only acts, but speaks for Yahweh.

10. Cf. the statements of Justin Martyr in chapters 6 and 11 of the first *Apology*.

11. Polycarp, bishop of Smyrna in the second century, is reported to have replied to the Roman proconsul's exhortation that he take the oath of allegiance to the emperor and curse Christ, "Eighty-six years have I served him, and he never did me any wrong. How shall I blaspheme my King who saved me?" Cf. 9:3 in the *Martyrdom of Polycarp*.

12. Mendenhall's "The Hebrew Conquest of Palestine" and his *The Tenth Generation* are interesting in their tracing of the logical results of the covenant understanding of Israel's relationship to God. Cf. also the very interesting treatment of all this by Gottwald in *The Tribes of Yahweh*.

13. It is Gerhard von Rad who, above all, set forth Israel's confession of its faith through interpretative recital of its own life as the basis of Old Testament theology. Cf. his *Old Testament Theology,* particularly Volume I. I opt for that understanding rather than the one of Eichrodt in his *Theology of the Old Testament*. Cf. the *excursus* at the end of Volume I for Eichrodt's critique of von Rad's method and conclusions.

14. Cf. von Rad's *Das formgeschichtliche Problem des Hexateuchs*.

15. Cf. von Rad, *op. cit*.

16. It should be noted that all Semitic literature is in origin and by nature oral, the written language consisting originally of consonants only and being really only a shorthand used to guarantee the accurate oral recital of what had been spoken or sung in the first place.

17. Cf. Noth's *Überlieferungsgeschichte des Pentateuch*. For the reconstruction of Israel's history here, cf. Noth's *History of Israel*.

18. The presence of the ark in the sanctuary of Jerusalem was *Israel's* assurance of the validity of that sanctuary for devotees of Yahweh, while, for the *Canaanites,* it was the sign of Yahweh's having assumed the authority of the ruler of the cosmos. What was probably originally an independent narrative of the fortunes of the ark through the period of the Philistine conquest and then the Davidic restoration of Israel is now found in I Samuel 4:1–7:2; II Samuel 6–7. That narrative may very well have come into being as the Israelite *hieros logos* for the sanctuary of Jerusalem, the official *apologia* for its status as the central sanctuary of Yahweh. Cr. Rost, *Die Überlieferung von der Thronnachfolge Davids*.

19. On the Yahwist epic (also called the "J" document because of the German rendering of the divine name as "Jahveh"), cf. standard introductions to the Old Testament literature: Anderson, *Understanding the Old Testament,* Gottwald, *A Light to the Nations;* Guthrie, *God and History in the Old Testament;* etc. Von Rad's exposition of the content and theology of the Yahwist is superb: cf. his *Theology of the Old Testament,* vol. I.

20. The question of how far the sources of the Pentateuch continue in the total narrative complex which is Genesis through II Kings is complex and much debated. In its final form the Bible itself divides the "former prophets" (Joshua—II Kings) from the Torah or Pentateuch (Genesis—Deuteronomy. That the division is artificial is widely recognized. Some speak of a Hexateuch (Genesis—Joshua) which narrates Israel's story through the conquest of Canaan and which is followed by a narrative of Israel's life in Canaan until the beginning of the exile. Others speak of a Tetrateuch (Genesis—Numbers) and of a

Deuteronomic History (Deuteronomy—II Kings). I prefer the solution set forth by Freedman in the article on the Pentateuch in the *Interpreter's Dictionary of the Bible,* namely that the J and E sources of the Pentateuch originally each, making use of various shorter materials already in existence when each of them was composed, carried the narrative down to the time in which it was written—J probably in the reign of Solomon, E probably following the Elijah/Elisha revolution in the northern kingdom. Why the Torah/Former Prophets division came about is obscure. It probably had to do with the ability of all in the post-exilic community to agree on the normative nature of Moses and his era for Judaism, but the inability of all to agree on how the post-Mosaic era in Canaan should be interpreted.

21. The narrative leading to Solomon's succession to the throne on the death of David is considered to be older than its present literary context and one of the earliest and most remarkable narratives in ancient literature (II Samuel 9–20; I Kings 1–2). It seems subtly to indicate that the succession of Solomon represented a victory for the "Canaanite" forces within David's court (Nathan, Zadok, Bathsheba, Benaiah) and a defeat of those "Israelite" forces who had backed Adonijah (Abiathar and Joab). Although Solomon's power held things in check during his lifetime, his disaffected former officer, Jeroboam, was ready to leave his Egyptian exile on Solomon's death to lead the revolt of those tribes located in the area where premonarchical Yahwism had been strongest against what they considered to be the Canaanizing apostasies of the Davidic dynasty.

22. Scholars gave the Elohist its name because it holds that the divine name, Yahweh, was first revealed to Moses, and, therefore never uses the name but only the Hebrew word for God—Elohim—in narrating the events of the pre-Mosaic era. The Yahwist, on the other hand, was given its name because of its referring to God by the name Yahweh from the very beginning of its narrative. On where the Elohist is located in the Bible and on its nature and content, cf. the references in note 20 above.

23. Although Mowinckel argued that E had originally had its own form of the primeval history (cf. *The Two Sources of the Predeuteronomic Primeval History (JE) in Genesis*), scholars are generally agreed that the E narrative did begin with Abraham. They are, however, not at all agreed on how J and E are to be disentangled from one another in Genesis 15. One source of the disagreement is the occurence of Yahweh (Lord) in Genesis 15:1, when (cf. the note just above) E holds that God was not known as Yahweh until the name was revealed to Moses. For reasons set forth in the note immediately following, however, I believe that E, while definitely holding that it was only with Moses that the name of Yahweh was revealed, understood the call of Abraham to be a prophetic call and therefore used the formula employed by prophets to claim divine inspiration: "The word of Yahweh came to me saying. . . . ." Thus, E is not claiming that Abraham knew Yahweh's name, but is beginning the narrative with its own interpretation of Abraham's call as being the first in a long line of prophetic calls.

24. E, in anticipation of what also was to be the position of Deuteronomy and the deuteronomic history of Israel (cf. von Rad, *Studies in Deuteronomy*), conceived of Israel's history as being held together by a succession of prophetic figures (covenant mediators) of whom Moses was the prototype. Those figures had consistently called Israel back from apostasy to the covenant with Yahweh, and the latest of them for E had been Elijah and Elisha who had recalled the northern kingdom of Israel from the Canaanizing bents of Omri and Ahab to the faithfulness of the dynasty of Jehu. For E, quite unlike J in which Yahweh is from the

beginning known as God of the cosmos, Yahweh's relationship to a people begins with the revelation of the divine name to the prophetic figure Moses. E could not, however, avoid J's previous establishment of the principle that what happened with Moses was the fulfillment of what had begun between Yahweh and Israel's ancient ancestors. So, E begins with Abraham, but interprets Abraham as a harbinger of the prophetic succession by the use of the established prophetic formula in Genesis 15:1. Once again, in the use of the formula, "the medium is the message" for those who have eyes to see.

25. The account of Josiah's reform is found in II Kings 22–23. Given the submission to Assyria of Josiah's predecessors, the cultic reform was also a declaration of political independence in which the cleansing of the temple of Assyrian influences meant that Yahweh was not subject to the Assyrian gods any longer. For the framers of the narrative (see the next note) Josiah represents a king of the Davidic line who is also a mediator of the covenent in the Mosaic tradition.

26. In its final form the account of Israel's life in the land of Canaan has clearly been edited so as to substantiate the theological views set forth in the book of Deuteronomy. It is in light of that that Old Testament scholars, while they differ on many details, are generally agreed in characterizing Joshua—II Kings as the deuteronomic history. Noth held that Deuteronomy—II Kings once existed separately as a complete work with Deuteronomy as the theological prelude as well as the narrative beginning of the history (*Überlieferungsgeschichte des Pentateuch*). Cf. von Rad's *Studies in Deuteronomy* and his article on Deuteronomy in the *Interpreter's Dictionary of the Bible*.

27. I am here following the theory of Frank M. Cross. Cf. chapter 10 of his *Canaanite Myth and Hebrew Epic*.

28. The Priestly Code sees the regulations for Israel's life as the people who render proper cultic service to the one, true God as having been revealed in ancient times ending with the final revelation to Moses. P is, therefore, confined to the Pentateuch, and is undoubtedly an early and influential factor in the process by which the Pentateuch (Torah) came, in separation from the narrative of Joshua—II Kings, to be regarded as fundamentally authoritative. On P, cf. the works mentioned in note 19 above.

29. It should be noted that, in the Hebrew Bible, Ruth is not a part of the narrative complex Genesis—II Kings. Ruth is a later, fictional writing critical of the exclusiveness of the post-exilic community under Ezra, and is in the Writings, the third and obviously later part of the Hebrew Bible—the Torah and the Prophets (former and latter) being the first two parts. The translators and compilers of the Greek Old Testament, the Septuagint, moved Ruth to where it seemed to fit into the narrative, and that is why we now have it between Judges and I Samuel. On the process by which the various sources came together to form Genesis—II Kings, cf. note 20 above and the works mentioned there.

30. Again, it should be noted that English translations of the Old Testament follow the order of the Greek Septuagint which rearranged the three Hebrew sections, Law and Prophets and Writings, so that all the narrative material came first followed by the poetic writings, with the prophets (the latter prophets) coming at the end in anticipation of the New Testament.

31. The work of the Chronicler, particularly with regard to the literary and chronological relationships of Ezra and Nehemiah to one another and to the work as a whole, presents its own problems to scholars. Because of the obviously primary nature of Genesis—II Kings, students and readers of the Bible are not as familiar with those problems as they are with the issues connected with Genesis—

II Kings. Cf. the articles on Chronicles and Ezra and Nehemiah by R. H. Pfeiffer in the *Interpreter's Dictionary of the Bible* and the volumes on I Chronicles, II Chronicles, and Ezra and Nehemiah in *The Anchor Bible* by Jacob M. Myers.

32. I prefer to use the word "myth" in the neutral way in which it is used by anthropologists, simply to denote a people's articulation by whatever means of its view of the nature of reality. Thus, I prefer not to characterize the cosmic epics of the Canaanites or Mesopotamians as "myths" and Israel's epics as non-mythical. Israel's view is not non-mythical. The point is that Israel's myth is significantly and radically different from the myths of its ancient Near Eastern neighbors. Rather than being cosmic and rooted in nature, Israel's myth is historical and eschatological. Rather than being hymnic (in the sense in which we have examined that term in chapter 1), Israel's is a *todah* myth.

33. Those who have eyes to see will recognize how dependent I am in what follows on the work of Gerhard von Rad, regardless of the extent to which I have made use of his insights in my own way.

34. Cf. von Rad, "The Theological Problem of the Old Testament Doctrine of Creation" in his *The Problem of the Hexateuch and Other Essays*.

35. E sees those dealings as beginning with Abraham, D with Moses. Cf. the discussion earlier in this chapter.

36. For two recent treatments of the passage and issues connected with it, cf. the commentaries on Genesis of von Rad in The Old Testament Library and of Speiser in the Anchor Bible.

37. It has to be admitted that significant roots of the pretentious western industrialism which has produced the ecological crisis now confronting us lie in ancient Israel's myth. It has also to be said, however, that the impetus for responsible dealing with that crisis is probably to be found in the prophetic dimensions of Israel's myth rather than in some romantic nature mysticism.

38. The flood story in Genesis 6–9 has provided a classic passage for assignment to Old Testament students to disentangle two sources, the differences between the characteristics of J and P being very obvious. Distinguishing between the two sources is not, however, important for our purposes here.

39. The epic is translated into English by E. A. Speiser in Pritchard's *Ancient Near Eastern Texts,* p. 72ff.

40. The custom *per se* originated so far back that recovery of the original reason for it is impossible. The important point is P's interpretation of what it means in light of Israel's reflection on its dealings with Yahweh.

41. Von Rad's treatment of God's covenant with Noah (Genesis 9:1–17) is superb along these lines.

42. Again, in terms of the issues present in the enterprise of Old Testament theology, it will be recognized that I am a follower of von Rad. Cf. his *Old Testament Theology,* particularly the section on methodological presuppositions in volume I.

43. Eichrodt's criticism of von Rad's Old Testament theology seems to me to tend to avoid the radical implications of *todah* theology. Cf. the *excursus* on the problem of Old Testament theology at the end of volume I of his *Theology of the Old Testament*.

Chapter 3 The Vision of the Prophets: A New Israel

1. It should be noted once again that the Hebrew Bible differs from English translations, which follow the Greek Septuagint, in the books included in the

prophetic collection. In the Hebrew Bible, Daniel, not really a prophetic book but a later apocalyptic writing, is included in the Writings at the end of the canon and not between Ezekiel and Hosea in the collection of prophetic books.

2. Many interpreters use the term "writing prophets" in order to distinguish those prophets for whom books are named from those who appear in the narrative books. I am not happy with that term because of its implication that the prophets were authors. They were not, really. They were speakers and doers whose words and acts were remembered and recorded in various kinds of ways. I prefer to use the term "canonical prophets" to designate those for whom books are named in the canon so as to avoid the implication that they were authors in any modern sense.

3. Cf. Bright, *History of Israel,* chapters 7–10, and Noth, *History of Israel,* part 3.

4. Cf. Breasted, *Ancient Times,* p. 100ff.

5. It is the Assyrian deportation of northern Israelites which has prompted endless speculations on what happened to the "ten lost tribes," including the unsubstantiated speculation that some of them ended up in Scandinavia and Britain—"Anglo-Israelism." The fact was that the Assyrians simply mixed the peoples they had conquered up with one another. That some kind of self–consciously Israelite population, if mixed with other elements, remained in the area of Samaria after the Assyrian conquest is recognized in a way reflecting Judahite prejudice in the narrative in II Kings 17:24–41. Prejudiced and distorted as that passage is, it does indicate the way in which the Samaritans of New Testament times—and, indeed, of the present—have a history going clear back to the northern kingdom.

6. A word about the nature of the exile is in order. Like the Assyrians before them, the Babylonians took measures to ensure that conquered peoples would not regain their power. Their method was to bring conquered kings and their courts (including their priests) to live in Babylon—where their royal status seems to have been honored. That meant that, even though exile was a profound spiritual reality, many Israelites still lived in Palestine during the exile. That explains why the Babylonian Jewish community was respected for its leadership (cf. the Babylonian Talmud), as well as the tensions that arose between those already in the land and those who returned with Nehemiah and Ezra.

7. The chronology of the canonical prophets is roughtly as follows: 750–700 Amos, Hosea, Isaiah, Micah; 609–580 Jeremiah, Zephaniah, Nahum, Habakkuk, Ezekiel; 538–400 II Isaiah, Haggai, Zechariah, Obadiah, Malachi, Joel. It should be noted how the three chronological groupings cluster around the historical upheavals attending the successive expansions of the Assyrian, Babylonian, and Persian empires.

8. On the cultic office of covenant mediator, cf. Guthrie, *Israel's Sacred Songs,* pp. 42–51, and the literature cited there.

9. Apparently the word "prophet" (Hebrew *nabhi'*) came into the vocabulary of the Israelites out of Canaanite culture, and originally denoted a person susceptible to ecstatic siezures which were taken to indicate the presence of divine power (cf. the "prophets" in I Samuel 9:9–13 and the use of the verb "prophesy" to describe Saul's irrational behavior in I Samuel 18:10). Since the office in question was charismatic in the broadest sense of that word, "prophet" came to be its designation. "Word" etymologically denotes that which lies outside and behind a given reality. Thus it denotes the divine assessment of what a situation, either one demanding a human decision or a set of historical events,

means. So the decalogue in Hebrew is "the ten words," and a prophet's pronouncement of the divine meaning of the expansion of the Assyrian empire is a "word."

10. Cf. chapter 1 of Guthrie, *Israel's Sacred Songs,* and especially p. 27 on how Psalm 81:6–7 moves from the subject being a "he" to a "you" and from the verbs being in a past tense to their being in a present tense. This psalm is very likely to have originated in the covenant cult.

11. This tradition about the nature of the prophetic office seems to be the one in which Hosea and Jeremiah and the prophet behind Micah 6–7 stand. Hosea 4, Micah 6:1–8, and Jeremiah 2:4–13 are examples of the *rib,* or controversy, form in which the prophet is following the covenant cult form found in Psalm 81. That a prophet like Jeremiah could engage in controversy with prophets who understood their office on the basis of the tradition discussed in the next paragraph of the text is indicated by Jeremiah 23:23–40 in which prophets who have the "word" are contrasted with those who have dreams and visions.

12. The Mari letters antedate Israel's prophets considerably, coming from the latter half of the 18th century B.C.

13. It is only in II Samuel 12:1–15a that Nathan appears as a "calling-to-account" prophetic figure, and that passage may be an insertion reflecting Israel's understanding of what a prophet *should* be. It can be omitted with the narrative proceeding very smoothly from 11:27 to 12:15b. Otherwise, Nathan delivers a Mari like dynastic oracle in II Samuel 7, and I Kings 1:8 associates Nathan with the "Canaanizing" party which backed Solomon as David's successor.

14. This understanding of the prophetic office seems to be to the fore in Amos and in the tradition underlying the book of Isaiah. Isaiah 6 and Isaiah 40 are often cited as examples of how a prophetic figure is admitted in vision to what is transpiring in the deliberations of the council of divine beings. I believe the same imagery underlies what must be the call visions of Amos in Amos 7:1–9; 8:1–3.

15. Note how, even back in the 9th century before the time of the canonical prophets, Elijah seems to embody the Mosaic covenant mediator type of prophet, Micaiah the type of prophet whose claim was to have been admitted to the deliberations of the divine assembly.

16. On the forms of the treaties and their relation to the covenant formularies of the Old Testament, cf. G. E. Mendenhall, *Law and Covenant in Israel and the Ancient Near East* and Klaus Baltzar, *The Covenant Formulary.*

17. Isaiah 1:2ff. and Jeremiah 2:4ff. are examples of the *rib* form in the prophetic literature. Psalms 50 and 81 are the only examples preserved from Israel's cult in the Psalter. While something of such an accusatory nature might at first glance be adjudged as grim and legalistic, what the *rib* was about in the context of ancient Near Eastern religion and culture was, in fact, good news. In a world which attributed worth only to the divine, heavenly realm and which viewed the gods as capricious and arbitrary, what the covenant and the *rib* liturgy were about was the consistent demand of a God who, precisely through demand, redeemed human existence from meaninglessness.

18. Although the prophets were unique and creative in ways which transcended the traditions out of which they came, they were still products of that tradition. We can only appreciate many of the nuances in the prophetic literature by undergoing the discipline of discovering what the hearers of the prophets just took for granted by participating in the culture which they shared with the prophets. The discipline of form criticism is what is employed by biblical scholars to attempt to see biblical passages in the context of the culture in which they originated.

19. The line in brackets has been added to the text, for both sentence structure and poetic meter require the conclusion that something has fallen out in the transmission of the text.

20. Again, the line in brackets has been added in order to keep the sense of the text. If this line is not added, the "in order to understand" of the final line of the passage would have to pick up on the "remember" six lines back. It does appear that this text has suffered in transmission. The bracketed "in Trans-Jordan" and "on this side" in the previous line do not represent an attempt to improve translation. They have been inserted simply to help the modern reader understand that the proper names have to do with places on opposite sides of the Jordan River and that the reference is to Israel's crossing into Canaan in the time of Joshua.

21. Cf. the "Prayer to Every God" in Pritchard, *Ancient Near Eastern Texts*, p. 391.

22. It should be noted that the above treatment of Micah 6:1–8, and particularly the interpretation of the meaning of verse 8, is that of the present author. It should not be taken as reflecting a generally agreed upon interpretation of the passage.

23. Again, cf. the references to "seers" in the Mari letters—Pritchard, *Ancient Near Eastern Texts*, p.482 (letter b). In the cultic literature of the Old Testament itself, Psalm 82 is probably in form the kind of communication of such a prophet of how victory was in store for a king's god that was delivered by such prophets as a result of visions of what had transpired in the heavenly court.

24. Isaiah's ready access to the king and his aristocratic tone have often been pointed out. What we have been saying about his background can serve to make all that more understandable. Isaiah, unlike Amos ("I am no prophet, nor a prophet's son"), may indeed have been a professional prophet before the call came to be a prophet in a sense for which he had not bargained.

25. The narrative in II Kings 19:35–37 (note that II Kings 18–20 and Isaiah 36–39 seem to be a narrative which got into the Bible in two different places) and Isaiah 37:36–38 holds that the Assyrians lifted the siege of Jerusalem because of Yahweh's miraculous intervention, and Herodotus (II, 141) in a vague way speaks of the Assyrians not proceeding to the conquest of Egypt because of a plague of rats among them. Reconstruction of the actual events of the Assyrian invasions is difficult (cf. Bright, *History*, 267–271, 282–287), but there is a strong tradition that Jerusalem was besieged and then saved in what seemed to be a miraculous way. That only undergirded the tradition that the sacred city was inviolable, made things difficult for Jeremiah a century or so later, and made the fall of the city to the Babylonians finally in 587 a terribly traumatic thing.

26. Again, here is an indication of the way in which Isaiah's ethos is clearly the city-kingdom of Jerusalem and the royal court of the Davidic dynasty.

27. I have added in verse 13 the bracketed words "any more than" just to capture better the poetic flow of the passage. I have also followed the Septuagint in the same verse in reading "fasting" instead of "iniquity"—that seems to make more sense in the context.

28. It should be noted that, in Hebrew, the word for "the Assyrian" is Ashur. Ashur *does* mean Assyrians(s), but it does so in a corporate way because it is also both the name of the city where the Assyrians originated and of the god whose devotees they are. Thus, given Isaiah's ethos in the royal court of Jerusalem and the mythology of the ancient Near East, there is a *double entendre* here. Yes, the Assyrian(s) are the rod of Yahweh's anger, but Isaiah's contemporaries would also have understood the words to mean that Yahweh, ruler of the cosmos and the assembly of the gods, was sending the subordinate god Ashur on mission of judgment.

29. It was Martin Noth who established the nature of pre-monarchical Israel as an amphictyony. Cf. his *Das System der zwölf Stämme Israels* and, in English, his *History of Israel,* pp. 85–138.

30. For the beginning of the understanding of this contrast I am indebted to James Muilenberg with whom I studied Old Testament in the forties. For a thorough treatment of what *goy* is all about, but one which does not do justice to the contrast I consider to be very important, cf. the article "Nations" by E. J. Hamlin in the *Interpreter's Dictionary of the Bible.*

31. Theologically in the Yahwist everything from the story of the Tower of Babel through the call of Abram in Genesis 12:1–3 is one pericope in which the parts depend on one another. Cf. von Rad's superb treatment in his *Genesis*, pp. 147–163. The fact that J and P are intertwined in the genealogy in Genesis 11 is not important for the overall theological implications of the passage in its finished form.

32. It is, of course, the case that elements connected with whatever form the story existed in before the Yahwist took it over for the Yahwist's theological purposes persist: cf. the divine jealousy of potential human power.

33. I translate the concluding words as I do because I believe they render the Hebrew better than the usual "every family of the earth." The Hebrew word usually translated "earth" is not *'erets* (geographical earth) but *'adamah* ("earth" in the sense of "soil" or "dust"). It is the word involved in the well-known "*Dust* thou art, and unto *dust* shalt thou return." So, the sense is not "people everywhere," but "all that humanity of every variety which arises from, is dependent on, and ultimately returns to the earth." The statement is not about some "missionary" effort, but about God's miraculous redemption of humanity in calling a piece of it to be simply human, and not defensively *goy*.

34. "Eschatological" is defined in many different ways. That is the case precisely because the Bible, Old Testament and New Testament alike, points toward the "last (Greek, *eschatos*) things." Everyone who seeks to interpret the biblical message *has* to define eschatology in some way. That, simply, is my point. A cosmic, cyclical, "myth-of-the-eternal-return" view of the final nature of things is not what the Bible has in mind. Things began somewhere and are going somewhere: that is the—implicit or explicit—biblical presupposition, however we come to terms theoretically with that presupposition.

35. It has long been recognized that there are two sources behind the narrative in I Samuel: one is variously characterized as pro-Saul, pro-monarchical, early; the other as pro-Samuel, anti-monarchical, late. For details on the issues involved, cf. commentaries such as the *Interpreter's Bible.* My own view is that the first of the sources is basically J, and the second E. Cf. note 20 to chapter 2.

36. Absalom, for those who can read between the lines of the narrative in II Samuel, was clearly playing on the discontent of Israelites with the Canaanite city-kingdom polity which had resulted from David's rise to power. II Samuel 15:1–6 is eloquent in its subtle setting forth of the issues:

> Absalom used to rise early and take his place where people entered the gate of the royal city. To anyone bringing a matter for judgment to the king Absalom would call out and say, "What *city* (Canaanite source of identity) do you come?" When one of them would say, "I am of such and such a *tribe* (Israelite source of identity) in Israel," . . . Absalom would say, "Oh that I were *judge* (not *king,* but ancient Israelite "prophetic" figure) in the land!"

That kind of play on the background of Israel was what lay behind the revolts of both Absalom and Sheba against David. It also was what led to the division of the kingdom after the death of Solomon.

37. Clearly Egypt played on Israel's inner tensions by providing refuge to Jeroboam during the reign of Solomon until Solomon was succeeded by the weaker, and less understanding of the issues, Rehoboam. Cf. I Kings 11:26–40 which would not be so lengthy if it were not for the editors' knowledge of the significance of what is being recounted there.

38. The story of the northern kingdom from Jeroboam I until Zimri was one in which a usurper's inheritor was assassinated so that no dynasty ever began. That continued to be the case not just because of political intrigue, but because of the "Israelite" bias against *goy,* "this-worldly," dynastic power.

39. Again, cf. von Rad, *Studies in Deuteronomy,* chapter 7.

40. *Midbar*, in Hebrew, means "desert", but also that "chaos" which lies outside the order brought to the world by kings designated by the gods. The play on words in a prophet like Hosea lies in the prophet's faith that Yahweh had created a people in precisely what, from a *goy* point of view, had been chaos.

41. The latter part of the passage clearly refers to Israel's assent to the covenant at Sinai after being rescued from Egypt. So, the opening verse has to be understood in that context. That is why I have rendered, "and will speak tenderly to her" in the way that I have. What the line literally says is, "And will direct a word to her heart." "Word" is the basis of Israel's covenant existence with God. "Heart" is the seat of understanding. That is the basis of my translating the line, "Will restore covenant meaning to her existence again."

42. Cf. von Rad, *Old Testament Theology,* volume II, p. 271ff.

43. That is the reason I left what the Hebrew literally says in my translation of Jeremiah 23:7–8: "the land of Zaphon." "Zaphon" is indeed the Hebrew word for "north," but the Canaanite literature from ancient Ugarit shows that it is the name of the mountain to the north of Palestine which is the home of the divine and demonic forces of the universe. Thus, here as in Jeremiah 1:13 it has overtones not caught by simply translating it "north."

44. Chapters 40 through 66 of the book of Isaiah come from prophets in the tradition of the original Isaiah (a "school?") who post-date the original prophet by about two centuries. Isaiah 40–55 (II or Deutero-Isaiah) seems to represent a response to Cyrus' taking of Babylon in 538. Isaiah 56–66 (III or Trito-Isaiah) seems to consist of various prophetic materials from after that time. It was Cyrus' policy, just as he gained favor in Babylon itself by restoring an ancient priesthood banned by Babylonian kings, to allow and even subsidize the restoration of the cults of various nations Babylon had conquered and whose kings and priests had been exiled to Babylon. Isaiah 41 seems to reflect a consequent debate about just which god really did send Cyrus with that policy. In 41:2–4,25–29 the Israelite prophet argues that it must be Yahweh because Yahweh is the only god who has consistently acted on the human scene in historical events. I would maintain that it is out of this argument that conscious monotheism begins to emerge in Israel.

45. The *Heilsorakel* seems to have been the priestly response of reassurance to a devotee who went to the sanctuary to lament misfortune and seek the help of the devotee's god, the equivalent of the absolution pronounced by a priest to a Christian penitent. The form was isolated by Begrich in his article "Das priesterliche Heilsorakel." Cf. Guthrie, *Israel's Sacred Songs,* pp. 143–144.

46. The other side of II Isaiah's monotheism (cf. note 44 above) is, I believe, a universalizing of Yahweh's action as a protector God who responds to human

cries of need. Cf. the discussion of thanksgiving in chapter 1 of this book and particularly the discussion there of *zedek,* "righteousness." By implication at least II Isaiah is insisting that *all* can participate in that "righteousness" which Israel originally knew in connection with rescue from Egyptian oppression and which is, at root, Yahweh's vindication of those in need.

47. The Chronicler even holds that already by the time of Josiah the monarchy had outlived its purpose and that Yahweh's will was now being done by other rulers than Israel's Davidic kings. In II Kings 23:29–30 the deuteronomic historians see Josiah as a heroic king who was tragically slain by Pharaoh Neco as he insisted on the independence of Judah. The Chronicler's interpretation in II Chronicles 35:20–24 is significantly different. There Josiah dies for seeking to defend a doomed nation in disobedience to the word of God spoken precisely by the Egyptian ruler.

48. That is obscured in English translations of the Old Testament in which, following the order of the Greek Septuagint, the work of the Chronicler comes after II Kings and before the Psalter. Nevertheless, it is the case that the work of the Chronicler, except for very few passages from Ezra and Nehemiah, is rarely read in Christian churches.

49. The Hebrew Bible really contains four great anthologies of prophetic material. That the Book of the Twelve (so it is designated in Jewish tradition) is an anthology is quite clear. What is not so clear initially is that Isaiah, Jeremiah, and Ezekiel are also anthologies. Each of them probably is the result of the life and continuing activity of prophetic "schools" which began with the master whose activity in a time of crisis started it all. That is clear with regard to the book of Isaiah (cf. note 44 above), and is most likely also true of the books of Jeremiah and Ezekiel. The Book of the Twelve probably is a collection of materials originating with some significant prophets whose "schools" were not as significant as those of Isaiah, Jeremiah, and Ezekiel.

50. For that way of stating it I am indebted to von Rad and his approach in volume 2 of his *Old Testament Theology.*

51. Autobiographical and biographical narratives are found in the books of the prophets sometimes in long sections, sometimes mixed in with recorded pronouncements of the prophets. Cf. passages such as the following: Amos 7:1–8:3; Hosea 1–3; Isaiah 6–8, 36–39; Jeremiah 1, 26–29, 36–39; Ezekiel 1–3, 8–11.

52. For a discussion of the issues involved in Hosea 1 and Hosea 3, cf. Pfeiffer, *Introduction to the Old Testament,* pp. 566–570.

53. We must remember that the books of the Old Testament, though varying in the intensity with which they were organized and edited, are the products of tradition. They do, in various ways, make use of writings which existed separately before the books as we know them came into being. So, not only is the same block of material included both in II Kings 18–20 and Isaiah 36–39, but the same is true of Isaiah 2:2–4 and Micah 4:1–3, of Genesis 12:10–20 and Genesis 20:1–9 and Genesis 26:6–11, and of other passages.

54. Cf. Sheldon Blank, *Prophetic Faith in Isaiah,* chapter 2.

55. My own theory is that Jeremiah 26–29, with various addenda in Jeremiah 30–35, is a memoir of Jeremiah which was preserved among the exiles in Babylon, while Jeremiah 36–45 is a memoir which originated among those who remained in Palestine after 587, some of whom fled to Egypt. The source of Jeremiah 36–45 is most likely Baruch, Jeremiah's companion and scribe.

56. Hans Shhmidt was the commentator who characterized the biographical material in Jeremiah in that way. Cf. his commentary.

57. My own view is that the servant songs in II Isaiah are later in composition that the context in which they now appear, that they represent a considered view of the vocation of Israel as God's servant which is the result of extended meditation on the lives and witness of prophets such as Isaiah and Jeremiah, and that they are like musical "rondos" at transition points in the great poetic/prophetic anthology which is Isaiah 40–55.

58. While it is now more than 30 years old, the most thorough survey of the various views taken of the suffering servant is still Christopher North, *The Suffering Servant in Deutero Isaiah*.

59. Cf. the way in which "Jacob" can be used as a synonym for "Israel" is such a way that the name of an individual is also the designation of a people. Cf. also note 28 above on how "Ashur" is a singular word denoting the God of Assyria but also can be used in such a way as to necessitate the translation "Assyrian*s*." The classic treatment of all this is H. W. Robinson, "The Hebrew Conception of Corporate Personality."

Chapter 4 Wisdom's Reinterpretation: Adaptation to Exile

1. Chapter 2 above deals with the successive stages by which the narrative of the Old Testament came into being. Cf. in particular footnote 20 to that chapter and Freedman's article on the Pentateuch in *The Interpreter's Dictionary of the Bible*.

2. The Psalter as we know it in the Hebrew Bible and translations thereof undoubtedly came into being by as complicated a process as did the narrative complex of the Old Testament. For what I take to be the ethos out of which the final collection came into existence, cf. Guthrie, *Israel's Sacred Songs,* pp. 188–193. Cf. also Sabourin, *The Psalms,* pp. 6–11, and Westermann, "Zur Sammlung des Psalters."

3. I have translated these verses quite freely in order to get at what I think is a conscious contrast in "river" imagery between the waters that make the city of God rejoice in Psalm 46 and *Babylon's* water in Psalm 137.

4. Cf. Pritchard, *Ancient Near Eastern Texts,* pp. 405–440.

5. I believe von Rad's treatment of wisdom to be the best and most sensitive available. Cf. his *Old Testament Theology* I, pp. 408–459 and his *Wisdom in Israel.*

6. Cr. Koehler's delightful description of the *sod* and what transpired there in his *Hebrew Man,* pp. 99–107.

7. Cf. von Rad's treatment of Genesis 37–50 in his *Genesis,* and particularly his "Epilogue to the Joseph Story" at the very end of that volume.

8. Cf. von Rad, "The Beginnings of Historical Writing in Ancient Israel" in *The Problem of the Hexateuch and Other Essays* for a superb treatment of the account of Solomon's succession to David's throne. For a treatment of that narrative which quite specifically sees its author as a wisdom teacher, see Whybray, *The Succession Narrative*. For wisdom influences elsewhere in the Old Testament, see Crenshaw, "Method in Determining Wisdom Influence upon 'Historical' Literature," and Terrien, "Amos and Wisdom."

9. Cf. von Rad, *Old Testament Theology,* pp. 428–429.

10. For a passage in Egyptian literature in which *ma'at* is simply translated "justice," cf. "The Instruction of the Vizier Ptah-Hotep" in Pritchard, *Ancient Near Eastern Tests*, p. 412, lines 85–95.
For passages in which *ma'at* is a goddess, cf. the first paragraph from the autobiography of Rekh-mi-Re, Pritchard, p. 213, and ix 7 of the hymns to the gods near the top of p. 372 in Pritchard.

11. The following section of this chapter is a restatement of what I set forth in *Wisdom and Canon,* and, in shorter form, in *Israel's Sacred Songs*.

12. The ancient Greek translation of the Hebrew Bible differs from the Massoretic Text, the Hebrew version accepted by the Jewish community since the early centuries of the Christian era, in that it contains some books not in the Hebrew (cf. II Esdras, Wisdom, Ecclesiasticus, Tobit, I and II Maccabees), variations of some things already in the Hebrew Bible (I Esdras), and the overplus of some books which are longer than the versions of them in the Hebrew (Judith, the rest of Esther, Baruch and Jeremiah's letter, the Song of the Three, Susanna and the Elders, Bel and the Dragon, and the Prayer of Manasseh.) When Jerome produced the Vulgate, the Latin translation which was used in the West until fairly recently, he used the Hebrew text and included the things over and above that in the Septuagint when ordered to do so by the Bishop of Rome. He is reputed to have termed the latter writings "apocrypha"—"obscure." At the Reformation the classical Protestant churches retained only the books in the Hebrew (but kept the Septuagint order), while the Roman Church kept the Vulgate. The Church of England held the Apocrypha to be of use for edification but not inspired in the same way as the rest of the Old and New Testaments, and included the Apocrypha as a separate collection in the Bible—not where its writings come in the order of the Septuagint.

13. I believe that the original Psalter consisted of what we know as Psalms 1–119, the beginning and the concluding psalms being wisdom poems. Furthermore, I see wisdom poems at points of organizational significance in the psalter, viz. Psalms 49, 73, etc. Cf. *Israel's Sacred Songs,* p. 190ff. I hope to do an article one day demonstrating this.

14. Cf. Jeremias, *The Central Message of the New Testament,* p. 70ff. The prayer itself is from a Mithras liturgy, but Jeremias quotes it in giving the background in the exilic and post-exilic periods of statements such as the one at the beginning of Hebrews, "God, who in different ways and and different times spoke *in the past* through God's servants the prophets, has *in these latter days* spoken through the Son." The statement implies a tradition of silence between the time of the prophets and the present.

15. Again, my translation is in many places conjectural, and represents an attempt to convey what seems to be the imagery of the poem. On the problems of the text, cf. the various commentaries on Job.

16. It should be noted that Hebrew has no neuter gender. All nouns are either masculine or feminine. That wisdom came to be personified as a female is probably due simply to the fact that the gender of the word is feminine.

17. In establishing a royal court of the kind that prevailed in the culture Solomon undoubtedly founded a school for the training of scribes and civil servants. Since education consisted to a large extent of learning "proverbs" which brought wisdom to bear on situations in life, it was through this that Solomon probably came to be associated with "the wise" and to be thought of as the patron of wisdom in Israel.

18. Again, commentaries can be consulted about the text. My translation sometimes verges on paraphrase, but it does so in order to emphasize what the text itself means in terms of what is being discussed here.

19. As the foregoing translation indicates, I prefer "little child." "Artisan" or "holder of things together" could be poetically parallel to "Yahweh's delight" in the immediately next line, but the following two lines use the parallelism of "reveling" or "playing," and the "child" imagery seems to me to go better with

that. It also, in accord with the theology of the preface to the book of Proverbs, makes more sense in terms of Wisdom's being subordinate to Yahweh.

20. I see the concluding lines as focussing in from the totality of creation to the earth itself to humankind. That is why I add the bracketed words [admittedly not there in the Hebrew] in order to make that clear.

21. That dualism which is often associated with gnosticism and traced to "Greek" roots can, in my opinion, be traced way back to the atmosphere present here in the preface to Proverbs. The question of where the dualistic personification, of Wisdom as well as the Adversary, comes from has never been satisfactorily answered. Albright (*From the Stone Age to Christianity*, p. 167ff.) opined that underneath the Proverbs 8 passage lay a very ancient, northwest Semitic tradition of a goddess of life and wisdom. No literature has been found to substantiate that. The imagery of Wisdom, particularly in Ecclesiasticus 24, is reminiscent of the Egyptian goddess Isis in some ways.

22. On Ecclesiasticus, cf. J. G. Snaith, *Ecclesiasticus*.

23. Simon II was high priest ca. 219–196B.C. His high priesthood did, in fact, represent the last flowering of the restoration of the temple cult begun under Nehemiah and Ezra. In 171 Antiochus IV Epiphanes interfered in things in a way that led, finally, to the Maccabean revolt.

24. For a commentary and a listing of the literature, cf. Winston, *The Wisdom of Solomon*.

25. On the book of Baruch, cf. Pfeiffer, *History of New Testament Times*.

26. Note how in Ezra 7:25 the book of the law of Moses is referred to as "the wisdom of God which is in your hand."

27. The term "normative Judaism" originated with G. F. Moore in his epochal work, *Judaism*. While more recent work has revealed the extremely variegated nature of Judaism in New Testament times and caused questions to be raised about the term, that rabbinic Judaism characterized by Moore as "normative" is what finally survived as the Judaism known in the modern world.

28. "Rabbi" is a term of respect: literally "My great one," and much like "Your honor." The latter is not a bad rendering, since the word denotes one who is a teacher skilled in the interpretation of the law of Moses.

29. Cf. Strack, *Introduction to the Talmud and Midrash*.

30. Cf. Danby, *The Mishnah*.

31. Cf. Strack, *op. cit.*, chapter XIII.

32. Cf. Baron, *A Social and Religious History of the Jews*, Vol. II *Ancient Times*, part II.

34. On I Maccabees, cf. Pfeiffer, *History of New Testament Times*, chapter XI.

35. Cf. Bouyer, *Eucharist*, chapters III and IV.

36. Cf. Baron's history, as well as much recent work on the background of the New Testament.

37. On the various "schools" within Judaism, cf. the works of Baron and Pfeiffer cited above.

38. On this understanding of Daniel, cf. von Rad, *Old Testament Theology* II, p. 301ff.

Chapter 5 Thanksgiving Reappropriated: The New Testament Canon

1. Krister Stendahl is fond of pointing out that St. Paul would not have understood at all the conception underlying the Prayer Book celebration of "The

Conversion of St. Paul the Apostle." In no way did Paul conceive of himself as having "converted" from one religion to another.

2. The bibliographical data on the book are to be found in the bibliography.

3. Cf. Koester and Robinson, *Trajectories through Early Christianity,* particularly chapter 4.

4. "Gnosticism" is derived from the Greek *gnosis,* which simply means "knowledge." It denotes an understanding and practice of Christianity as the secret knowledge through which human beings can be spiritually liberated from ignorance and illusion and find their own identity with the divine. Cf. the articles on "Gnosticism" in the *Interpreter's Dictionary of the Bible* and in the supplementary volume of the IDB.

5. Cf. Koester, "GNOMAI DIAPHOROI," in *Trajectories through Early Christianity.*

6. For Judaism "orthodoxy" has to do with *practice,* not with belief or doctrine or theological position.

7. The literature on Paul and the Pauline writings in the New Testament is vast indeed. For an introduction to the issues, cf. the articles on "Paul the Apostle" in the *Interpreter's Dictionary of the Bible* and the supplementary volume to the IDB.

8. For Paul the historical reality "Jesus" seems to be focussed completely in the crucifixion. That seems to be because the history into which Paul and the Corinthian Christians have been swept up, the history which is the medium of God's revelation and presence, began when the self-emptying death of Jesus led to the crucifixion which was the beginning of that history. Subsequent Christian reflection on the experience to which Paul witnessed located the beginning of the reality further and further back: Mark located it at Jesus' baptism, Matthew and Luke at Jesus' birth, John before creation in the being of God.

9. This translation, or paraphrase, represents an attempt to convey what the words are really saying in light of their context.

10. There are, of course, complicated questions about the composition and order of the Corinthian correspondence: cf. the various introductions and commentaries. How those problems are solved does not, however, affect the main thrust of the argument here.

11. Cf., for example, Romans 1:1–3; I Corinthians 1:17; II Corinthians 4:3; Galatians 1:6ff.; Philippians 1:5; Colossians 1:5; I Thessalonians 1:5; II Thessalonians 1:8.

12. In spite of the use of Paul's writings by such people as Luther in later Christian controversies, the basic issue is not "freedom vs. legalism" or "faith vs. works" in some abstract, theoretical, doctrinal way. It is, and we are far enough into our argument now for the words to have meaning, *todah* and all that that means vs. *torah* and all that that means. A lot of later arguments have really distorted the issue into an advocacy of one kind of *torah* over against another.

13. Cf. Robinson's chapter 3 in *Trajectories through Early Christianity.*

14. Cf. MacRae, "Nag Hammadi," in *Interpreter's Dictionary* of the Bible and the literature cited there.

15. Even if the minority of critical scholars who consider Matthew to predate Mark and Mark to be a precis of Matthew be correct, the argument here is not affected. It is the existence of Q as a reality which is basic to what we are saying.

16. Luke's form of Q seems to most scholars to reflect more the form of the original. Cf. Neirynck on "Q" in *Interpreter's Dictionary of the Bible,* supplemental volume.

17. Cf. Ezra 7:25.
18. Cf. Schmitals, *Die Gnosis in Korinth*, p. 45.
19. Again, cf. Koester's "GNOMAI DIAPHOROI" in *Trajectories through Early Christianity*.
20. Note how the narrative of Jesus' life and death seems, in Matthew, to be organized around five didactic discourses by Jesus (cf. Johnson's introduction in *Interpreter's Bible*, volume 7, p. 246ff.).
21. That statement about Aegean Christianity is not meant to be ideological, not made out of a "heresy-versus-orthodoxy" stance. It is simply descriptive.
22. Thus, it is not just that Mark omits, on the whole, Jesus' teaching—as is so often pointed out. Mark really omits *everything* found in Q. This is true whether Mark is the earliest gospel, as most believe, or was extracted from an early form of Matthew. Whatever the origin of Mark in relation to the other gospels, it seems consciously to dissociate itself from the interpretation of Jesus found in Q.
23. For an explanation of the issues, cf. Rowlingson, "Synoptic Problem," *Interpreter's Dictionary of the Bible*.
24. It should be noted that the *content* of the teachings, even in Q, is basically eschatological, more in line with *todah* than *torah*, even if the *form* of Q implies something else which is to affect the content when we come to something like the Gospel of Thomas.
25. From "The Problem of History in Mark," p. 135.
26. For other "gospels," cf. James, *The Apocryphal New Testament*.
27. The Greek work basically denotes a straight rod or bar, comes to be used of a ruler in drawing straight lines, and then comes to have the meaning of "standard' or "norm" or "official" as in "canon" of Scripture.
28. This translation of the famous passage is admittedly a free one. It is, however, the case that the concluding verse is the climax of what is said in verse 23 ff. I have tried to render those verses in such a way as to make it clear how they find their meaning in verse 28.
29. There is substantial, though by no means universal, agreement that Ephesians is not a writing of Paul himself but the work of a disciple who sets forth the Pauline themes, possibly as an early introduction to the collection of the letters of Paul.
30. In the same way that Paul does so—quite possibly sarcastically—in the opening chapters of I Corinthians, Ephesians uses wisdom vocabulary in setting forth the work of God in the Church in history. What is at issue, the passage implies, is the nature of *true* wisdom.
31. Again, I have been free in translating a passage so rich in its allusions and meaning that translation is difficult if all that is there is to come through. The imagery is based on the wall which barred non-Jews from entrance to the inner precincts of the temple on which signs said, "No one of another race is to proceed within the partition and enclosing wall around the sanctuary; and anyone arrested there will be himself to blame for the penalty of death which will be imposed as a consequence."
32. For being led to this kind of understanding of Paul and Romans I am indebted to Munck, *Paul and the Salvation of Mankind*. The English translation of Munck's title is unfortunate both for its sexism and for its failure to capture the flavor of the original *Paulus und die Heilsgeschichte*. "Paul and God's Redemptive Course of Events" would have been better.
33. Cf. the various commentaries on Mark 1:1. A comparison will indicate that whether "beginning" refers to the preaching of John the Baptist or to Jesus' life and death and resurrection as recounted in the gospel is an open question.

34. The footnotes to Mark 16:8–20 in the New English Bible summarize the issues very well.

35. I have translated *onoma* "story" rather than "name" in view of the connotation of "fame" or "reputation" or "record" which the word "name" bears in Hebrew, and in other languages as well. The preposition does bear the overtones of "into," so I have interpreted the prepositon and the word "name" together in a "*todah*" way for which I think there is justification.

36. Cf. Conzelmann's *The Theology of St. Luke* for an interpretation of Luke-Acts which, unlike so much New Testament scholarship, transcends "Jesus piety" and takes the perspective of the early Church seriously. Even though I do not finally agree with Conzelmann's results, he is dealing with the real issues. Again (cf. note 32 above) the English translation of the title of Conzelmann's work distorts the issue being dealt with. *Die Mitte der Zeit* has to do with eschatology, not "theology," with the significance of the course of events which include Jesus and the Church rather than an abstract, doctrinal position.

37. The ultimate origins of the Fourth Gospel seem to lie in a complicated Judeo-Hellenistic background of which we really had no hints before the discovery of things such the Qumran scrolls. For an introduction and bibliography, cf. Cross, "The Dead Sea Scrolls," p. 657ff. in *Interpreter's Bible,* volume 12, and Smith, "John, Gospel of," in the supplementary volume to *Interpreter's Dictionary of the Bible*.

38. Cf. Dodd, *According to the Scriptures*; Lindars, *New Testament Apologetic*; Shires, *Finding the Old Testament in the New*.

39. The New Testament, particularly in the Fourth Gospel, does speak of "Jews" as over against Jesus and his followers, and that does lead to the reprehensible anti-Semitism for which the Christian Church has been responsible down through history. I do believe that a careful study would indicate that that atmosphere is definitely post-Paul.

40. Cf. von Rad, "Typological Interpretation of the Old Testament," and the last section of the second volume of his *Old Testament Theology*.

41. Paul states the contrast as being between Abraham's faith and Moses' *torah,* but that is his way of making the point in a pre-historical-critical age.

42. We really know about Marcion, who lived in the second century, through refutations of his teaching and writing, particularly those of Tertullian. In one sense, Marcionism, which outlasted its originator for a long time, triumphed subtly even if the *content* of its teaching was refuted and died out. It was responsible for the shifting of concern from the shape of the Church's liturgical self-identification to the question of the official *book* and which writings should make it up.

Chapter 6 Eucharistia: The Canon Underlying the Canon

1. Of course, there was substantial agreement on which books formed the canon of scripture very early on. But it was really only at the time of the Reformation that, in the Protestant Confessions and the Council of Trent and the Thirty-nine Articles, official ecclesiastical statements were made on the question.

2. Cf. Mendenhall, "The Hebrew Conquest of Palestine."

3. It should be noted that, in the earliest Church, Baptism *included* the sealing with the Spirit which came to be known in the West as "confirmation."

4. It was precisely, as I see it, emphasis on mastering the *teaching* that distinguished gnosticism from normative Christianity.

5. Cf. Price and Weil, *Liturgy for Living,* p. 103ff.

6. The Apostles' Creed originated as a baptismal confession of faith, legend having it that the various phrases in it originated with the twelve apostles. It is used at the daily office and in a Eucharist at the time of burial as a reminder, daily and at the time of death, of the faith in which Christians live. On the creeds, cf. J.N.D. Kelly, *Early Christian Creeds.*

7. Cf. Price and Weil, *Liturgy for Living,* p. 222ff.

8. It was Dix's *The Shape of the Liturgy* which set forth the "shape" of the eucharistic action as what was central to the nature of the Eucharist. Discussion of the nature of the "shape" has gone on since the publication of that important work, but that the form—the agenda—is what is basic is clear. Cf. the Order for Eucharist, p. 400ff., in the 1979 Book of Common Prayer of the Episcopal Church in the U.S.

9. A basic bibliography is found on pp. 335–336 of Price and Weil, *Liturgy for Living.*

10. Cf., *inter alia,* chapters II–IV of Bouyer, *Eucharist.*

11. Cf. Bouyer, p. 1.

12. For a discussion of all this, cf. Bouyer, chapter VI, and particularly p. 158ff.

13. Cf. Bouyer, p. 169.

14. Cf. Bouyer, p. 13.

15. Cf. its restoration in the 1979 American Prayer Book.

16. It is undoubtedly the case that the historical consciousness by which western culture is characterized came into being under the influence of the biblical point of view as mediated through people like Eusebius and Augustine and Orosius. Cf. on this vast and interesting subject, *inter alia,* Auerbach, *Mimesis;* Loewith, *Meaning in History; Van Leeuwen, Christianity in World History.*

17. The sketch which follows is, in many ways, presumptuous and foolhardy, coming as it does from one whose special competence as a student of history is not in the era discussed. It hastily covers many things on which volumes of work have been done. Yet I do believe it to convey a true larger picture.

18. Cf. Patterson, *God and History in Early Christian Thought.*

19. The following are the generally recognized ecumenical councils: Nicea (I) 325 A.D., Constantinople (I) 381, Ephesus 431, Chalcedon 451. Eastern Orthodox, Roman Catholics, and Anglicans in varying degrees recognize others, but the great conciliar age runs through the fifth century.

20. Cf. Bouyer, chapters XI and XII.

21. There are valid arguments against the concept of a "Christendom" which prevailed in western culture from the time of Constantine until the Reformation and Renaissance. The concept does, however, denote a reality which existed in distinction to what preceded and followed it.

22. For this, and many other suggestive insights, I am grateful to Voegelin, *Order and History I: Israel and Revelation.*

23. Cf. note 1 above.

24. On the Apocrypha, cf. Dentan, *The Apocrypha: Bridge of the Testaments.*

25. It was Marshall McLuhan who opened the eyes of many of us to this factor in our cultural history. Cf. *Understanding Media* and *The Gutenberg Galaxy.*

26. This is why revision of the *book,* liturgical revision in that sense, is always traumatic for Anglicans, but even more so in a revision like the 1979 American Prayer Book in which "shape" rather than "book" is recognized as the basic thing and alternative sets of words are given to accompany the "shape."

27. The literature on all this is vast. For an analytical history, cf. Barraclough, *An Introduction to Contemporary History.*

28. Cf. Gooch, *History and Historians in the Nineteenth Century,* particularly the opening chapters.

29. Cf. Vico's discovery of Augustine and Orosius as a means of understanding reality: *The New Science.*

30. Cf. Butterfield, *The Origins of Modern Science,* p. 7.

31. The problem is not merely one for Christians. The gap between our culturally inherited value systems and the decisions now necessary in economic, technological, and political spheres is so vast as to defy solutions. Cf. C. P. Snow, *The Two Cultures.*

32. I first gained an insight along these lines a long time ago from the writings of D. R. G. Owen, *Scientism, Man and Religion* and *Body and Soul.*

33. The literature on historical study of the Bible and Christianity is vast. Harvey's *The Historian and the Believer* represents a Bultmannian attempt to deal with the issues. I find Roberts' *History and Christian Apologetic* a cogent setting forth of all the issues.

34. Again, the literature which could be cited in vast. Cf. Koch, *The Growth of the Biblical Tradition.*

35. Bouyer, *Eucharist,* p. 5.

36. Cf., *inter alia,* Bouyer, *Liturgical Piety; Prayer Book Studies;* Shepherd, *The Liturgical Renewal of the Church;* Spielmann, *History of Christian Worship;* Srawley, *The Liturgical Movement.*

37. Such a vision of the fundamental vocation of the Church came to me in the lecture "Community and Communion" by Bayne in *The Optional God,* pp. 46–50.

Bibliography

Albright, William F. *From the Stone Age to Christianity*. Garden City: Doubleday (Anchor Book), 1957, 2nd ed.

Anderson, Bernhard W. *Understanding the Old Testament*. Englewood Cliffs: Prentice-Hall, 1966, 2nd ed.

Auerbach, Erich. *Mimesis: The Representation of Reality in Western Literature*. Garden City: Doubleday (Anchor Book), 1957.

Baltzar, Klaus. *The Covenant Formulary in Old Testament, Jewish, and Early Christian Writings* (tr. David E. Green). Philadelphia: Fortress Press, 1971.

Baron, Salo W. *A Social and Religious History of the Jews*. New York: Columbia University Press, 1952.

Barraclough, Geoffrey. *An Introduction to Contemporary History*. Baltimore: Penguin Books, 1967.

Bauer, Walter. *Orthodoxy and Heresy in Earliest Christianity* (ed. Robert A. Kraft and Gerhard Krodel). Philadelphia: Fortress Press, 1971.

Bayne, Stephen. *The Optional God*. Wilton: Morehouse-Barlow, 1980.

Begrich, Joachim. "Das priesterliche Heilsorakel," *Zeitschrift für die alttestamentliche Wissenschaft* LII (1934), 81–92.

Blank, Sheldon. *Prophetic Faith in Isaiah*. New York: Harper, 1958.

Bouyer, Louis. *Eucharist: Theology and Spirituality of the Eucharistic Prayer* (tr. Charles U. Quinn). Notre Dame: University of Notre Dame Press, 1968.

———. *Liturgical Piety*. Notre Dame: University of Notre Dame Press, 1954.

Breasted, James H. *Ancient Times: A History of the Early World*. Boston: Ginn and Co., 1914.

Bright, John. *A History of Israel*. Philadelphia: Westminster Press, 1959.

Butterfield, Herbert. *The Origins of Modern Science: 1300–1800*. New York: Macmillan, 1960.

Conzelmann, Hans. *The Theology of St. Luke* (tr. G. Buswell). New York: Harper, 1961.

Crenshaw, J. L. "Method in Determining Wisdom Influence upon 'Historical' Literature," *Journal of Biblical Literature* 88 (1969), 129–142.

Cross, Frank Moore. *Canaanite Myth and Hebrew Epic: Essays in the History of the Religion of Israel.* Cambridge: Harvard University Press, 1973.

———. "The Dead Sea Scrolls," *Interpreter's Bible* 12. Nashville: Abingdon, 1957.

———. "Notes on a Canaanite Psalm in the Old Testament," *Bulletin of the American Schools of Oriental Research* CXVII (1950), 19–21.

Dahood, Mitchell. *Psalms I-III* (*The Anchor Bible* 16–17A). Garden City: Doubleday, 1966–1970.

Danby, Herbert. *The Mishnah.* London: Oxford University Press, 1933.

Dentan, Robert C. *The Apocrypha: Bridge of the Testaments.* Greenwich: Seabury Press, 1954.

Dix, Gregory. *The Shape of the Liturgy.* Westminster: Dacre Press, 1945.

Dodd, C.H. *According to the Scriptures.* London: Nisbet, 1952.

Eichrodt, Walther. *Theology of the Old Testament* (tr. J. A. Baker). Philadelphia: Westminster Press, I 1961, II 1967.

Frankfort, Henri, *et al. The Intellectual Adventure of Ancient Man.* Chicago: University of Chicago Press, 1946. (Subsequently reprinted as a Penguin paperback under the title, *Before Philosophy.*)

Freedman, David Noel. "Pentateuch," *Interpreter's Dictionary of the Bible* III. Nashville: Abingdon Press, 1962.

Gooch, G. P. *History and Historians in the Nineteenth Century.* Boston: Beacon Press, 1959.

Gottwald, Norman K. *A Light to the Nations: An Introduction to the Old Testament.* New York: Harper and Row, 1959.

———. *The Tribes of Yahweh: A Sociology of the Religion of Liberated Israel,* 1250–1050 B.C.E. Maryknoll: Orbis Books, 1979.

Grant, Robert M. "Gnosticism," *Interpreter's Dictionary of the Bible* II. Nashville: Abingdon Press, 1962.

Greenberg, Moshe. *The Hab/piru.* New Haven: American Oriental Society, 1955.

Gunkel, Herman, and Begrich, J. *Einleitung in die Psalmen. Die Gattungen der Religiösen Lyrik Israels.* Göttingen: Vandenhoeck and Ruprecht, 1933.

Gunkel, Herman. *The Psalms: A Form-Critical Introduction* (tr. Thomas M. Horner). Philadelphia: Fortress Press, 2nd printing 1969.

Guthrie, Harvey H., Jr. *God and History in the Old Testament.* New York: Seabury Press, 1960.

———. *Israel's Sacred Songs: A Study of Dominant Themes.* New York: Seabury Press, 1966.

——— . *Wisdom and Canon: Meanings of the Law and the Prophets.* Evanston: Seabury-Western Theological Seminary, 1966.

Hamlin, E. J. "Nations," *Interpreter's Dictionary of the Bible* III. Nashville: Abingdon Press, 1962.

Harvey, Van A. *The Historian and the Believer.* New York: Macmillan, 1966.

Hurd, John. "Paul the Apostle," *Interpreter's Dictionary of the Bible Supplementary Volume.* Nashville: Abingdon, 1976.

James, M. R. *The Apocryphal New Testament.* Oxford: Clarendon Press, 1953 (corrected edition).

Johnson, Aubrey. *Sacral Kingship in Ancient Israel.* Cardiff: University of Wales Press, 1955.

Johnson, Sherman E. "Matthew," *Interpreter's Bible* VII. Nashville: Abingdon Press, 1951.

Justin Martyer. *First Apology. Library of Christian Classics I: Early Christian Fathers.* London: SCM Press, 1953.

Kelly, J. N. D. *Early Christian Creeds*. New York: Longmans Green, 1950.
Koch, Klaus. *The Growth of the Biblical Tradition: The Form-Critical Method*. New York: Charles Scribner's Sons, 1969.
Köhler, Ludwig. *Hebrew Man*. London: SCM Press, 1956.
Koester, Helmut. See Robinson, James. M.
Kraus, Hans-Joachim. *Psalmen. Biblischer Kommentar* XV. Neukirchen: Verlag des Erziehungsverein, 1960.
———. *Worship in Israel* (tr. G. Buswell). Richmond: John Knox Press, 1965.
van Leeuwen, A. T. *Christianity in World History* (tr. H. H. Hoskind). New York: Scribner, 1964.
Lindars, Barnabas. *New Testament Apologetic: The Doctrinal Significance of the Old Testament Quotations*. Philadelphia: Westminster Press, 1962.
Loewith, Karl. *Meaning in History*. Chicago: University of Chicago Press, 1949.
McLuhan, Herbert Marshall. *The Gutenberg Galaxy: The Making of Typographic Man*. Toronto: University of Toronto Press, 1962.
———. *Understanding Media: The Extensions of Man*. New York: McGraw-Hill, 1964.
Mendenhall, George E. "The Hebrew Conquest of Palestine," *Biblical Archaeologist* XXV (1962), 66–87.
———. "Law and Covenant in Israel and the Ancient Near East," *Biblical Archaeologist* XVII (1954), 26–46, 49–76.
———. *The Tenth Generation: The Origins of the Biblical Tradition*. Baltimore: Johns Hopkins University Press, 1973.
Moore, George Foot. *Judaism in the First Centuries of the Christian Era: The Age of the Tannaim*. Cambridge: Harvard University Press, 1927.
Mowinckel, Sigmund. *The Psalms in Israel's Worship*. Nashville: Abingdon Press, 1962.
———. *The Two Sources of the Predeuteronomic Primeval History (JE) in Genesis*. Oslo, 1937.
Munck, Johannes. *Paul and the Salvation of Mankind* (tr. Frank Clarke). Richmond: John Knox Press, 1959.
Myers, Jacob. M. *I Chronicles, II Chronicles, Ezra and Nehemiah* (*Anchor Bible* XII, XIII, XIV). Garden City: Doubleday, 1965.
Neirynck, F. "Q," *Interpreter's Dictionary of the Bible Supplementary Volume*. Nashville: Abingdon Press, 1976.
North, Christopher. *The Suffering Servant in Deutero-Isaiah*. London: Oxford University Press, 1948.
Noth, Martin. *The History of Israel* (2nd edition). New York: Harper, 1960.
———. *Das System der zwölf Stämme Israels*. Stuttgart: Kohlhammer, 1930.
———. *Überlieferungsgeschichte des Pentateuch* (2nd edition). Stuttgart: Kohlhammer, 1948.
Owen, D. R. G. *Body and Soul*. Philadelphia: Westminster Press, 1956.
———. *Scientism, Man and Religion*. Philadelphia: Westminster Press, 1952.
Pagels, Elaine. *The Gnostic Gospels*. New York: Random House, 1979.
———. "Gnosticism," *Interpreter's Dictionary of the Bible Supplementary Volume*. Nashville: Abingdon Press, 1976.
Patterson, L. G. *God and History in Early Christian Thought*. New York: Seabury Press, 1967.
Pfeiffer, Robert H. "Chronicles," *Interpreter's Dictionary of the Bible* I. Nashville: Abingdon Press, 1962.
———. "Ezra and Nehemiah," *Interpreter's Dictionary of the Bible* II. Nashville: Abingdon Press, 1962.

———. *History of New Testament Times with an Introduction to the Apocrypha*. New York: Harper, 1949.
Pope, Marvin H. *El in the Ugaritic Texts*. Leiden: Brill, 1955.
Prayer Book Studies. New York: Church Pension Fund, 1950–1976.
Price, Charles P., and Weil, Louis. *Liturgy for Living* (*The Church's Teaching Series* V). New York: Seabury, 1979.
Pritchard, James B. (ed.). *Ancient Near Eastern Texts* (2nd edition). Princeton: Princeton University Press, 1955.
Purdy, A. C. "Paul the Apostle," *Interpreter's Dictionary of the Bible* III. Nashville: Abingdon Press, 1962.
von Rad, Gerhard. "Deuteronomy," *Interpreter's Dictionary of the Bible* I. Nashville: Abingdon Press, 1962.
———. *Old Testament Theology* (tr. D. M. G. Stalker). New York: Harper and Row, I 1962, II 1965.
———. *The Problem of the Hexateuch and Other Essays* (tr. E. W. Trueman Dickman). London: Oliver and Boyd, 1966.
———. *Studies in Deuteronomy: Studies in Biblical Theology* IX (tr. D. M. G. Stalker). London: SCM Press, 1953.
———. "Typological Interpretation of the Old Testament," *Interpretation* XV (1961), 174ff.
———. *Wisdom in Israel* (tr. James D. Martin). London: SCM Press, 1972.
Richardson, Alan. *A Theological Word Book of the Bible*. New York: Macmillan, 1951.
Roberts, T. A. *History and Christian Apologetic*. London: SPCK, 1960.
Robinson, H. Wheeler. "The Hebrew Conception of Corporate Personality," *Werden und Wesen des alten Testaments* (*Beihefte zur Zeitschrift für die alttestamentliche Wissenschaft* LXVI). Berlin: Giessen, 1936.
Robinson, James M. "The Problem of History in Mark," *Union Seminary Quarterly Review* XX (1965), 131ff.
——— and Koester, Helmut. *Trajectories through Early Christianity*. Philadelphia: Fortress Press, 1971.
Rost, Leonhard. *Die Überlieferung von der Thronnachfolge Davids*. Stuttgart: Kohlhammer, 1926.
Rowlingson, Donald T. "Synoptic Problem," *Interpreter's Dictionary of the Bible* IV. Nashville: Abingdon Press, 1962.
Sabourin, Leopold. *The Psalms: Their Origin and Meaning*. New York: Alba House, 1970.
Schmitals, Walter. *Die Gnosis in Korinth* (*Forschungen zur Religion und Literatur des Alten und Neuen Testaments* XLVIII). Göttingen: Vandenhoeck und Ruprecht.
Shepherd, Massey H., Jr. (ed.) *The Liturgical Renewal of the Church*. New York: Oxford, 1960.
Shires, Henry M. *Finding the Old Testament in the New*. Philadelphia: Westminster Press, 1974.
Smith, D. M. "John, Gospel of," *Interpreter's Dictionary of the Bible Supplementary Volume*. Nashville: Abingdon Press, 1976.
Snaith, John G. *Ecclesiasticus* (*The Cambridge Commentary on the New English Bible*). London: Cambridge University Press, 1974.
Spielmann, Richard M. *History of Christian Worship*. New York: Seabury Press, 1966.
Strawley, J. H. *The Liturgical Movement: Its Origin and Growth*. London: Mowbray, 1954.

Strack, Hermann L. *Introduction to the Talmud and Midrash*. New York: Meridian Books and the Jewish Publication Society, 1959.

Terrien, Samuel L. "Amos and Wisdom" in Anderson, Bernhard W. and Harrelson, Walter (eds.), *Israel's Prophetic Heritage*. New York: Harper, 1962.

Thomas, D. Winton. *Documents from Old Testament Times*. New York: Harper (Torch Book), 1961.

Vico, Giambattista. *The New Science* (tr. and ed. Bergin, Thomas G., and Fisch, Max H.). Garden City: Doubleday (Anchor Book), 1961.

Voegelin, Eric. *Order and History* I: *Israel and Revelation*. Baton Rouge: Louisiana State University Press, 1956.

Westermann, Claus. "Zur Sammlung des Psalters," *Zeitschrift der Deutschen Morgenländischen Gesellschaft* CXI (1961), 338–389.

Whybray, R. N. *The Succession Narrative: A Study of II Samuel* 9–20; *I Kings* 1–2 (*Studies in Biblical Theology 2nd Series* IX). London: SCM Press, 1968.

Weil, Louis. See Price, Charles P.

Winston, David. *The Wisdom of Solomon* (*Anchor Bible* XLIII). Garden City: Doubleday, 1979.

Index of Biblical References

Index